SAMUEL H. MAYO

Los Angeles Valley College

A HISTORY OF MEXICO

From Pre-Columbia to Present

Prentice-Hall, Inc., Englewood Cliffs, New Jersey 07632

Library of Congress Cataloging in Publication Data

MAYO, SAMUEL H
   A history of Mexico.

   Bibliography: p.
   Includes index.
   1. Mexico—History.   I. Title.
F1226.M38   972   77-18989
ISBN   0-13-390203-X

To Robby and Jenny,
my two children,
with love.

© 1978 by Prentice-Hall, Inc., Englewood Cliffs, N.J. 07632

Printed in the United States of America

10 9 8 7 6 5 4 3 2 1

PRENTICE-HALL INTERNATIONAL, Inc., *London*
PRENTICE-HALL OF AUSTRALIA PTY. Limited, *Sydney*
PRENTICE-HALL OF CANADA, LTD., *Toronto*
PRENTICE-HALL OF INDIA PRIVATE LIMITED, *New Delhi*
PRENTICE-HALL OF JAPAN, INC., *Tokyo*
PRENTICE-HALL OF SOUTHEAST ASIA PTE. LTD., *Singapore*
WHITEHALL BOOKS LIMITED, *Wellington, New Zealand*

Contents

Contents   v

Preface

Mexico's rich and diverse antecedents find root in the myriad Indian cultures which dominated the horn-shaped land for more than ten thousand years. In 1521, a handful of Spanish conquistadores with the aid of steel, firearms, horses, European diseases, Indian allies, and Indian legend, abruptly terminated the exotic Indian civilizations. Spain introduced into Mexico, European civilization with the cross and the sword operating in tandem. The three hundred years of colonial rule did not eliminate the Indian culture or ways of thinking and living; instead the Spanish and Indian cultures became inextricably interwoven. One hundred years after the movement for independence from Spain, Mexico experienced a violent revolution (some believe an extension of the movement for independence), from which modern Mexico slowly and laboriously emerged. In the last twenty years, Mexico has experienced phenomenal and unprecedented growth as a modern industrial power. It is this complex, diverse, and often contradictory history that I have attempted to relate in *The History of Mexico*.

My aim has been to capture some of the excitement of Mexico's past and to engender a feeling of enthusiasm in the reader about Mexico's history. Where possible, I have sought out events and quotations that would impart the richness, the diversity, and the human quality that could help the reader gain a greater understanding of the Mexican nation.

This book was part of an overall project which included scripting, filming, and hosting a forty-five half hour television series on the History of Mexico, and the project lasted for more than three years. During this time, we researched and filmed in both Spain and Mexico, a task that was not completed without the aid of so very many people.

I am particularly indebted to my three research associates who provided me with detailed research on various phases of Mexico's history. They are Professor Leslie Lewis on the colonial period, Professor Abraham Hoffman on the national and revolutionary eras, and Philip Boucher, a U.C.L.A. Teaching Assistant, on the modern-industrial period. I am also indebted to three U.C.L.A. professors who acted as content advisors and who read and edited the original narrative. They were Professor E. Bradford Burns on the Colonial period, Professor Robert Burr, Dept. Chairperson, on the national period and Professor Henry B. Nicholson of the Department of Anthropology, on the pre-Columbian.

In addition, all of the material was read and edited by Tom Mossman, Director of K.L.C.S. TV; Gumercindo Zuñiga and Jim Nunn of K.L.C.S. TV. Professor Solomon Modell and Professor Angelo Villa, both of Los Angeles Valley College, read and edited the material contained in the chapters on the Spanish heritage.

I wish also to thank various agencies of the Mexican government for their cooperation, including the Office of the Consul-General of Mexico in Los Angeles and the Mexican Consul General, Fernando Fernandez Farina; the *Instituto and Museo Nacional de Antropología e Historia*; the *Consejo Nacional de Turismo* and its Western Regional Director, Mr. Manuel Muñoz Avina; *Aeromexico* Airlines; the audio-visual section of the *Secretaría de Educación Pública*; *Canal 13* in Mexico City; and Mr. José Lieberman of radio station XEGM and KLOVE, who also provided valuable assistance. I wish also to thank the various agencies of Spain, including Tourism, the archival section of the Lonja in Seville, and Iberian Airlines. I would like also to thank those persons in Mexico who consented to personal interviews, including Fausto Zapata, Press Secretary to President Luis Echeverría Alvarez; Antonio Calderón Martinez, Director General of Commerce; Fernando Garza, Press Secretary to former President Gustavo Díaz Ordaz; to my late friend, José David Alfaro Siqueiros, the world renowned muralist; and to my good friend, the always most gracious Dr. Maynard Geiger, O.F.M., a leading Catholic historian and Director of the Santa Barbara Mission Archives.

A special thanks also to the Division of Instruction of the Los Angeles Community College District, and especially to Dr. Louis Hilleary, who offered a great deal of encouragement.

I have deep gratitude to my wife Leslee, and my children Robby and Jenny, all of whom showed infinite patience, support, and love throughout the many hours of research and writing. In creating a project of this proportion, errors are inevitable and responsibility for them must finally rest with me.

SAMUEL H. MAYO

THE UNITED STATES OF
MEXICO

0   100   200   300   400
Miles

CHAPTER 1

A Land of Contrast

On July 10, 1519, over 450 years ago, Hernán Cortés, the great conquistador, wrote to his Queen Juana and her son Emperor Charles V, just four months after he arrived in Mexico. The letter was written in Veracruz, but the description of the country was surprisingly accurate and filled with excitement:

> "The coast is completely flat with sandy beaches. . . . The country inland is likewise very flat with most beautiful meadows and streams; and among these are some so beautiful that in all Spain there can be none better. . . .
> ". . . and in certain places . . . runs a great range of the most beautiful mountains, and some of these are exceedingly high, but there is one which is much higher than all the others from which one may see a great part of the sea and land; indeed it is so high that if the day is not fine one cannot even see the summit, for the top half of it is all covered by cloud. . . . When the day is very fine one can see the peak rising above the cloud, and it is so white we think it to be covered in snow. . . ."[1]

Hernán Cortés landed on the flat and sandy beach of the Rio Antigua, just north of Veracruz. During the months of preparation for what would be his historic march into Mexico's interior, he built a fortress on the island in the harbor of Veracruz which he named San Juan de

[1] A. R. Pagden, Trans. & ed. *Hernan Cortes' Letters From Mexico.* (New York: Orien Press, 1971) pp. 28-29.

Ulúa. From that island he could look westward and see Mexico's highest mountain peak, the snow-covered Citlatépetl, more commonly known as Orizaba. At 18,700 feet, Orizaba is probably the most striking geographical formation in this land of contrast.

While Mexico's territory under Spanish rule was considerably larger, even today it occupies some 760,000 square miles, making it the fifth largest Republic in the Western Hemisphere—about one fourth the size of the United States. Mexico's northern limits begin at the international boundary at California, which is one marine league south of the port of San Diego. From there it moves west to the confluence of the Colorado and Gila rivers. The line then runs in an approximate southeast direction to the Rio Grande at El Paso and Ciudad Juárez. It then follows the Rio Grande as it winds its way to the Gulf of Mexico. In the northwest lies the rather desolate peninsula of Baja California which is divided into two of Mexico's thirty-one states. This dry and arid peninsula extends southeastward for a distance of 800 miles. Except for a few agricultural areas and the tourist centers of Tijuana, Ensenada, and La Paz in the south, Baja California has been sparsely inhabited, both historically and today. At the head of the peninsula is the agriculturally prosperous Mexicali Valley, which comprises the southern half of California's Imperial Valley. These valleys are below sea-level and are filled with alluvial Colorado River deposits forming a delta, which is constantly expanding. The peninsula is separated from the mainland of Mexico by the shrimp-rich Gulf of California. Mexico's mainland contains some of the most striking geographical features in the western hemisphere. Perhaps the most outstanding is the massive central plateau. The Mexican Plateau or Altiplano Méxicano may be viewed as a giant incline plane which tilts upward from the international border. At the Ciudad Juárez/El Paso border, the mesa or plateau is scarcely four thousand feet high. But by the time it reaches south of Mexico City, it has virtually doubled that elevation. The plateau is not smooth—rather it is dotted with discontinuous blocks of mountain ranges that give it a rugged character.

On either side of the Plateau are rugged mountain ranges running generally in a north-south direction. They grow in ruggedness and height as they move south. On the eastern side of the nation is the Sierra Madre Oriental—the mother mountain of the east. This is an old range that separates the flat coastal areas from Mexico's interior. Its counterpart on the western coast is the Sierra Madre Occidental—the mother mountain of the west. The Sierra Madre Occidental is generally higher; more rugged; younger; and more prone to turbulent volcanic and earthquake activity.

In the fall of 1943, a Tarascan farmer, Dionisio Pulido, discovered a column of smoke emanating from a cornfield in a valley, located in the state of Michoacán. Suddenly, the whole field erupted, a new volcano was born, and within eighteen months the volcano's cone rose almost two thousand feet above the valley floor. In the process two villages were buried and more than four thousand people were forced from their homes. Within a few months, the Church of San Juan de Parícutin (named after the village) had its entire first floor buried by hardened lava. In just seven months, only the bell tower remained. The interior of the church filled with hardened lava is mute testimony to the violent activity of the rugged mountain range known as the Sierra Madre Occidental. And these massive ranges that are located on either side of the *Mesa Central,* have also been a barrier to communication and hence to cultural exchange. Is it any wonder then, why Mexico has developed as a culturally fragmented nation in its developing years?

It is on the great Mexican Plateau that the majority of peoples have lived from the earliest settlements to the present. In the vast *Altiplano Méxicano* there are large basins of interior drainage called bolsones— literally big purses (or big bags). These bolsones capture the light-to-moderate rainfall in the *Altiplano Méxicano* and make the land fertile; and in a nation that depends on agriculture for its sustenance, fertile land was of first importance. Even today, the great population centers of Mexico—except for the industrial and mining regions—are in bolsones. Jalisco in which the city of Guadalajara is located, Queretaro, Gunajuato, San Luis Potosí, Morelia, Aguascalientes, Puebla, Oaxaca, and the heart of the nation, Mexico City, are all in bolsones.

The south central bolson of Toluca is a good example. The land there is fertile and conducive to growing a number of agricultural products. But Toluca has a pattern to it which is common to most of Mexico's agricultural areas. The land is tilled by farmers who live in the city of Toluca—or in nearby villages. They travel each day from their homes to till the outlying fields. At sunset, there is a long trail of farmers returning to their homes to share in the social life that towns have to offer. This pattern was established in Pre-Columbian times and reinforced during the Spanish occupation. Agricultural Mexico does have its regional differences. The people with the large sombreros and white muslin clothes are from southern states such as Morelos where the principal products are corn or maize, beans, squash, and other truck-farm products. Traditionally, they have supplied themselves and the urban centers of south central Mexico.

In the north much of the land is used for cattle raising. Since the arrival of the Spaniards, beef has been a major product of the vast northern plains. And the dress of the people reflects that heritage. Many still wear the stetson hat, high heeled boots, and the *chaparreras* or chaps. This was the traditional uniform of the vaquero—the forerunner of the

North American cowboy. And still there are other variations in the life-style and dress of those engaged in agriculture such as in the southern highland area of the state of Chiapas. In the city of San Cristobal de las Casas the Chamulas and Zinacatencos still wear centuries-old Indian dress styles. This area of heavy rainfall is excellent for coffee growing and as a result, coffee is one of Mexico's most successful exports.

But not all of Mexico is agriculture. There was a limited amount of mining before the Spanish conquest, but the colonizers from Europe turned mining into a profitable industry. Mining generated wealth, so the search for silver and gold was of prime importance to the Spaniards and the marginal areas that were lightly settled suddenly became centers of activity. Boom towns were born or died as the fortunes of the mine dictated. Some endured, supported by the extensive resources of proxi-mate mines. A good example is the beautiful colonial town of Guanajuato. The beauty of the town's structures results from the opulence of those who profited from the mines in the region, some of which are still producing today.

In more recent years, new centers have developed because of indus-try or the exploitation of abundant natural resources such as iron ore and oil. The coastal area of Michoacán has experienced a rapid influx of people in order to staff the largest industrial complex yet built in Mexico, Las Truchas steel works. Las Truchas is an example of the massive industrial development Mexico has experienced in the last two decades. Iron ore from the nearby mountains is transported to the mill for conver-sion into steel; and the steel will be used for myriad products that will either be sold domestically or exported throughout the world.

By far the most important developing industry in Mexico is petro-leum. Traditionally, this area on the gulf coast has been the center of Mexico's oil industry. From Reynosa along the international border, past Tampico, Posa Rica, Veracruz, Minatitlan, to Ciudad Pemex bordering on the Yucatan Peninsula—the entire Mexican Gulf Coast has been explored and exploited. In recent years, however, Mexico has invested large sums for the exploration and development of its petroleum and petrochemical industry. Exploration has extended to twenty-three of its thirty-one states; and estimates of Mexico's oil reserves now exceed sixty billion barrels. Her oil reserves are said to be the second largest in the world. Mexico's Secretary of Natural Resources estimated that as Mexico moves into the 1980's, she is expected to have the world's fifth largest petrochemical industry. The international need for petroleum under-scores the importance of Mexico's petrochemical industry, and signals the rising importance of Mexico in the world community of nations.

Presently Mexico exports a little more than 115,000 barrels of oil per day, approximately ten percent of its total production. The other ninety percent is used domestically as fuel and to support a growing industrial complex, which includes burgeoning systems of transportation and communication.

The two mountain ranges that trisect Mexico, the Sierra Madre Occidental and the Sierra Madre Oriental, have hampered commerce and communications. But in recent years, these and other barriers are being overcome by the extension and modernization of Mexico's transportation system. Mexico's ports of trade, where for centuries the great sailing ships of Spain traded products for gold, have now been modernized to handle giant oil tankers and merchant ships. Most foreigners think of Acapulco as a tourist paradise. But it is also a major seaport where goods produced by Mexican industry are shipped to North and South America and to the countries of Asia. For almost three hundred years, the Manila galleons sailed from Acapulco to the Philippines. It took six months to complete the seven thousand mile journey. The galleons were laden with gold and silver to exchange for silks, spices, ivory, china, and other finery from Asia. Today, these ships carry railroad cars, automobiles, diesel engines, busses, sewing machines, and thousands of spare parts to trade for photographic and electronic equipment and other manufactured goods not yet produced in Mexico.

On the Gulf Coast of Mexico is the seaport of Veracruz. During the colonial era it was the major trading center for New Spain. In that respect, nothing has really changed. North of Veracruz is the port city of Tampico; and to the south is Coatzacoalcos, or the Port of Mexico. But neither can match the volume and variety of products that are shipped in and out of Veracruz.

One of the great problems that has faced Mexico for centuries is the distribution of goods that arrive in these seaports. A major step toward solving that problem was accomplished in 1873, with the inauguration of the first railroad line from Veracruz to Mexico City, a marvel of engineering accomplishment. Starting in Veracruz, the line then climbed nine thousand feet above the coastal plane across the Sierra Madre Oriental to the Mesa Central. This marked the beginning of railroad construction which accelerated rapidly during the rest of the nineteenth century. Lines were built in a north-south direction connecting with lines north of the Rio Grande. And while the railroads are necessary for the movement of goods, they are also important for the movement of people. Tourism is a major source of income for Mexico, and the railroads are essential for the movement of tourists. At the Ferrocarrils Nacional Station in Mexico City, modern trains depart every day en route to all parts of the Republic. Tourists and vacationers fill these trains throughout the year.

In recent years Mexico has improved and modernized existing highways. It has also constructed multi-lane turnpikes such as the one which runs from Mexico City to Puebla—a distance of about eighty-five miles. These turnpikes are financed by the government and paid for by a toll charge.

The construction of modern highways has also opened up isolated regions. The highway which now traverses the entire length of the Baja California Peninsula is an excellent example. The government hopes these highways will increase tourism and trade, and will improve the economy of the poorer outlying regions.

Natural barriers have also been overcome through the development of aviation. Mexico City International airport is located just twenty miles outside of Mexico City. Its facilities accommodate thousands of people arriving from and departing to cities throughout Mexico—and the entire world. In the past, travel from Europe was reserved for the wealthy who could afford the time and expense of luxurious ocean liners. Today, thousands arrive on airlines, at a price within the grasp of many working Europeans. Tourism in Mexico has achieved an international reputation.

Until the last decade, most vehicles were imported from the United States or Europe. But Mexico is now manufacturing its own automobiles, busses, and railroad trains. In compliance with the law, all automobiles sold in Mexico must be 100% assembled in the nation. More than eighty percent of Volkswagen's component parts are manufactured at the Volkswagen plant in the state of Puebla. The percentage is even higher for the Renault plant in Monterrey.

When I was in Mexico in 1961 and 1962, generally the busses used for highway transportation were imported from the United States. City busses were often United States World War II surplus. Today most of these have been replaced with vehicles which are manufactured in Mexico. Bus transportation in Mexico is inexpensive and comfortable. Modern Dina busses service every part of the Republic. And busses are essential to commuter transportation within the cities.

The cities in Mexico reflect a regional diversity of a nation whose heritage included Indian civilizations mixed with the European cultures. Many of the cities have a heritage dating back hundreds of years, and others have the flavor of a recent frontier boom town, such as Tijuana. It is located just across the international border from the city of San Ysidro, California. It could be called a frontier town; and the fact that the population there is rapidly increasing, gives it the quality of a boom town. Except for the bull ring, the jailai stadium, and a few plush hotels, Tijuana is a town of small shopkeepers selling everything from paintings to perfume. Tijuana is an example of a northern frontier city which is reflected even in the music and the dress. The music is Norteño—which includes a small accordian and a wooden block beaten with drumsticks—and the dress is decidedly cowboy with boots, jeans, and stetsons.

The city of Veracruz lies in the middle of Mexico's gulf coast, and the structures and inhabitants are quite different from those in Tijuana. In 1520, Veracruz was the first city established by the Spaniards. Its architecture reflects that colonialism, as do the dress and mannerisms of the people. The main square or plaza is very similar to plazas found in Spain. And the church and the public buildings also mirror a style imported from Spain. Cowboy boots and stetsons will not be seen in this city. Instead, these people wear white pants, and a shirt called the guayabera. And the music? Well, it too is different. Instead of the Norteño accordian and wood block, the Veracruzanos play the harp, the *guitarras de golpe,* and the *vihuela*—a small guitar which sounds much like a harp. Their music is a mixture of Spanish and Caribbean tied together with Pre-Columbian Totonaca.

Some cities in the interior of Mexico reveal their strong Indian heritage. Oaxaca is such a city. The architecture is decidedly Spanish-colonial—but the culture is just as strongly Indian. Market day in Oaxaca is held every Saturday. Early in the morning, people come here from all over the countryside and from their homes in the city, to sell and exchange their wares. The market differs little from the ones that were held in the days before the Spanish conquest. Even the dress and faces of the participants carry that heritage; the faces appear Indian, but the dress is early European peasant.

These and other cities throughout the republic testify to the regional differences of this land—in the architecture, the people, their dress, their art, and their music. But one city encompasses most of these regional differences; and yet it is one of the most modern and cosmopolitan centers in the entire world—the heart of the nation, La Ciudad de Mexico. Mexico City rests on a major bolson which is thirty miles wide by forty miles long. It is located at the southern end of the great Mexican Plateau in the Anahuac Valley. In Pre-Columbian times, that is before the arrival of Columbus, the city stood on an island in the middle of Lake Texcoco; and it was called Tenochtitlan. Even then, it was the economic and social center of the Azteca—and time has only increased its importance as the economic, social, political, and cultural center of the nation. Generally, regional costumes are replaced by a shirt, tie, and jacket. Like any big city, there is a constant movement of people hurrying to and from work, searching through the markets, or merely sauntering through one of the city's many parks such as the one at Chapultepec. Like no other cosmopolitan city, contrast characterizes Mexico. The mercado, or market, in the Merced district, contains stalls that are very similar to those seen in reproductions of the great Azteca markets. The vendors hawk their wares to anyone within listening range. Contrast Merced Mercado to a modern supermarket on Avenida Insurgentes. Shopping carts are pushed through isles stocked with packaged goods in an air-conditioned building.

In the factories of the city, employees work on assembly lines con-

tributing their labor to manufacture finished products they might never
see. Contrast that to a glass-blowing works in Mexico. The workers create
a finished product which reflects years of artistic talent inherited from
those who brought the art to America centuries ago.

Again the contrast may be seen in the music. At Garibaldi Square,
the mariachis gather nightly. Residents who might wish a mariachi group
for a party at home, marriage, a birthday, a graduation, a reunion, or any
other event have their pick at Garibaldi Square. The music of the mariachi
is emotional and it is a mixture of European and Indian. On the other
hand, one might wish to witness the ancient and mysterious music of the
Pre-Columbian civilizations. Inside the theatre—known as Palacio de
Bellas Artes, the Palace of Fine Arts—you can reserve a seat to watch the
highly respected Ballet Folklorico de Mexico. Or one might wish to return
on another evening and listen to the Mexican Symphony Orchestra.

This magnificent city also contains examples of the most beautiful
and *avant-garde* art in the world. Most familiar to the tourist would be the
National University of Mexico. The library, executed by the artist Juan
O'Gorman, is a mosaic of millions of small tiles fitted together to illustrate
the great sweep of Mexican history. And there are many other public
buildings that are decorated with murals contributed by artists of international renown. Public hospitals, and Social Security Buildings are decorated with murals that incorporate both Indian and Spanish themes. But
murals are not limited to government buildings—at a movie theatre on
Avenida Insurgentes are the mosaic murals of the world-renowned Diego
Rivera.

Mexico City is developing into a megalopolis of interconnecting
cities and suburbs. Many of them are designed to serve the needs of the
rising middle class. In the suburb of Ciudad Satelite—or Satellite City—
the homes are modern, and there are massive shopping centers where
one could get lost among the many consumer goods now available to the
Mexican people. Some neighborhoods within the city mirror the opulence of the wealthy residents. In the Lomas section of Mexico most of the
homes were constructed during the Diaz years, and the architecture is
decidedly Spanish Colonial. But in the section known as the Pedrigal, near
the University of Mexico, are the wealthy homes that have been constructed within the last thirty years. The innovative architecture is an
example of the creativity of the nation.

The contrast of colonial and avant-garde may be seen within the
center of the city as well. In the Zocalo, or the central plaza, is the National
Palace—the colonial residence of 62 viceroys. And diagonally across from
the Palace was the home of the conquistador, Hernán Cortés.

Amid these timeless Colonial structures are modern hotels and
office buildings that rise over fifty stories above the ground: The *Hotel de*

México, the National Lottery Building, and the Latin American Tower. The Tower is forty-six stories of glass and it literally floats on flexible pilings that are driven deep into the earth.

Nowhere is this contrast more clearly seen than at the Plaza of the Three Cultures—at Tlatelolco. In front are the remains of an Azteca pyramid—a symbol of the Indian contribution. Next to the pyramid is one of the first Catholic Churches built in Mexico City—it represents the Spanish contribution. And the magnificent office building behind the church is a large government building which houses the Department of Interior—it represents the Modern. In the middle of this plaza is a plaque. Its words tell the story of Mexico's intellectual and emotional ideal.

> "In 1521, Tlatelolco, heroically defended by Cauhtemoc, fell under the power of Hernan Cortes. It was neither a victory nor a defeat, but the painful beginning of the mestizo people, which is Mexico today."

CHAPTER 2

The Hunter from Tepexpan

Ancient man probably settled in Mexico because it was in the path of his migration south; and because the land was so well suited to his basic needs for survival, he stayed. The high valley of Mexico was especially desirable. More than a mile high, the air was crisp and clear. All around were lakes, forests, grasslands, and swamps, greatly enhanced by a beautiful springtime climate.

The numbers and variety of animals together with the vegetation and climate motivated the early migrant-hunter to remain. Because small arrow points and sharpened flints have been found, it is believed he killed and ate small game such as rabbits and birds. But it was the big game animals, now extinct, that tantalized his taste.

Because hunting took more than one person to kill these animals, it engendered group interaction and fostered group cooperation. There were a plethora of animals, especially deer-like animals with forked horns, called pronghorn antelope. There were also a variety of elephants including the gigantic woolly mammoths. There were giant armadillos, a superabundance of large bison, camels and even horses. Horses, which early became extinct on this continent, were not found again until the Spaniards reintroduced them in the period of the conquest.

The discovery of these extinct animal remains tell a great deal about the diet of ancient man. The bones show they were killed in a community hunt, and then scraped and eaten.

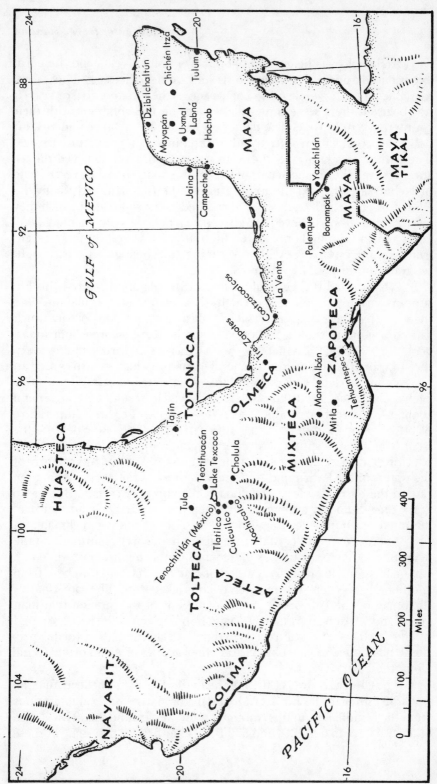

FIGURE 1.

Archaeologists believe that about two million years ago the earth experienced a general cooling—the result, a series of ice ages. The technical name given the whole period of ice ages is the Pleistocene. For years it was believed there were four ice advances on this continent with their counterparts in Europe. The names given each ice advance told how far down the ice sheet purportedly advanced during that particular ice age. The earliest was known as the Nebraskan—and it was believed the ice sheet covered the northern part of the continent down to the present state of Nebraska. The next three, the Kansas, the Illinoian, and finally the Wisconsin, each had ice sheets that reached to the states after which they were named. It was believed the Wisconsin reached its peak about 25,000 years ago and receded only eleven thousand years ago. But more recent evidence suggests many cycles of warming and cooling and at least eight separate and distinct ice advances.

What caused this general cooling off of the atmosphere—this life support envelope around the earth—is a matter of speculation. One theory is that there was a reversal of the earth's magnetic polarity which caused a general cooling. Another, submitted by George Simpson, a geologist of the 1920's, is that there was an increase of carbon monoxide in the atmosphere. This caused a general warming, which in turn caused an increase in the cloud cover around the earth. The increased cloud cover eventually blocked out the sun's rays which resulted in a general cooling—the eventual product, ice! A decrease of the earth's temperature of only five or six degrees could result in an ice age. How delicate the balance of the atmosphere! More recently, a group of scientists at Columbia University have theorized that the ice ages were caused by a mixture of the waters of the Pacific and Atlantic with those of the Arctic. What then caused these ice advances? We don't really know for certain. But we do know they did occur and generally when they occurred—and that man migrated south in order to escape the ravages of the frigid climate.

There are a number of theories about man's arrival throughout the hemisphere. Some say he was indigenous to this hemisphere while one person has gone so far as to suggest that man may have arrived here from another solar system via an interstellar rocket ship! The late Charles Chapman of the University of California was of the opinion that man arrived by raft or boat from Asia, island hopping across the Pacific carried by the Japanese and California currents. As substantiation for his proposal, he pointed to jade objects and other articles of Asian origin found along the Pacific Coast.

The Church of Jesus Christ of the Latter Day Saints believes that the Book of Esther in the Book of Mormon summarizes several migrations from the Middle East to this continent. One was around 2,200 B.C.—the other two were in 600 B.C. and 580 B.C. They believe that some of these people came across the Pacific on rafts and boats while others sailed across the Atlantic either around Cape of Good Hope or through the Straits of Gibraltar. While the Mormons do not deny the possibility of collateral land migrations from Asia, they believe that a large number—maybe even a majority of the American Indian population—came in these three ocean migrations. And what about the islands of the Pacific? They believe that the similarities of those people to the American Indian proves they sailed to these islands from America. They point to Thor Heyerdahl's *Kon Tiki* to prove the feasibility of the Pacific crossing; and to prove the feasibility of the Atlantic crossing, there is Heyerdahl's *Voyage of The Ra*—the journal of the passage of a papyrus boat from Gibraltar to the Bahamas in the Caribbean. Many books have been assembled picturing the similarities of Indian artifacts, art, and even religious attitudes to those found in the ancient Middle East.

Nevertheless, archaeologists and anthropologists generally believe that man crossed the Bering Straits—and that he, like the migrating animals, was searching for a warmer, more habitable climate.

But when did this migration take place? Again more controversy! Until recently archeologists dated man's arrival between 10 and 25,000 years ago. The late Dr. Leaky said it might have been in excess of 100,000. But of this date there is little evidence. Dr. Jeff Bada of the University of California at Scripps Institute of Oceanography with his new dating method of *racemization* dates a find near Oceanside, Calif. at approximately 50,000 years ago. According to Dr. Bada, all living organisms have only left handed amino acids. After the organism dies, these left handed amino acids convert to right handed ones, *at a set rate,* until there is an equal amount of both left and right handed amino acid molecules; at which time the process ends. This process of conversion is called racemization. By feeding a sample of the once living organism through an electronic analyzer, one is able to determine the ratio of right to left handed amino acid molecules, and therefore, the antiquity of the once living organism. Dr. Bada used his process of racemization dating to determine the antiquity of a human skull found in 1929 at the Del Mar Cliffs, near Oceanside, Calif. He concluded that Del Mar Man was in excess of 48,000 years old. This has caused the scientific community to re-examine their assumptions about the arrival of man in the Americas.

If ancient man did migrate from Asia during one of the ice advances—or even in a period of cooling or warming—the likelihood was that there was a land bridge across the Bering Strait making foot travel possible. This land bridge probably resulted from a general lowering of the sea level caused by excessive deposits of ice on the land. The amount of water in the ocean can be significantly diminished if water is taken out of the rain cycle. This happens when water is stored in huge ice deposits on the land . . . which lowers the ocean and provides a land bridge. It is also believed that Alaska was never completely glaciated so there were ice-free land routes along which man could travel. Not all persons would necessarily need to walk either. They could have traveled in small boats, hugging the coast as they moved slowly and deliberately south. There is also strong archaeological evidence that early man moved all across present day Alaska and Canada. As a hunter, he foraged south along a number of routes following the animals as they sought a warmer climate.

When we think of ancient man we tend to picture a hairy, heavy browed, semi-upright man who communicated by grunting and flailing his arms wildly about. While we don't know how Mexico's early inhabitant gesticulated or communicated, we have a pretty good idea of what he looked like. Except for his dress and social customs, he couldn't be distinguished from many people of today. He was a little shorter than modern man; and in general had a broader forehead, but racial and cultural mixtures that might resemble him are common to our present day racially miscegenated populations.

Early man in the Western hemisphere is termed proto-Mongoloid which means Asian in appearance. But what has puzzled anthropologists is that if man did come from Asia then why the absence of many genetic features in the American Indian which are so common to Asians. Mongoloid features generally include an absence of body hair and a large face with a great deal of fatty tissue deposits. The forehead is smooth with hair that is straight and black. The cheekbones are pronounced and high. The chin is usually small, and the nose is broad and flattened. The eye has the well known Asian eye-lid or epicanthic fold which falls directly over the eye protecting it from sun and glare. But the American Indians, or Amerinds as they are called, do not show or manifest all of these specialized Mongoloid characteristics. Many Amerinds have small faces, some body hair, indistinct cheekbones, pronounced or convex noses, and wavy hair. Furthermore, many Amerinds have deep set eyeballs without the Asian or epicanthic lid. What is really puzzling is the almost total absence of Type B blood in the American aboriginal. Why this void when 20 to 40 percent of all Asians have Type B blood? In two separate studies, Joseph E. Birdsell and A. E. Mourant discussed the contradictions in physical features and blood types of the Amerinds or American Indians. Birdsell uses the term Amurians to refer to some ancient "root population." This so called "root population" gave rise to many branches of modern man. The Mongoloid is one. Another is the Australian aborigine. Still another is the Ainu of northern Japan. Thus, the Mongoloid very well might be a cold-adapted offshoot of the Amurian root. It might be that the original migrants to this continent were not the cold-adapted Mongoloid but the root Amurian who had some, but not all, Mongoloid features. Hence the contradiction that he is Mongoloid but he is not

Mongoloid. Or, he is similar but different. Some American Indians have relatively large faces but lack the Asian eyelid. Others may have the Asian eyelid but not high and pronounced cheekbones. Still others may have straight black hair, but pronounced convex noses. Thus while the inhabitants of a very cold Asia adapted their bodies to the cold climate—the migrants to warmer America had no need to adapt genetically to the cold. Again, the similarities and yet the differences. And as to the blood differences—there are several possibilities, but two could have worked in tandem. First it is possible that by random accident, the early Amurian migrant lacked the Type B blood. Secondly, it may be that the new environment favored Types O and A over Type B, therefore, Type O and A became predominant. And remember much could have changed because the Amerinds have had more than one-thousand generations for genetic adaptation. Not even the miscegenation caused by the Spanish conquest altered this absence of Type B blood—for Spain also lacked the B blood group. In terms of today's speeds, early man moved at the snail's pace of 18.3 miles per year. It took him approximately eighteen thousand years to travel the eleven thousand miles from the Bering Straits to Patagonia, which is the southernmost tip of South America. Over these many years and long miles much could have influenced changes in our migrant. Mutations or random changes in the genetic structure develop fresh genetic structure. If this random change, which occurs at a chance rate of one for every fifty to one hundred thousand persons, is favorable, it will be reproduced. If, however, geographic, climatic, or social hardships are not favorable to the new genetic material, chances are it would not survive and reproduce. This is an example of natural selection. Thus, the surviving or strongest genetic changes mix with other genetic groups to give the divergent variations we find in the Amerind.

　　　Probably one of the most astonishing variances, although cultural, is language. In his investigation of Pre-Columbian Latin American linguistics, Paul Rivet says there are at least 123 linguistic families. One catalogue lists 260 languages in Guatemala and Mexico. Because language is such a unique and complex code, it is safe to assume that there were a number of root languages belonging to early man. While it is difficult to ascertain the numbers of these root language families or groups, it is almost impossible to discover their population numbers. Demographers, who study population, have submitted a wide range of Pre-Columbian population figures in their attempt to approximate the census prior to the arrival of Columbus for all of the Americas. Estimates range from six million to one-hundred million inhabitants. The larger figure was submitted by a historian and a political scientist at the University of California at Berkeley. They estimated that in the *late* 15th century Central Mexico had almost twenty-five million inhabitants or roughly what the area supports today!

　　　So the first man of Mexico was probably Mongoloid or, as anthropologist Ernest Hooton reported, an admixture of some Australian, Negro, European, and Alpine with the Indian. He was a migrant, to be sure a slow moving traveler, but a migrant nevertheless. He traveled in small groups, probably along several routes. He also hunted in groups— no doubt seeking large game. He might have spoken anywhere in the neighborhood of two hundred and sixty languages. And he probably liked the plants, animals, land and climate of Mexico, particularly of its high central valley. It must have been ideal for a community hunt, made even more magnificent by the ice covered peaks of Popocatépetl and Ixtaccíhuatl. For years, anthropologists believed that early man must have rested in the valley of Mexico in his move south. They believed it, but they couldn't prove it. Then in 1945, while workers were digging a ditch for a tubercular hospital near Mexico City, they found some huge bones. The engineer in charge was called and he notified an archeologist. It was determined that the bones belonged to an imperial mammoth. The excitement was heightened when an obsidian flake, possibly shaped by man, was found near the fossil skull of the mammoth. Obsidian, or volcanic glass, was used by early man for his weapons and tools. The geologists Dr. Helmut de Terra of Mexico and Dr. Hans Lundberg of Canada, along with several Mexican archaeologists searched the area for other mammoth remains. They dug two pits. In the first they found only damp earth. But the second pit contained the skeleton of a man. Because of the composition of the layers of earth above him, his age was estimated to be between eight and ten thousand years. His discoverers called him "The Man of Tepexpan"—although that in itself may be a misnomer, since some now believe our "man" might be a woman. Tepexpan was the first solid evidence that people had existed and hunted the large extinct animals of the valley of Mexico. This first resident or poblador of Mexico was fifty-five to sixty years old, short in stature, but differing very little from his descendants today. Other archeologists questioned the methods used in dating and excavating Tepexpan and our first poblador remained suspect until several years later.

Dr. Pablo Martínez del Río, head of the Department of Prehistory in Mexico, had earlier discovered a fossilized elephant at Santa Isabel Iztapan. He decided to re-examine his find. Only two miles from Tepexpan, the Iztapan site could prove decisive in authenticating Tepexpan man. After several days of excavation around Iztapan, a flint spearhead was discovered pointing into the elephant. Parts of an obsidian scraper, combination tool and knifeblade and a chalcedony scraper and dart point were also found. (Chalcedony is a milkish-white translucent quartz rock.) No doubt the hunters had killed the mammoth, cut and scraped his hide and then scraped the flesh from the bones. Dr. Pablo Martínez del Río concluded that Iztapan was killed by Tepexpan's contemporary. And even if Tepexpan remained suspect, man's existence in Mexico at least ten thousand years ago was a fact.

Tepexpan and Iztapan were only two of literally hundreds of sites found in the Valley of Mexico. Each of the many sites reveals something new and different about these early hunters as they developed into the first settlers and farmers of Mexico. Dr. Helmut de Terra has classified the sedentary complexity of early man on a developmental scale ranging from least complex or "industry" to mid-complexity or "culture" to great complexity or "civilization." The oldest "industry" in the Valley of Mexico is San Juan Industry which dates from eight to twelve thousand years ago. A handful of obsidian artifacts used for killing and scraping extinct animals represent this period.

In 1958, Chalco Industry was discovered. Its stone hearth, grinding stones, obsidian tools accompanied an almost complete human skeleton which was dated between six to seven thousand years ago. Obviously, the milling stone meant the use of grain and this with the heavy hearth told us that man had become at least partly sedentary.

Art objects or paintings of early man are lacking in most of the very early archaeological sites. The earliest object discovered, in 1870, was made from a vertebra of an extinct llama or camel. It was carved to look like the head of a coyote or wolf, and is more than 3,500 years old. It is named after the valley in which it was found, Tequixquiac. Dr. Frederick Peterson believes that early man, somewhere between Tepexpan at 10,000 years and Tequixquiac approaching 3,500 years, produced representative art—but it is yet to be found. Around 5,000 to 3,000 B.C. our early hunter decided to settle down and become sedentary. He added implements of war to his early flints and scrapers.

Probably the most important item which elevated him to the status of a culture was nothing more than a stick. It is called a *coa,* and our early settler poked a hole in the ground with it to drop in a kernel of corn. This began planned agriculture. Once our early poblador did this, he inadvertently invented the division of labor. No longer did every member of the community need to spend his waking hours hunting for food. Now, one person could feed more than himself and therefore free his comrades for other more specialized jobs, such as: warriors, governors, priests, athletes, artists, and builders, and a host of other specialized occupations. Hence we find in sites dated after 2,000 B.C. items that Dr. Paul Kirchoff calls the accouterments of culture. These include agricultural items as the coa or chinampa culture, which is the construction of floating lake gardens. Also included is the cultivation of cacao and seed for oils and the Maguey or century plant for fibres and pulque, an intoxicating drink.

Blowguns, wooden and obsidian swords, shields, cotton padded armour suits, and other items of war were developed. Body adornments such as lip plugs, ear plugs, necklaces, turbans, and heeled sandals appeared in increasing numbers.

As the *poblador* became more settled, he invented the codex or a picture book which was folded in accordion style—back and forth. In these codices he recorded other inventions of his culture such as numbering systems and hieroglyphic writings. Hieroglyphs are figures, objects, or abstract drawings which are used to represent words, sounds, or even abstract ideas. He also recorded great deeds of his rulers, his warriors, and the battles they fought. Codices contained maps of his surroundings and areas through which his traders and warriors traveled and fought. Stelae, which are monuments carved from stone, were introduced. These stone monuments recorded complex, significant events such as cataclysms, birthdays, and unlucky days. And also carved from stone were calendars.

Cultured man not only danced and held religious ceremonies but he began the practice of animal and human sacrifices. To accommodate his religion, he built massive stepped pyramids covered with complex and intricate carvings and bas reliefs of that which he worshipped. Attendant to the pyramids were extensive ball courts with stone rings placed high along the walls. The ball game was religious and difficult. Surrounding his religious centers he built irrigation projects and terraced the hills in order to cultivate his food. For access and protection of his agricultural units he built roads and drainage canals.

Three ancient sites are representative of this Formative or Pre-Classic period. The earliest is Tlatilco, settled in 1,200 B.C. This site produced a great deal of pottery that appears both functional and decorative. In addition to plain cylindrical and globular vessels there were female figurines with stumpy arms and legs. There were unclothed figurines with elaborate ornamentation and headdress—and those of animals as well. The second site is Copilco which flourished around 900 B.C. It was discovered under lava beds near the University of Mexico in the Pedregal section of Mexico City. In addition to a graveyard, a number of pottery figurines were found resembling those of Tlatilco. But by far the most exciting site is Cuicuilco. This stepped circular pyramid is also located next to the University. The pyramid is sixty feet high and 370 feet in diameter with four separate tiers. It was topped with horseshoe altars which probably housed idols or representations of gods. In 1957, the University of California at Berkeley did extensive excavation at Cuicuilco. They found at least four more pyramids, one even larger than the exposed one. It had an adobe surface with at least seven tiers. Cuicuilco, which is dated at 600 B.C., is extremely difficult to unearth since the entire area was covered by lava at around 200 B.C.—the result of a massive eruption from the volcano Xitli.

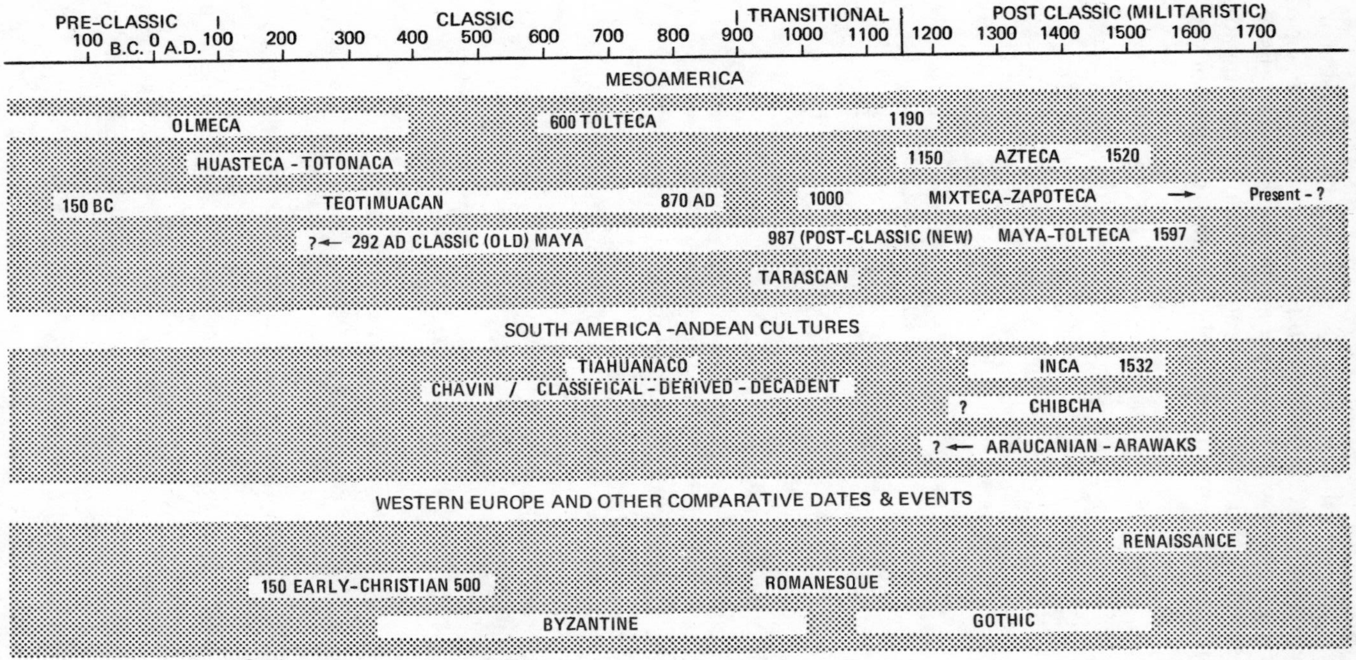

PRE-CLASSIC | CLASSIC | TRANSITIONAL | POST CLASSIC (MILITARISTIC)

100 B.C. 0 A.D. 100 200 300 400 500 600 700 800 900 1000 1100 1200 1300 1400 1500 1600 1700

MESOAMERICA

OLMECA
HUASTECA - TOTONACA
150 BC
TEOTIMUACAN
600 TOLTECA
870 AD
?← 292 AD CLASSIC (OLD) MAYA
1000
987 (POST-CLASSIC (NEW) MAYA-TOLTECA 1597
TARASCAN
1190
1150 AZTECA 1520
MIXTECA-ZAPOTECA → Present - ?

SOUTH AMERICA -ANDEAN CULTURES

CHAVIN / CLASSIFICAL :DERIVED - DECADENT
TIAHUANACO
INCA 1532
? CHIBCHA
? ?← ARAUCANIAN - ARAWAKS

WESTERN EUROPE AND OTHER COMPARATIVE DATES & EVENTS

150 EARLY-CHRISTIAN 500
BYZANTINE
ROMANESQUE
GOTHIC
RENAISSANCE

Greeks

1600 B.C. – 1150 B.C. Mycenaean Peru
1150 B.C. – 850 B.C. Dark Age
850 B.C. – 334 B.C. Hellenic Age
400's B.C. – Golden Age
460 – 430 B.C. – Age of Pericles
334 B.C. – 146 B.C. – Hellenistic Age
146 B.C. – 395 A.D. – Roman Control

HOLY ROMAN EMPIRE – 962 A.D. (Otto the Great)
to 1806 (dissolved by Napoleon)
JEWISH EXODUS – Circa 1250 B.C.
AGE OF THE PYRAMIDS 2,700 – 2,500 B.C. (EGYPT)
FIRST WRITING – MESOPOTAMIA – Circa 3,500 B.C.
START OF AGE OF METALS – 3,500 B.C.
THE WHEEL – Circa 4,000 B.C.
ALEXANDER "THE GREAT" OF MACEDON 356 – 323 B.C.

JULIUS CAESAR 60 – 27 B.C.
MOHAMMED 570 – 632 A.D.
FIRST CRUSADE 1096 A.D.
GENGHIS KHAN 1167 – 1227
MAGNA CARTA 1215
MARCO POLO 1271 (RET'D 1295)
JOHANN GUTENBERG – 1456

FIGURE 2.

19

These three sites reveal something of man's early settlement in Mexico. They represent the Preclassic period of Mexico's archaeology. These and other sites, along with fossils and artifacts are the records of man's entry into America and his slow but steady evolution from nomad-hunter to industry to culture and finally the abstract complexities of Civilization.

CHAPTER 3

The Magicians

Religion was a driving force of the people known as the Olmeca. They brought the developing cultures a step closer to the abstract complexity of civilization. The Olmeca left a colossal stone head, and today we are still wondering if this is how the Olmeca looked. If so, why were they so different from the other peoples of the valley of Mexico, and where did these strangers come from?

As the early migrant-hunter turned settler, he passed through a period of discovery and invention. He had introduced a whole array of weaponry, tools, ornamentations, and representations of deities. The coa transformed him from a hunter-gatherer into a farmer. He had learned the need to cooperate from his early experience with the hunt, and that spirit of cooperation extended to man the farmer, man the settler. At first he settled in villages, and they were small. The total Pre-Classic population of the villages of El Arbolillo, Tlatilco, and Zacatenco, in the valley of Mexico, was not more than two hundred people. These early farmers planted corn or maize as their main crop. They ate their harvest and threw the corncobs into refuse piles outside of their homes. Farming did not turn them into vegetarians however, for these rubbish heaps also contained bones of "boar, deer, jaguar, coatimundi, ducks, turkeys, iguanas, fish, and turtles."

At the site of Tlatilco, two hundred and three burial sites were unearthed. The graves tell us that these people believed that death was a transition to an after life. In addition to the deceased, the burial sites contained obsidian points, pottery, and a host of figurines to accompany him to his after life. If these figurines depict the inhabitants of Tlatilco, then they tell us something about the way they looked as well as how they lived. Their clothes? well—they were rather abbreviated. They did wear necklaces, hair ornamentation, and they painted or tattooed their bodies. Their ears were pierced—and stretched—and the lobe filled in with a large stone or clay plug. The nose was pierced and also duly ornamented.

The burial of these items with the deceased indicate that these people and the people of El Arbolillo and Zacatenco all believed in an after life. Of the two hundred and three burials at Tlatilco more than one hundred and sixty, or seventy-eight percent, contained offerings. El Arbolillo and particularly Zacatenco did not have nearly that high a percentage of offerings placed in the burial sites. But it is possible since many of these graves were dug up by contemporary inhabitants, that objects were also disturbed and "floated" from earlier to later graves. Thus, despite the absence of offerings in some of the grave sites, most or all of the sites may have had offerings at one time.

These early farmers lived a rather simple life with little outside influence. They developed their tools slowly and used materials which were easy to work. Clay, bone, wood, and obsidian were used extensively. In addition to clay bowls, they made vessels from calabash gourds and they wove baskets and simple mats on which they could sleep. Whatever changes occurred in the culture took place gradually and at a leisurely pace.

Our early farmers remained relatively undisturbed for several centuries, but experienced a dynamic change in their society. An influx of peoples from the south, west, and east changed the culture of these simple farmers dramatically. Probably the *most* dramatic change was the increase in the number of villages and the general population of the Valley of Mexico. Affected by the mystical and religious practices of these new arrivals, the life styles of our early farmers went through a significant transition. Professor Frederick Peterson in his book, *Ancient Mexico,* called these new immigrants "The Magicians." They were dominated by ritual song, dance, and chanting. They were obsessed with weird, eerie, monstrous, and unnatural representations of man, animals, and gods. Their figurines were distorted and designed to be frightening. (Some of the heads showed apparent mutilation and the skulls of these figurines display a cleft, or a large depression in the back, or are pointed at the top.) The mouths were large and animal-like and the teeth have dental mutilation. Bodies were twisted and contorted and the genital region enlarged out of proportion to the body. The skeletons of these people indicate that mutilations were not limited to jade figurines but practiced on people as well. Apparently, the human skull was artificially deformed and the teeth were mutilated.

The magicians brought with them a worship of a feline or jaguar god. Guessing from the figurines of shamans or priests, the priests probably wore jaguar masks painted with white stripes. They carried rattles and wore capes made of jaguar skins. Tall hats topped their heads, and the costumes were probably designed to elicit fear and respect. The populace wove cotton into cloth, made cradles for their children, and worked jade and other green stone into a fine art. But added to their ability to create was an ability to destroy. Burial sites reveal tortured human sacrifice. Limbs were severed and heads decapitated or smashed. Multiple burials lead one to believe that both adults and children were sacrificed, either to appease the gods or to accompany an important soul to his after life.

Who were these people that disturbed the peaceful existence of our early farmers and how long did their magic influence last? The last part of the question is easier to answer than the first. The "magicians" appeared about 1,000 B.C. and maintained their influence to around 650 B.C. by which time they had merged with the farmer population and ceased to be a separate entity. Who they were is manifestly more difficult to answer. Archaeologists generally agree that much of the pottery and facial design of the figurines indicate that the magicians might have been Olmeca. But there is no certainty. Olmeca influence appears throughout south central Mexico, but clearly their greatest influence was in three major sites in the states of Veracruz and Tabasco, on the Gulf Coast—San Lorenzo, La Venta, and Tres Zapotes. Recent radiocarbon dating has confirmed Olmeca culture in this region at 1200 B.C. Other aspects of the Olmeca people have evoked considerable controversy among anthropologists and archaeologists. Whether they were the inventors of hieroglyphic writing, religious ceremony, and the ritual bar-dot calendar, is still a matter of argument and disagreement. The prominent Mexican archaeologist Ignacio Bernal in his book, *The Olmec World,* wrote these words:

"Actually I believe that the first signs of civilization are to be found on the Gulf Coast, in the area I call 'Metropolitan Olmec.' These first signs of civilization occur not only there but also at sites such as Monte Albán and those in the highlands of Guatemala, which are not tropical and possess an entirely different habitat, even though they may be contemporaneous with the efflorescence of the Olmecs. But why then should we not suggest that it was at Monte Albán, or better still the Valley of Oaxaca, where this civilization was born? My answer is that there are not antecedents there. On the other hand, these do exist in the Olmec area of the Gulf Coast. Of course proof may be lacking there because of lack of exploration, but at the present time we must rely exclusively upon the facts we know and not attempt to reach completely theoretical conclusions based on future discoveries.

Therefore I accept provisionally the hypothesis of the birth of civilization on the tropical coast."[2]

Along this tropical coast lie the three important Olmeca sites. West of the Papaloapan River, in the state of Veracruz is the site of Tres Zapotes. To the southeast is San Lorenzo. Farther south and east, in the state of Tabasco, at the mouth of the Tonala River is the Olmeca site of La Venta. The annual rainfall of these areas ranges from a low of 74 inches to a high of 122 inches. The regions where some of these sites are located are covered with tall vegetation and impassable jungle. Yet it was out of this jungle that the Olmeca apparently carved a civilization with monumental artwork that surpasses the imagination, and replete with farmland, albeit sometimes flooded. Corn, beans, and squash, harvested in Tres Zapotes today, were the staples of Tres Zapotes of yesterday. Each year, the clearing of jungle was begun in March and the cuttings were burned in May, the driest month. The ground, now covered with ashes, was planted in June, the first rainy month. During the growing season, the fields had to be weeded at least twice to battle the ever-growing jungle. From mid-November to mid-December the crop was harvested, and this slash and burn method of farming began again. This is so a second or winter's crop could be sown in January and harvested between May and June. And so the constant agricultural battle continued.

Beyond the sculptures the Olmeca left behind, we have no way of ascertaining their physical characteristics. The humid jungle soil, high in acidity, quickly destroys skeletal remains which could have definitively told us something about the inhabitants.

Probably the most spectacular—and best known—Olmeca art form are the colossal stone heads found in these sites along the Gulf Coast. The first was discovered in 1862, and since then fourteen have been added to the list. The most important ones were the monumental stone heads, some of which are over eight feet tall and are carved from a single piece of basalt or grayish-black volcanic rock. Each represents hours of labor and dedication on the part of the sculptor or sculptors; and each of these monoliths has its own unique characteristics. Most have a cap and head-band carved into the stone, with the ears uncovered and delineated. On first glance they resemble old fashioned football helmets. On some, braided hair appears to hang over the headband, and the look of the eyes is stern and imperious. The eyelid on some appear to have the epicanthic fold or Asian eye lid while the nose is broad and flat. The cheekbones are high and pronounced while the face is wide and jowly. The thick lips are shapely and the chin is pronounced. Is this what the Olmeca looked like or

[2]Ignacio Bernal, *The Olmec World*. Doris Heyden and Fernando Horcositas, trans. (Berkeley: University of Calif. Press, 1969), p. 13.

were these representations of gods, their rulers, or "other" peoples whom they deified? The key that unlocks the door to the mystery may never be found and we may forever be filled with speculation.

Just inland from the coast, in the state of Tabasco, La Venta has always been exciting because of its early pyramid which could be the oldest in Mexico. Because the site was occupied from 1000 to 600 B.C., it predates the construction of the pyramid of Cuicuilco in Mexico City. The pyramid of La Venta is 420 by 240 feet and 100 feet high. It is built in a rectangular area which is aligned on an axis of about eight degrees west of true north. The entire court is enclosed by low mounds, with another similar court attached to the north. The mounds on the northerly court are topped with upright pillars of naturally cut basalt.

The excitement of La Venta was heightened in 1959 and 1960 when the excavation of several mounds revealed an exquisite archaeological find. After digging through layers of clay and slabs of serpentine rock and greenish colored stones, a mosaic pavement was discovered. The mosaics were formed to represent a stylized jaguar face. This may have ultimately evolved into the god Tlaloc later worshipped by the Azteca and other civilizations. It is estimated that the amount of serpentine in these various pits weighed about 5,000 tons and was carried by water from a source which was more than 350 miles away. Even more startling, this material must have been carried on the backs of individuals to and from the water's edge, for there is no evidence of the use of beasts of burden. One of the pits contained sixteen Olmeca figurines made of jade with polished ax blades forming a background. Why were these items created and then obviously buried at the moment of creation?

Could it not be that these art works constituted an offering to the earth, so sacred that they were never to be seen by humans again?

These and other figurines, most of jade and serpentine, remain objects of vast speculation; as does the transportation of twenty-ton blocks of building stone. The fact that these stones were moved through swamps and marshes from their source in the mountains more than sixty miles away suggests an impressive knowledge of engineering. But other than the deformities of their figurines which were similar to those of Tlatilco, little is known of these people who the Azteca later called the Olmeca. Olmeca is a Nahuatl word which means people of the land of rubber. By 400 to 250 B.C., the Olmeca sites of the Gulf Coast were abandoned and the jungle was triumphant again. But Olmeca influence continued in these and other areas for as late as the fifth century A.D.

Many centuries later, another group called by the Aztecs the Olmeca, flourished with their great capital in the highland area of Cholula. These people are called by archaeologists the Historical Olmeca to differentiate them from the earlier Archaeological Olmeca. The Historical

Olmeca had a very different art style which is related to the Tolteca-
Azteca, and other later Post-Classic Art styles of Mexico. The colossal
heads and baby-face figurines of the Archaeological Olmeca disappeared
centuries before. The great archaeological site of Cholula indicates Historical Olmeca influence. This area, which has a pyramid larger than
Cheops in Egypt, shows successive occupations of seven different cultures, one of which was Olmeca. They mixed with the other peoples of
Cholula, and may have remained there as late as the twelfth century A.D.
Legend has the invading Tolteca, from the central highlands, expelling
the Olmeca from that area.

By 250 B.C. the Archaeological Olmeca lost their identity as a viable
culture, and their art styles disappeared. Their influence beyond the Gulf
Coast continued and touched upon other developing cultures. By 800
A.D., in the late Classic period, the Tolteca exerted major influence in
south central Mexico. But one major culture stands out as bridging the
gap between the Olmeca and the Tolteca—the great culture of
Teotihuacan which began in 150 B.C. and was destroyed in 750 A.D. It
acts as a link between the Pre-Classic and Post-Classic period of Mexico's
Pre-Columbian story.

The renowned anthropologist Eric Wolf described the Classic
period as that period in which a new priestly ruling class exerted their
influence through the power of their gods. This power was expressed in a
number of ways. One was through the authority of the calendar—which
represented not only dates and important events of the past—but also
could predict the future. The Classic period may really be considered a
theocratic period as well. Art was another way the theocrats exerted their
power. In his work, *Sons of the Shaking Earth,* Eric Wolf wrote:

> "This art is often called 'Classic.' The term 'Classic' is a stylistic term; it
> indicates that during this period there was not only a florescence of society
> but also a florescence in the forms of expression employed by this society. It
> is ultimately a term that refers to a culmination, a fruition of art forms; and
> indeed the Mesoamerican Theocratic period is such a period of culmination
> and fruition. Yet artistic style is inherently difficult to express in words, just
> as it is very difficult to evaluate. It is all too easy to let oneself be guided by
> Occidental notions of fulfillment in art, and to associate Classic florescence
> with sobriety and purity of line, while ascribing decadence to a love for
> riotous expression."[3]

San Juan de Teotihuacan was apparently the largest and most dominant Theocratic center of the late Pre-Classic and Classic periods of
Pre-Columbian Mexico. It is thirty miles northeast of Mexico City in

[3]Eric Wolf, *Sons of the Shaking Earth* (Chicago: Univ. of Chicago Press, 1959),
p. 90.

a semi-dry valley. The site was not only important to its contemporaries but also to the Tolteca and Azteca who followed. Long after it was destroyed and abandoned, the Azteca went there to worship—and possibly to bury their honored dead. By 700 A.D. this influential city covered more than 2,000 acres. The entire site is dominated by two massive pyramids with many smaller pyramids, mounds, and platforms throughout the entire area. The largest of the two is called the Pyramid of the Sun. The outer stone work appeared to be economically irreparable. Believing another layer of stone existed beneath the first, a peeling process was begun around the turn of the century. Much to the shock of the project director, when the outer stonework was removed, it revealed not another layer of stone but a pile of earth. As the rains began to dissolve the core of the pyramid, it was hurriedly covered with a new layer of stone which bears little resemblance to the symmetry of the original structure. Even so, the pyramid of the sun and the smaller pyramid of the moon have been the object of much comparison and speculation. Because ancient legend says that gods lived there and the sun and the moon were created there, the site is extremely important. The similarity between the Pyramid of the Sun and the Cheops pyramid in Egypt is surprising. Cheops measures 226.50 meters at the base while the Pyramid of the Sun measures 225.00 meters. Cheops is 144.32 meters high while the Pyramid of the Sun measures 65.00 meters without its temple and 75.00 meters with it. Keeping it mind the problem of reconstruction, the similarity is amazing—almost exactly the same measurements at the base and almost half the height of Cheops. It is estimated that the Pyramid of the Sun, which contains about 1,300,000 cubic yards of earth, took 10,000 people twenty years to build. Either the faith of the people or the power of the priests must have been enormous. Yet there is a vast difference between the Egyptian pyramids and those of Mexico. The pyramids of Egypt were constructed from stone blocks and were primarily dedicated as tombs for the rulers. The pyramids of Mexico, on the other hand, were generally made of earth and rubble with only a cut stone facade. And more important is the function of the Mexican pyramid which served as a base for a temple which was placed at the top of the huge mound.

The smaller Pyramid of the Moon was reconstructed in 1968, in time for Mexico's presentation of the Olympics. A much better restoration was done. Another fascinating structure at Teotihuacan has been called both the Citadel and the Precinct of the Feathered Serpent. At the eastern end of this citadel, precinct, or plaza is the Temple of Quetzalcoatl. It is covered with a massive facade of rows of plumed serpents with feline fangs. Between these are rows of the rain god Tlaloc. There are also carvings of undulating serpents and conch shells throughout the entire facade. The conch shells suggest the inhabitants traveled to the sea.

The major area of Teotihuacan lies along a central track, some sixty yards wide. It is called the Avenida de los Muertos. This avenue begins at the Pyramid of the Moon and runs past the Pyramid of the Sun, and the Precinct of the Feathered Serpent. The entire length of the avenue appears to be lined on both sides with civic and religious structures, and the homes of wealthy residents. There also appears to be a number of residential areas which connect to the Avenue of the Dead by narrower streets. People lived here in small quarters and crowded conditions. Yet each of these residential areas has a religious center patterned after the main center—but on a smaller scale. This leads one to believe that these smaller communities had a measure of independence, and acted as satellites to the major center of Teotihuacan. On each side of the large pyramids there are huge open squares which have been ascertained as locations for markets. The archeologist René Millon of the University of Rochester carried out extensive archaeological research of Teotihuacan over a period of twenty years. He points out that there were hundreds of courtyards and forecourts in Teotihuacan—all of which must have collected massive amounts of water during the rainy season. In addition, the homes of those who could have afforded them were without windows. They contained rectangular openings in the ceiling to provide for light and air. Rain must have fallen into these structures so how was inundation prevented? Each structure was provided with ingenious central rectangular wells from which ran conduits. These conduits emptied into a main drainage ditch which ran the length of the site to a nearby river. This drain carried away both water and waste, and kept the streets and alley ways free from flooding.

René Millon sees Teotihuacan as the largest archeological site in the entire Western hemisphere with literally thousands of structures and a population of more than 200,000 people. Teotihuacan was neither built in one generation nor by one root culture group. The actual construction of the site shows at least three and possibly four main levels of construction—with a number of sub-levels in each of the main ones. The city itself shows careful planning at each stage of construction. The entire area covers more than seven square miles and there is evidence that not all of the inhabitants lived in the central city or in the apparent satellites. Farmers may have lived in thatched or mud huts located on the surrounding farmland. The entire site is so massive and so complex that there must have been a great deal of order and a powerful centralized authority. The immensity and prevalence of the religious structures indicates that authority was vested in a priest-ruler class—an aspect common to the Classic period. And so powerful was this priest-ruler class that the influence of Teotihuacan extended far beyond its borders. One sees this influence as far south as Guatemala City. Near the City is the site of Kaminaljuyu. In

500 B.C. it had been a flourishing commercial center, but by A.D. 400 the people of Kamianaljuyu experienced the shock of invasion and occupation. By whom? The best guess is by the warriors of Teotihuacan—an exceptionally long distance to move an army at that time.

Then there is the incomprehensible religious center of El Tajín. Located in the northern part of the state of Veracruz, it was built around 600 A.D. It is a fascinating center and the pagoda-like temples and niches look suspiciously Oriental. But this site also shows some influence of Teotihuacan. In fact Teotihuacan's influence extends far beyond these two diverse areas in time and scope.

By 800 A.D., the grand design of Teotihuacan came to an end. The red, black, and yellow painting with designs of mythological insects and butterflies was replaced with a procession of animals. These predatory beasts are feline representations that are stern, threatening, and oppressive. They could represent a drastic change. But why? Warriors from outside? Revolution from within? A sign from the gods? The answer is locked in the mute silence of the wild beast murals. Fangs bared and claws extended, a dripping symbol hangs below the mouth. In front there is a reversed question mark hieroglyph which appears to defy the viewer from penetrating the secret of the procession of the animals.

Within a half century after its creation the great city of Teotihuacan was literally put to the torch. The burned brick and gray-black ash mixing with inexorable mounds of earth and weeds, have added the destruction of time to the destruction by man.

By A.D. 870, the metropolis of Teotihuacan, once bustling with activity, now stood abandoned, left to the forces of nature. Within a few years, a new people came to the abandoned city to bury their dead. The pottery and offerings buried with their dead tell us that these new people were the Tolteca of Tula. The Tolteca came as a new warrior civilization that the archaeologists believe were, in part, born out of the ashes of the once great metropolis which, as the name Teotihuacan tells us, was "the place of the gods."

CHAPTER 4

One Reed, Our Prince, The Serpent of Precious Feathers

Less than a thousand years ago, a sacrificial victim lay on a stone slab located high above the Temple of the Warriors at Chichen Itzá. A high priest stood over him and a long obsidian knife flashed in his hand. With a single stroke the knife was brought down and the chest cavity split open. The heart was wrenched from the body and offered to the god, Chac Mool. The sacrifice done—the gods were appeased! And the Tolteca once more believed that the beneficial forces of nature would continue.

Sacrifice to a god or gods has been part of many civilizations. In Genesis, Chapter 22, the Bible tells us that God ordered Abraham to sacrifice his son Isaac in the Land of Moriah as a burnt offering to the Lord. As Abraham was about to fulfill the command, an angel of the Lord appeared and provided Abraham with a ram instead. God had been convinced of Abraham's sincerity and true fear of Him. So the ram was slain and offered.

In Mexico, human sacrifice did not begin with the Tolteca. It was merely acquired by them from earlier cultures such as the Olmeca. And when the Tolteca disappeared, human sacrifice continued in various forms with subsequent civilizations, such as the Azteca or the later Maya. If sacrifice has been a part of man's existence throughout the world, and it appears that it has, what then has he gained from it? The reward varies. In Mexico, propitiating the gods was a strong motivation, although not the only motivating factor. Early Mexicans believed that the gods sacrificed themselves so that man might exist. Therefore, it was man's duty to reciprocate and to sacrifice himself so the gods might exist. In some cases, such as with the Tolteca, they believed that the gods needed human sacrifice so they would be strong and able to perform their miracles. Without human sacrifice, the rain god Tlaloc would become weak and unable to bring water. Without rain, the crops would die; and so would civilization. The Tolteca also acquired a sacrificial ceremony which belonged to an adversary civilization, the Huaxteca. It involved a ceremony which symbolized a reciprocal fertility between man and earth—a symbolic sexual intercourse which returned life to the earth from which it came. The sacrificial victim was tied to an upright rack and the chest above his heart was painted white. As warriors danced around him, they shot arrows into his body and permitted his blood to drip upon the ground, thus fertilizing the earth from which came the sustenance of man.

The god Xipe Totec, meaning "Our Lord the Flayed One," was another member of the Tolteca sacrificial pantheon. This was the god of vegetation, and was associated with the rites of spring. His representation in clay was brought to life by warriors and priests. After the victim was sacrificed, his body was flayed or skinned. The skin was draped over a priest as a part of the rite of spring. In the ceramic image one can see the limp hands and fingers lying over those of the priest underneath. Through the mouth of the flayed one, we see the mouth of the living priest. (An Eastern anthropologist recently published a thesis in which he postulated that the sacrifice, particularly the later Aztec sacrifice, actually developed out of a need for protein—and that the Aztecs were in fact cannibalistic.)

While human sacrifice has been pervasive with man, it has not always been accepted by him. This was even true of the hierarchy of the period we are discussing. While a contemporary written record does not exist, the period is replete with legend preserved by the oral tradition. Much of this became part of Azteca folklore, and was later told to Catholic priests who wrote down these stories in Nahuatl—at that time the predominant language of Mexico. There is a famous legend which involved an attempt to terminate human sacrifice and to replace it with offerings of animals, insects, and objects. The story also describes the birth and deification of one of Mexico's most famous kings and deities, Quetzalcoatl—the feathered serpent.

The legend begins in 900 A.D. with the arrival of the Tolteca in Mexico. They were part of the Tolteca-Chichimeca-Otomi group of semi-nomads. Their leader was Mixcoatl or Cloud Serpent. One day, as he was hunting deer, Mixcoatl beheld a woman for whom he felt an immediate attraction. In fear, she ran. Mixcoatl attempted to stop her by shooting some arrows at her which to his surprise and admiration she parried away with her bare hand. She became known as Chimalma or shield hand—and was taken by Mixcoatl as his wife. Their child, some say conceived by a form of immaculate conception, was named Our Prince, or Topiltzin. Because he was born on the day of Ce Acatl or one reed, he became known as Ce Acatl Topiltzin. His father Mixcoatl was killed by his own brother before Topiltzin's birth and his mother Chimalma died in the process of childbirth. Thus, the great personage of Ce Acatl Topiltzin began his life without parents and had to be reared by his grandparents.

Early orphaned, our legendary hero is said to have attended a school for priests at Xochicalco, a site just south of Mexico City where the Pyramid of the Great Plumed Serpent may be seen today. So priestly, so pious was Ce Acatl Topiltzin that the high priest gave him the name of a god, Quetzalcoatl, or plumed serpent. So now Ce Acatl Topiltzin became known as Ce Acatl Topiltzin Quetzalcoatl—or born on the day of One Reed, Our Prince, The Plumed Serpent or the Serpent of Precious Feathers. And thus the confusion, or synonymy of the man and the god. Upon reaching manhood, Ce Acatl Topiltzin Quetzalcoatl avenged his father's death by slaying his treacherous uncle. Topiltzin Quetzalcoatl then assumed the leadership of the Tolteca. It was he who attempted to initiate cultural and religious reformation at Tula, the Tolteca capital. Legend continues that he welcomed a new and friendly people to the Toltecas. These immigrants were called the Nonoalca, or those who cannot speak correctly, and may have been the survivors of Teotihuacan. They apparently had a facility for sculpture and pottery making, and their work manifested a brief artistic florescence at Tula. In addition, Topiltzin Quetzalcoatl developed new and improved methods of agriculture and metallurgy and ways of making gold and silver ornaments. And for all of this the Tolteca loved and respected him. Fray Bernardino de Sahagún, who wrote the story of Topiltzin Quetzalcoatl at the time of the Conquest, recorded the words of the Azteca praising the man/god, the Plumed Serpent. The following version of this story may be found in Father Diego Durán's work, *The Aztecs:*

> "Quetzalcoatl reigned in Tula. Everywhere were abundance and happiness. Pumpkins were so large that a man could hardly embrace them with his arms. The ears of maize were wonderfully long, like the grinder of a metate. Corn was to be found everywhere scattered on the ground as if it were worthless. Ears of corn that were not perfect were used to light the fires. Cotton grew in colors: red, yellow, pink, purple, green, light green, reddish yellow, and spotted like a jaguar. All these colors it had by nature; it came out of the earth that way; it grew that way; no one had to dye it.
>
> Also there were birds of precious feathers: turquoise colored, shining green, yellow, their breasts the color of flame—precious birds of all colors, singing wondrously. And there grew the finest chocolate everywhere. The

Toltecs possessed so many precious stones and gold that they did not know what to do with them. All the inhabitants of Tula were rich and happy; they never knew poverty or sorrow; nothing was ever lacking in their homes."[4]

It was in the area of religion that Topiltzin Quetzalcoatl met with his greatest resistance. But Quetzalcoatl's attempts to end human sacrifice and to substitute animals, insects, and objects caused fear and confusion. And he desired to worship the benevolent Quetzalcoatl, the god of his father, instead of the principal Tolteca god Tezcatlipoca. Later, Azteca legend was to view the upheavals of the world as the result of a constant struggle between the benevolent Quetzalcoatl and Tezcatlipoca the god of the night, of the wicked, and of the wizards. Legend says that Tezcatlipoca and two other gods tricked Topiltzin Quetzalcoatl into looking into a magic mirror which made his body look old and wrinkled.

" 'My son, Quetzalcoatl, Precious Serpent, I have come to greet you. And I have come so that you may see your own body.' 'Why have you gone to so much trouble, O little grandfather?' Answered Quetzalcoatl. 'Where do you come from? What is this you say about my body?' 'O my child,' responded Tezcatlipoca, 'My priest, I am your servant and I have come from the slopes of the mountain of Nonohualco. Behold your body! My child, look at yourself, know yourself. You will now appear upon the mirror!' "

Seeing his ugliness Topiltzin feared that his subjects would no longer respect him and flee from Tula.[5]

" 'If my vassals could see my ugliness they would flee,' said Quetzalcoatl when he beheld himself in the mirror. His eyelids were swollen, his eyes were sunken in their sockets, and his face was bloated! He hardly looked like a man! 'My vassals will never see me,' exclaimed Quetzalcoatl, 'I will remain here alone!' "[6]

The three evil gods then prepared a stew for Topiltzin Quetzalcoatl made of "tomatoes, onions, chile, beans, and corn." They also prepared intoxicating liquor for him brewed from the maguey. He ate the stew but refused the pulque in fear of becoming drunk.

" 'I will not drink it,' he cried out. 'I am fasting. Perhaps it will kill me!' 'Just taste it with your little finger; it is angry pulque, it is strong pulque.' With his little finger Quetzalcoatl tasted it. 'Little grandfather,' he said, 'I am going to drink three cups of it!' 'You will drink four!' exclaimed the wizards. Soon they gave him his fifth cup. And when he had drunk they gave each of his

[4]Diego Durán, *The Aztecs* (New York: Orion Press, 1964), p. 326.
[5]Durán, p. 327.
[6]Durán, p. 327.

vassals five cups. Then Ilhuimecatl taught Quetzalcoatl a new song. 'This, my house of precious feathers! This, my house of red sea shells! I will have to abandon it, alas!' "[7]

After much prodding, he drank, became intoxicated and asked that his lovely sister be sent to him.

" 'Go, bring my sister, Quetzalpetlatl, Precious Mat, the priestess! She and I are going to drink together!' And so, his messengers went to the mountain of Nonohualco, where she was doing penance. 'Quetzalpetlatl, Precious Mat, daughter,' they said, 'Noble lady, you who live doing penance, we have come to take you away. Quetzalcoatl, the priest, awaits you, so that he and you may be united'. 'It is well, little grandfather, little messenger,' she answered, 'let us depart!' "[8]

When he awoke from his intoxication he realized that his drunken and incestous behavior had brought him shame and the loss of piety. Weeping and wailing he left Tula, together with his followers, as a self inflicted punishment.

" 'O wretch that I am,' moaned Quetzalcoatl. 'Let this day not be numbered among those I have spent in this my house. Ah, that I could remain here, but how can I? My body has become of clay! I have only anxiety and the desires of a slave! Nothing but anguish is left for me now!"
And when he had finished speaking, all his vassals and servants were also filled with sorrow and they wept.
'O little grandfather, O servant,' exclaimed Quetzalcoatl. 'I am going to abandon the city. Conceal everything, hide all we had possessed—Gladness, richness, all our possessions and wealth!' "[9]

Finally, he arrived at Cholula, in the present state of Puebla. He remained there with his followers for the next twenty years living among the descendants of the Olmeca. The chronicles say that he then journeyed to Coatzalcoalcos in the State of Veracruz with four young priests to whom he taught his doctrines. From here, on the date of Ce Acatl, he went to the place of Black and Red Painting promising to return from the east on the date of his departure, Ce Acatl. How fortuitous it was for Hernán Cortes that he should land in the place he called La Villa Rica de Vera Cruz—on the exact year of Ce Acatl, 1519. It is entirely possible that Topiltzin Quetzalcoatl went to the region of the Maya—Chichen Itza—

[7]Durán, p. 328.
[8]Durán, p. 328.
[9]Durán, p. 329.

for the Maya chroniclers show him arriving as Kukulcan—which is feathered serpent in Maya—in the years between 987 and 1000. But in this legend of Quetzalcoatl, the man and the god became one and inseparable. It is the legend of a man/god that is messianic—almost Christlike. For many who saw Hernán Cortes land on that fateful day in 1519, it was a prophecy fulfilled. Whether the massive influence of the Tolteca throughout Mexico was the result of one man, Topiltzin Quetzalcoatl, or whether it was the result of Tolteca military prowess, is difficult to ascertain. Nonetheless, from about 1000 A.D. on, Tolteca influence throughout south central Mexico and Yucatan is pervasive. It can be seen in the gods, in the art, the architecture, and the very life styles of the people.

The record of events between Topiltzin Quetzalcoatl's self exile and the last ruler of the Tolteca at Tula is almost nonexistent. The name of this last important ruler indicates that despite the departure of Topiltzin, the worship of the god Quetzalcoatl continued. The last king of the Tolteca was named One Snake Big Hand Plumed Serpent, or Ce Coatl Huemac Quetzalcoatl. For fifty of his sixty years as ruler of the Tolteca there was relative peace and calm. True, there is evidence of increasing militarism, but it was the last ten years of Huemac Quetzalcoatl's reign that were the most turbulent. From 1158 until his downfall ten years later, Huemac Quetzalcoatl suffered irreparable reverses. Drought and subsequent crop failure led to famine and a loss of faith by the masses. Even the legend about why the drought took place is damning to Huemac Quetzalcoatl. The story says that he was playing the sacred ball game with the god Tlaloc. Huemac won, but refused his reward of corn. Instead he wanted rich feathers and jade. Tlaloc, who was offended, honored his request but out of anger withheld the rain so the crops would not grow. Thus, he proved that corn is far more precious than rich feathers or jade.

Added to the problems of drought and internal dissension, Huemac and the Tolteca faced invasion from the north. The Chichimeca, driven south by the drought, challenged the disintegrating Tolteca society. General social fear intensified reliance on the military. There was an increase in war-like representations. Stelae and friezes of warriors and warrior priests replaced the earlier sculptures of Tolteca gods. Commerce and religious authority characteristic of the earlier Tolteca was replaced by a tightly knit militarism. The new militarism required loyalty and tribute and sought expansion and political subjugation through warfare.

The proud Tolteca traced their lineage to a mythical city or area of perfection called Tollan. They saw the city of Tollan as their claim to superiority. Even those who were hired mercenaries claimed they also were from Tollan, as did many of the conquered peoples who were incorporated into the Tolteca. The Tolteca in two hundred years had established political and religious dominance over a wide area north of

the great center of Teotihuacan. Their agricultural settlements pene-
trated into the unsettled areas to the north—as far as the present states of
Durango and Zacatecas. But the dividing line between the sedentary
agricultural settlements of the Tolteca and the nomadic hunter-gatherers
was always ill-defined, constantly shifting and changing. Undoubtedly,
the Tolteca incorporated some of the nomadic hunters into their mercenary military forces. But this was dangerous because it left the way open
for ambitious warriors to establish their own hegemony over productive
settled areas. Is it possible that this top-heavy mercenary militaristic
society the Tolteca created for their own safety and protection led, finally,
to their own downfall?

Legend of what happened to the Tolteca and why Tula was destroyed tells of a dissident group from within and an invading force from
without. And that is essentially what happened. The warrior class, exacting unreasonable tribute, made it impossible for peripheral settlements to
remain loyal and to exist. This was aggravated by ambitious mercenaries
in the provinces over whom control was almost impossible. Besides their
ambitious princes, there was the ever present threat from the less civilized
barbarians from the north, the Chichimeca. Chichimeca means dog
lineage or decendants of the dog, or in the pejorative sense, son of a dog.
Among the Chichimeca, probably the best known group was the Azteca.

The term Chichimeca is questionable since it was used as an insult by
factions of this invading culture. But events are often couched in rich
folklore. The eventual downfall of One Snake Big Hand Plumed Serpent
is a good example of myth symbolizing events. Heumac Quetzalcoatl
ordered a subservient culture, the Nonoalca, to bring him a woman four
hands wide in the buttocks. When they did, Huemac said: "Do you call
that four hands wide? Go out and find me another!" Feeling insulted, the
Nonoalca revolted and finally left Tula in 1168. Perhaps the rebellion of
the Nonoalca precipitated rebellion among the Tolteca themselves. For in
the same year of 1168, Huemac fled from Tula to Chapultepec—which is
now Chapultepec Park in Mexico City—and there he remained until his
death in 1174 from suicide or murder. With the exile of Huemac and his
eventual death, the great city of Tula fell victim to the invading barbarians
from the north, the great Chichimeca. Tula was destroyed by these
invaders, and little of the original magnificence of the city remains. In the
center of the area that has been excavated stands the Temple of the
Morning Star. Archeologists have placed on top of this pyramid, as
though guarding the remnants of this once great civilization, massive
stone carvings of Tolteca warriors. They stand as mute evidence of the
magnificence and power of the ruling warrior priest class of Tula. Most of
the facades and friezes which once covered the pyramids and buildings of
Tula have been destroyed. But on one part of the Temple of the Morning

Star, an interesting frieze remains, which gives us some evidence of the splendor of Tula. Displayed are rows of eagles feeding on human hearts. Alternating with the rows of eagles are walking jaguars, testimony to the feline cult so common throughout Middle America. In addition there are large columns with friezes of warriors with feathered headdress. Their ears are adorned with square ear plugs and they wear breastplates in the design of stylized butterflies. They wear wristlets and in their hands they carry curved swords and spear throwers. Wide bands wrap their knees, and on their feet are sandals decorated with feathered serpents.

These warrior representations and those on the Pyramid of the Morning Star are but a small amount of the archaeological evidence that could be available if extensive excavations are started. There are ball courts, extensive halls, and houses connected with passageways. But the vast area surrounding the central city contains many mounds that have yet to be excavated.

And what about the power vacuum created in south central Mexico by the collapse of the Tolteca? It was filled by two groups. The area in and around Mexico City was occupied and developed by groups of the Chichimeca. One such group was led by a warrior named Monster, or Xolotl. The codices tell us that he and his followers brought the bow and arrow to Mexico. From here, the stories become confusing and sometimes contradictory. Much is couched in legendary folklore. But we see a picture emerging. That of a semi-barbarian group of warriors and nomad hunters who conquer but become subjugated by the stronger social sys-system. The conquerors are the Chichimeca, and the stronger social system is that of the Tolteca. What finally emerges is the city of Mexico and the fabulous Aztec civilization.

Meanwhile, in the area south of Mexico City, other groups were developing independently. The Mixteca or Cloud people had occupied the area of Puebla. Four hundred miles further south, the Zapoteca were establishing their centers at the now famous archaeological sites of Mitla and Monte Albán. In time the Mixteca and the Zapoteca would clash and the Cloud People, as the Azteca called them, would prevail. The ruling family of the Zapoteca then fled the area of Oaxaca and moved to the Isthmus of Tehuantepec. But only temporarily, for such was the pattern of conquest and reconquest of these Pre-Columbian people. Even today, there are Zapotecan enclaves in the area of Oaxaca, where Spanish remains unspoken and where the culture remains unique.

The stubborn Zapoteca, who were never cowed by the powerful Azteca, left behind the extensive ruins of Mitla and Monte Albán in the area of Oaxaca. Monte Albán, which shows some Olmec stylistic influence, later became a major Zapotecan center. This vast and important center overlooks the city of Oaxaca. The man-made rock platform on which the site is built is 3,117 feet long and 1,476 feet wide. The site itself is 1,300 feet above the valley of Oaxaca floor and it is magnificently adorned with stone carvings of so-called dancers and calendar glyphs. There are ball courts, courtyards, pyramids and tombs. The great numbers of tombs suggests that important persons from surrounding areas were brought here for burial. Because there is no water source at this site, those who remained there must have depended on water carriers to supply the center with its needs. And the purpose of this great center, even today, is not known.

By 1300, Monte Albań was abandoned in the face of the Mixteca invasions. To the Valley of Oaxaca, the Mixteca brought with them the predominant Tolteca culture which was spreading throughout south-central Mexico. The Tolteca as a nation-state had disappeared, but the cultural flourescence which they began centuries before continued.

The Zapotecan center of Mitla, also in the Valley of Oaxaca, continued as a Zapotecan stronghold for almost another century. Finally, it too was temporarily abandoned as the Zapotecan rulers retreated to the Isthmus of Tehuantepec. Mitla is unique among all of the Pre-Columbian cities. Unlike others of this period, the buildings are not built on pyramids. They rather form a compound of low roof buildings surrounding a central quadrangle. The buildings exude a feeling of immensity that is contrasted sharply with the minute stone mosaics covering the walls of these structures. Over twenty varieties of patterns all emanate from a single motif, a stepped spiral which is a stylized head of a serpent. It is said that Mitla, with its cave-like rooms, represented the spirit of the inner earth. It was also the residence of a sacred priest who was ubiquitous and all powerful. This priest, called the "Great Seer," had the power to place himself in a trance and communicate with the gods and transmit the messages of the gods to the faithful.

After the decline of Mitla, the Zapoteca maintained their stronghold in Tehuantepec, only to be challenged again years later by the emerging Mexica-Azteca at Mexico City. Ironic, is it not, that the Azteca failed in their attempt to permanently conquer the Zapoteca because they united with their former enemies, the Mixteca in a combined effort to ward off Azteca domination. And so the cycles of predominance and conquest continued.

But the demise of Tula did not mean the demise of the Tolteca. Just as the earlier Olmeca spread their people and influence throughout south central Mexico so did these Tolteca. The area around Lake Texcoco and the Valley of Mexico was heavily influenced by the Tolteca culture. The Tolteca laid the foundation for Mexico City upon which the Axteca later expanded. Tolteca influence was manifest as far south as the Yucatan Peninsula. The Mayan city of Chichen-Itza shows strong Toltecan influence in its art and architecture. Chichen-Itza has at least two distinct stages of development. The second stage is strikingly similar to the Theocratic-Military period at Tula. The arrival of the Tolteca at Chichen-Itza is also incorporated in Mayan folklore which tells of a man/deity who brought a cultural flowering to the city. He was called Kukulcan, which in Mayan means feathered or plumed serpent.

CHAPTER 5

"One Imix, Eight Pop"

The following are the twenty days of the Mayan religious calendar: Imix, Ik, Akbal, Kan, Chicchan, Cimi, Manik, Lamat, Muluc, Oc, Chuen, Eb, Ben, Ix, Men, Cib, Caban, Eznab, Cauac, Ahau. The Maya also had a secular calendar of eighteen months plus the five unlucky days of Uayeb. This gave them an accurate solar year of 365 days—a remarkable achievement which only the ancient Egyptians rivaled.

As social systems become more complex and stratified, as technology increases and thinking becomes more diverse and abstract, nomad-hunter becomes classified into industry—industry becomes culture, and culture is more likely to be called a civilization.

Unquestionably, the Maya constituted one of the most complex and sophisticated Pre-Columbian civilizations. In addition to having all of the artifacts and tools of an industry and culture, the Maya perfected a partially phonetic hieroglyphic system of writing which to this day has only been partially deciphered. Much of this writing was recorded in accordion or screen-style folded bark paper which served as books. This is called by modern scholars a codex or, in the plural, codices. The early Spanish priests saw the codex as heretical and in their desire to destroy all traces of paganism they destroyed irreplacable Maya codices which might have acted as a Rosetta Stone, or cipher with which to unlock the secrets of the Maya. A number of Spanish priests were guilty of this senseless destruction, but Bishop Diego de Landa stands out as the most infamous of all. He wrote: "We found a large number of books of these characters, and as they contained nothing but superstition and lies of the devil, we burned them all, which the Indians regretted to an amazing degree and which caused them great anguish."

But Landa did admit that those codices were filled with information; in his discussion of education he wrote: "The high priest appointed priests for the towns . . . examining them in the sciences and ceremonies . . . provided them with books and sent them forth. And they employed themselves in the duties of the temples and teaching their sciences, as well as in writing books about them. The sciences they taught were the counting of the years, months and days, the feasts and ceremonies, the administration of sacraments, the fateful days and diseases, and antiquities, and how to read and write with letters and characters with which they wrote, and drawing which illustrated the meaning of the writings."[10]

All that remains today are a few scattered and undeciphered codices and thousands of glyphs carved into the stone stelae and ornate temples. Despite all the volumes of books written on the Maya—probably more than any other Pre-Columbian civilization—the amount of definitive knowledge is limited. The speculations and disagreements are unlimited.

It is generally believed that Maya civilization began in the Peten area of Guatemala around the birth of Christ. This dating might appear to be a little late. And it probably is. It is believed the area was occupied by Maya progenitors for about 3,000 years before that. But there is general disagreement about where Maya cultural antecedents began. The late Sylvanus Morley, a scholar on the Maya civilization, felt the Peten area in Guatemala was the most likely place. He singled out two sites in this area to prove his point. They contain early Maya calendrical dating. A limestone stelae from Tikal is dated at 292 A.D., while only eleven miles away at Uaxactun there is a stelae with a dating of 328 A.D. But work done by the Mexican archaeologists Miguel Covarrubias, Alfonso Caso, and many others points the finger of origin to the Olmeca of Veracruz. This theory is becoming increasingly popular among archaeologists as earlier datings of bar-dot calendars are found in this region. Nonetheless, archaeologists date the beginning of Maya history at 292 A.D. Anything before this is considered Maya prehistory and is extremely difficult to document.

The great Maya civilization is divided into two separate and distinct periods which archaeologists call the Classic and Post-Classic. The Classic consists of literally hundreds of sites that encompass three distinct time periods. These periods span from 320 A.D. to 987 A.D. All of the great centers of the Classic period were abandoned and have fallen into ruin.

[10]From Frederick Peterson, *Ancient Mexico: An Introduction to the Pre-Hispanic Cultures* (New York: Capricorn, 1962) eighth impression, p. 233.

Today, four sites stand out as representative of the various periods of the Classic. They are Tikal in Guatemala; Bonampak in the Mexican state of Chipas; Palenque in the state of Chiapas; and Tulum on the far eastern shore of the Yucatan Peninsula. Tulum spanned both the Classic and Post-Classic periods as did several other sites.

The three most characteristic sites of the Post-Classic are Chichen-Itza, Mayapan, and again Tulum. All three are located in northern Yucatan. Of the three, Chichen-Itza stands out as the largest and most important Maya center. In the northern area of the Yucatan, near the port of Progreso, there have been recent and extensive excavations in a center known as Dzibilchaltun. The buildings are not as impressive here as with the other three sites. Nonetheless, the discovery of artifacts and other remnants of Mayan civilization may some day reveal much about these mysterious people.

At all of these sites, the Maya had a tradition of erecting massive stone stelae or stone pillars. On these they not only recorded dates but also events which represented the actual daily lives of the Maya. They painted exquisite frescoes which are extremely valuable in learning about Maya society. Both Classic and Post-Classic may have had highly structured societies that at times acted independently and other times were under control of another. At the head of each city-state was a chief who normally received his power by primogeniture in perpetuity. That is, the eldest son by the principal wife—if he were capable—would inherit the mantle of power forever and ever. Although he was advised by a council of principal chiefs, priests, and other important persons, he exercised the final authority over internal and external affairs. He appointed the chiefs of the secondary or associated centers and villages; and it is believed that he might also have exercised a certain amount of religious authority.

Each center had an elected war chief—a sort of secretary of defense. He commanded a permanent militia that was called upon only in the event of an emergency—such as the defense of the city. When not engaged in active service, the militia returned to their homes and carried out their normal community activities. The Classic period, once believed to be relatively peaceful, was in fact highly militaristic. Their weapons, however, were limited to wooden and obsidian spears and swords. The bow and arrow were not introduced to the Maya until the Post-Classic period.

There were five major classes in this great civilization: the nobles, the priests, the merchants, the mass of the common free people, and the slaves. At the top was the nobility which included the local chiefs of the dependent capitals. They received a salary and collected tribute. The chief exercised executive, legislative and judicial powers. He governed with the aid of two or three of his counselors. Laws were enforced with fines to be paid in cotton or cacao beans. The most severe form of punishment was slavery.

Second to the nobles were the priests. Their power must have been great for they were not only responsible for ceremonial activities but also they were the mathematicians and astronomers as well. With the Maya ability to generally forecast certain natural phenomena, the priests' supernatural powers must have appeared awesome. The priesthood itself was structured with assistants who were responsible for various aspects of religious ceremonies such as conducting the heart sacrifice. J. Eric Thompson, a foremost Maya scholar, believes that the status of the priests must have been greater than that of the nobles themselves.

Maya religion spoke of a creator god, a supreme diety called Hunab Ku. As in other Pre-Columbian religions, the Maya viewed their gods dualistically. There were good gods and bad gods. Or to put it another way, the benevolent and the malevolent. The benevolent gods maintained life-sustaining systems and brought thunder, lightning and rain. They made the earth fertile and brought forth the crops and favored the sustenance of life. The malevolent gods brought drought, or hurricanes and floods, and instigated conflict and war.

The Maya generally believed in thirteen heavens or skies, each stacked one upon the other and each controlled by a particular god. There were also nine underworlds, each controlled by a malevolent god. The lowest was the domain of the god of death, Ah Puch. To receive favor from the gods they must be appeased and the Maya had a number of ways of accomplishing this. Probably the best known was through the sacrifice of offerings to the gods. Offerings were made in the form of precious items of gold, silver, copper or jade. Or they could also be foodstuffs— corn, beans, tortillas, fruits, tobacco, or even animals. Human sacrifice was still offered, but in many instances it consisted of merely drawing blood from various parts of the body such as the ear, cheeks, tongue, lower lip, or genitals and sprinkling that blood on the idols which represented the god. Although Hunab Ku was the supreme being, the creator of all things, it was his son, Itzamna, that played the major role in the Maya pantheon. Itzamna is pictured as a toothless old man with sunken cheeks, and an aquiline nose. He oftentimes wears a beard. Itzamna, the god of the skies and of day and night, was the most benevolent god. His antithesis was the most malevolent, the most evil god of death, war, and human sacrifice, Ah Puch. He is usually represented by a skeleton, with rattles and bells, and is accompanied by a dog, an owl and a moan bird—a special kind of owl; three animals of evil design.

Chac, the god of rain, also occupied an important place in the Maya pantheon. He controlled wind, rain, thunder and lightning. Because of his power, he was the god of fertility and agriculture. Practically all of the more recent Maya sites have elaborate representations of Chac. And he looks suspiciously like Talaoc who was so pervasive in Teotihuacan. His face is depicted with a jutting curlique snout and either two prominent teeth or a row of feline teeth. Itzamna, Ah Puch, and Chac are only a few of the many gods which the Maya worshipped in both the Classic and Post-Classic periods. But one of the most important gods was added after the later period of the Post-Classic. He was Kukulkan, which in Maya means plumed serpent. His arrival in Chichen Itza and Mayapan roughly corresponds to the legendary departure of Topiltzin Quetzalcoatl from the Tolteca capital of Tula. Was it, in fact, a historical reality turned legend? Could Kukulkan have actually been the self-exiled Toltecan prince, Ce Acatl Topiltzin Quetzalcoatl?

Human sacrifice, flaying, and even ritual cannibalism became part of the later period of Maya. This was probably encouraged by the Tolteca arriving from the Mexican highlands. One of the most sacred repositories for sacrifice was the sacred cenote or well at Chichen Itza. Beginning in 1905, the cenote has been repeatedly dredged and explored. Searchers have found myriad items made from gold, copper, and jade in addition to a number of human skulls, both male and female. The finds have included "masks, cups, bells, pendants, bracelets, ear-rings, buttons, rings, ceremonial hatchets, beads from a necklace, and pendants in jade, wooden spear throwers, a sacrificial knife, fragments of cotton fabric, bone or shell ornaments, and pellets of copal." Since the Maya had almost no metallurgy, the high incidence of metal objects at the cenote of Chichen Itza suggests the well must have been a place of sacred pilgrimage. And it had attracted peoples from areas far to the south and from the Valley of Mexico to the north.

The entire life of a Maya was involved in religion. He was born into religion, he lived it, and he died in religion. Paul Rivet, the noted anthropolist, wrote: "Without exaggerating, it can be said that every moment as well as every act of his existence was associated with ceremonies, the necessity for which was impressed on his mind in an uncompromising manner. The day of the sacred year of 260 days when he was born, as it were determined his destiny, decided which gods were favourable to him and which were hostile."[11]

Religion involved literally everything. Birth, the way a child was carried, puberty rites, marriage, illness, health, and finally death, all had religious significance and involved religious ritual and ceremony. Some believe that religion exacted so much sacrifice and tribute from the people that they revolted against the priesthood and caused the downfall of the Old Empire.

The largest class of people were engaged in agriculture, primarily the cultivation of maize. And farming was not a simple matter. Much of the land which the Maya cultivated was either jumgle thicket or heavy forest. First, the trees had to be cut down and burned. Seeds were then

[11]Paul Rivet, *Mayan Cities*, trans. Miriam and Lionel Cochan (London: Elek Books, 1960), p. 80.

planted in the ashes that remained. Harvesting was done collectively in the middle of the rainy season.

In addition to maize, the Maya planted cacao, beans, calabashes sweet potatoes, tomatoes, manioc, peppers, and a number of other root foods and spices. Cotton was also cultivated and the fibre of the cactus, commonly called sisal, was used to make rope and material.

The Maya also hunted and ate birds, deer, and the peccary, a piglike animal. They domesticated the turkey and a fat, hairless and barkless dog. This was in addition to the hounds they kept to aid in the hunt. They developed a stingless bee from which they obtained honey—which served both as a food and the base for an alcoholic drink.

In addition to feeding their families they had to support the nobles and priests. This burden was increased by the extraction of heavy tribute and oppressive offerings to the gods. The farmers lived in little villages clustered throughout the agricultural area. Their homes were of sticks covered with a clay or adobe and topped with a thatched roof. Some of the people were engaged in the construction of buildings, pyramids, and stelae. Others quarried rock and transported the material to the construction sites.

The average man and woman awoke at four or five in the morning and lit the household fire by means of boring a stick of hardwood into a softer wood. After a simple morning meal of either tortillas and beans or just a liquid paste made of ground corn called atole, most men went to the forest to work the land. Others went out to hunt or engage in other occupations. For the women, practically the whole day was spent in the preparation of food. The maize was shelled, cooked, ground, and patted into tortillas. The main meal, an hour before sunset, was comprised of "tortillas, beans, eggs, a little meat, vegetables, and chocolate. . . ." After the meal the men took daily hot baths in wooden basins, hollowed out of a cedar trunk. One more light meal was eaten before bedtime at eight or nine o'clock.

For the slaves, who were prisoners of war, orphans, or criminals, daily life was comprised of unceasing labor. They were beasts of burden, not only for the construction of pyramids and temples, but also for carrying heavy loads of water long distances—sometimes from distant underground sources. Their rights and privileges were limited and they were (virtually) bought and sold

Thus we have found a complex social and religious structure, which contains the hallmarks of civilization. Aspects of technology are also indicators of civilization. Three stand out: writing, chronology, and the resultant knowledge of astronomy.

It is in the area of writing that the Maya excelled. Yet this is the aspect of Maya civilization of which we know the least. Of the thousands of codices which were written by the Maya, only three remain. One is divided in two parts and both parts together are in the Museo de América ín Madrid. The other two are located in Paris and in Dresden. The Dresden Codex concerns astronomy more than others, but is also religious and ritualistic—as are the other two in Paris and Madrid. After much study, experts have been able to decipher the hieroglyphs to the extent that Maya mathematics and astronomy may be understood. The Maya employed a vigesimal or base 20 system rather than our decimal or base 10 system. Using bars as five and dots as one, the Maya counted vertically from the bottom up. Each number appearing above the previous one represented a number twenty times larger. They also used the zero—although known in ancient Mesopotamia—long before Western Europe. The zero was diagrammed by a shell. Thus one could write the number twenty by placing a dot on top of a shell. Keep in mind that each number or set of numbers above the previous one was twenty times greater. So a dot above a shell has a value twenty times greater than the dot which is one. Since it appears on the second line up, it is worth twenty. The number twenty-seven would be a bar and two dots on the lower level. That

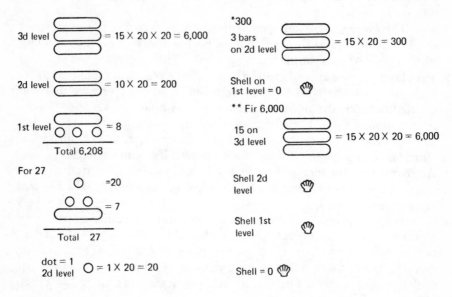

FIGURE 3.

equals seven. Then place a dot only on the next level. That's your twenty unit. Twenty plus the original seven is twenty-seven. Let's look at 300. Place your shell on the first level, then place three bars totaling fifteen on the second level. Ah, but the second level is times twenty. So we get twenty times fifteen or three hundred. Simple, no? Well, if you put fifteen on the third level and placed shells at the first two levels, you would get fifteen times twenty times twenty or a sum total of six thousand.   The Maya also had numerical glyphs represented by a series of head designs—portraits of gods—numbering one through twenty. Of the more than 850 glyphs catalogued, about one-third have been tentatively deciphered. This, of course, includes the bar-dot numerical system. It is assumed that the bar-dot system is fully understood. But there is disagreement. Upon close inspection, one finds the empty spaces in the bars and dots either left blank, or filled-in. Some of the spaces have hash marks, crescents, dots, x's crosses, and other designs. Are these spaces merely decorative or do they have numerical or ideological value? The secret might be forever locked in the stone on which these designs have been carved. Perhaps some day a "Rosetta" stone or deciphering tool may answer this perplexing question.

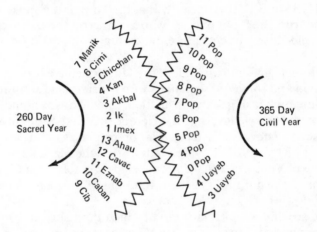

FIGURE 4. Diagram of how the two Maya Calendars operated together. Adapted from Sylvanus G. Morley. *The Ancient Maya,* revised by George W. Brainerd. stanford University Press, third edition, 1956, p. 234. Drawing made by Samuel Mayo.

Astronomy and chronology were inextricably a part of the Maya system of writing. Both had a religious orientation or basis. The Maya were deeply interested in dating and this has helped to give us a clearer picture of their life patterns. At first, they had a sacred or ritual calendar with a basic year of 260 days. Later it was coordinated with a solar year calendar of 365 days. The 260-day year had thirteen "weeks" of twenty days each. Each of the twenty days had a *name*, just as each of our seven days of the week has a name, and was combined with thirteen numbers. For example, since the first day was called Imix, one could have a date of One Imix, Two Imix, up to Thirteen Imix.

Coupled with this religious-ritual calendar was a non-religious solar-based calendar of 365 days. The solar or secular calendar had eighteen "months" or periods of twenty days each for a total of 360 days. Added at the end were the five unlucky days of Uayeb. Chronological dating was often represented by a meshing of both the religious and the secular/solar calendars. As for example, the first of the eighteen periods was named Pop. Hence, we could have the dating of One Imix, Eight Pop. Because the two calendars were used together in a sort of "Calendar Round," it took fifty-two years before identical month-day combinations would again reappear. And to make matters more complex and yet remarkably accurate, the calendars were put together to form the Maya "Long Count Calendar," an astonishing achievement for then and now.

While there is disagreement on the earliest known Maya (date) several scholars have placed the beginning of their calendrical dating at August 11, 3114 B.C. It is uncanny that the Maya often spoke of having originated from the four "Bacabs" who came across the seas to escape the floods. Some Bible students place the dating of the great flood at 3000 B.C.

With their mathematic ability, the Maya calculated the movements of the moon and some of the planets with considerable accuracy. In the study of lunations, using Maya calculations, modern astronomers, with all their advanced knowledge, show a difference of only one day in 300 years. The Dresden Codex also has a calendar of the planet Venus which covers a period of 384 years. The Codex tells us that the Maya knew that "five revolutions of Venus, or 2,920 days, equaled eight solar years." And Maya calculation of the durations of the revolutions of the planet Venus varies only slightly from recent calculations.

And so, this complex civilization which flourished in two separate and distinct periods leaves us with as many questions as we have answers. The hieroglyphs on the pyramids, temples, stelae, and codices are augmented by several Maya language histories recorded phonetically in Latin alphabet after the conquest. Out of the ruins of these massive cities, archaeologists and anthropologists are attempting to reconstruct the life and history of a most significant people. Each day new and important information is uncovered which might someday complete the puzzle of the great Maya civilization.

CHAPTER 6

The People
of the Fifth Sun

There are many myths and legends concerning these people called the Aztecs. Some describe the pyramids they built, the wars they waged and the human sacrifices they made. It has been said that their Emperor Montezuma was terrible and savage in his deeds. But the Aztecs were far more complex than these simple stereotypes lead us to believe. They had a great civilization with a rich and varied history. Fortunately, much of this history was preserved and recorded for us by early priests, conquistadores, Spanish chroniclers, and the Azteca themselves.

Our best information on Azteca society comes from the Franciscan father, Fray Bernardino De Sahagun. This remarkable priest arrived in Mexico shortly after the conquest in 1529. He began to learn Nahuatl while sailing to New Spain from six Aztecs who were being returned home. For the next thirty years he interviewed Aztecs and then wrote down their statements in phoneticized Nahuatl. Of the many volumes he recorded, twelve remain. But they are the foundation of our knowledge of the Azteca.

The Azteca believed they originally came from a place called "the region of the seven caves" or Chicomoztoc. They migrated south to the place called Aztlan which meant either "the land of the Heron or crane," or "place of Whiteness." But the god Huitzilopochtli told them they were the chosen people and to continue their wanderings until they came to an

island in the middle of a lake. Here they would find an eagle perched on a
cactus in the act of devouring a serpent, and it would be here they should
build a great city. The Azteca must have entered Mexico around the
middle of the twelfth century, and after years of wandering and warring
they arrived at Chapultepec about the year 1300. Chapultepec in Nahuatl
means grasshopper hill. For twenty-five years the Azteca hunted, fished,
and fought off hostile tribes. In 1325 they crossed to an island in the
western portion of Lake Texcoco. Here they found the eagle devouring
the serpent while perched on a cactus. They knew the prophecy of
Huitzilopochtli was fulfilled so they built a pyramid and temple to him on
that spot. In honor of the high priest Tenoch and the god Huitzilopochtli,
who was also called Mexitli, they named their new city the place of the god
Mexitli and possibly the priest Tenoch, or Mexico-Tenochtitlan. Tenoch
can also mean "next to or at the stone cactus." Tenochtitlan is the site of
modern Mexico City and the National Cathedral is built on the same spot
where the pyramid and Temple Mayor precinct once was located.

But reality does not always square with legend. And the truth is that
the Azteca were not the chosen people looking for the signs of
Huitzilopochtli—rather they were barbarian marauders who served as
mercenaries employed by the Tepaneca of Azcapaz to protect their merchantmen and their trade routes. When they became strong enough, they
challenged their Tepaneca employers and established Azteca rule over
this great merchant center. Thus by 1473, the fledgling city of Tenochtitlan, one of the three major cities of the great Aztec empire, had gained
control over the older commercial center of Tlatelolco.

Still, the Azteca had not yet gained predominance over the Valley of
Mexico. Tenochtitlan was fast becoming the military center of a Triple
Alliance which included the city of Tlacopan and the cultural center of
Texcoco. From Tenochtitlan marched the military thrust of the imperial
Mexica-Azteca. They considered themselves the chosen "People of the
Sun" and believed they were "destined by Huitzilopochtli to become
masters of the world and instruments for the fulfillment of his will." To
return the favor of the gods, they offered them "the magic substance of
life," human blood—through human sacrifice—which was practiced on a
massive scale in the latter years of Azteca rule. (In 1977, an American
anthropologist even advanced the theory that human sacrifice among the
Azteca was really for the purpose of obtaining needed protein for an
expanding population.)

Until 1500, it was Texcoco that prevailed as the cultural and intellectual center of the triple alliance. This uneasy alliance with the militaristic
Mexica-Azteca did not prevent the Texcocans from bringing a cultural
flowering to the valley under their fabulous king, Nezahualcoyotl—which
means fasting or hungry coyote in Nahuatl. Under this great poet-

philosopher the Valley of Mexico experienced a golden age of learning and development.

Nezahualcoyotl promulgated a series of laws which were considered fair and just for the time. In engineering, Texcoco was far ahead of its time. It became a rich agricultural unit. With the construction of dams, canals, and irrigation systems, marginal land was made productive. A massive dike which bore the name of Nezahualcoyotl was built across the lagoon of Lake Texcoco, which not only insured fresh water entering the irrigation system, but prevented the flooding of Tenochtitlan.

Nezahualcoyotl had a reputation for being talented, wise, creative, and a law giver. His code of laws became a standard legal code for the civilization. His exquisite open-air bath cut into natural rock had a view of the lake. He cultivated his botanical gardens, and maintained a harem of more than one hundred wives. But it was in poetry that he has achieved a lasting fame. Several of his poems were translated into Spanish and they form a part of the national literature of present day Mexico. The following is a sample of Nezahualcoyotl's poetry:

> When you depart from this life to the next, oh King Yoyontzin,
> The time will come when your vassals will be broken and destroyed
> And all your things will be engulfed by oblivion . . .
> For this is the inevitable outcome of all powers, empires, and domains;
> Transitory are they and unstable.
> The time of life is borrowed,
> In an instant it must be left behind.[12]

Unfortunately, by 1500 the Mexica-Azteca had gained control over this great society of Texcoco. Now Azteca influence—merchant and military—extended far beyond the centers of Tenochtitlan, Tlatelolco, and Texcoco. The merchantmen, the Pochteca, together with the military carried the Azteca banners throughout Middle America.

Examining the life of a Pochteca merchant might give one some insight into the Azteca society. This merchant was a prominent man and his name was Coatl. He was the head of an Azteca Calpulli, which some have called kinship or familial clan and others believe was a clan responsible for the distribution of goods and services. Coatl saw himself as the head of a far flung family whose members resided as far away as Guatemala. As the head of his Calpulli, the Pochteca was the nominal owner of a vast area of land, far more than he himself could cultivate. So in order to find the human resources necessary for successful agriculture, Coatl sent a number of letters to the members of his family throughout

[12]Miguel Leon Portilla, *Aztec Thought and Culture*, trans. Jack Emory Davis (Norman, Oklahoma: University of Oklahoma Press, 1963), p. 72.

Mexico. In these letters, he invited these people to come and be active members of his Calpulli.

If the family member accepted, he traveled on foot to the residence of Coatl who lived in Cuernavaca, surrounded by waterfalls, lush growth, and a mild climate averaging 75°. A Spaniard described some other Azteca homes which might serve as our example. The main house was of

> "stone and lime with several tall chambers and great patios. The flat [roof was] made of good wood, the walls were so well polished that the first Spaniards to see them thought they were made of silver. The floors were of mortar, perfectly levelled and polished. Many houses had towers and roof crests, an atrium with trees, and an orchard with pools. The largest houses had two doors, one leading to the street and the other to the canal or canoe passage. Neither entrance had wooden doors because doors were not used, believing that their houses were well defended by the severity of their laws against thieves. To keep people from peering inside they had the entrance covered with a reed curtain."

When his new farmer arrived, Coatl allowed him to build his family's dwelling onto the main house, thus forming a compound of buildings not unlike today's townhouses. But the Pochteca were merchants, not gentlemen farmers. There were two kinds of tradesmen, the local merchants and the export-importers. Coatl was not a local shop keeper for, as always, romance and status were connected with trading over long distances. The local traders dealt with items of relatively low value—utilitarian items. Practically the same rules that applied to trade in Pre-Columbian Mexico still exist today—and so do some of the markets. In Toluca, thirty miles from Mexico City, the market that flourished five hundred years ago still flourishes today. Every Friday, the local merchants bring their wares to sell or to trade. Most of the times are of small value—mainly food and handicrafts. There are fruits and vegetables, sausages, wine, blankets, needle work, and hand woven baskets. The large market has canvas covered stalls, encompassing an area of four square blocks, about the same size as in the days of the Azteca. And most of the Indian merchants follow the rules that have existed for centuries. For example, most will not sell their wares outside of the market, or on non-market days.

But Coatl would never have been found selling in a regional market. He was an export-importer. As a result, he had wealth and fame. He or his subordinates traveled great distances trading items of great value—items for the nobility. From Tenochtitlan they exported "slaves, rich clothing, gold and precious stones, obsidian, herbs, red ochre, cocyineal dye, copper bells, and skeins of rabbit fur." These items were traded from the Gulf lowlands all the way to Guatemala. From there he imported the rich feathers of the Quetzal bird, "turquoise, jade, jaguar skins, feather cloaks, shirts, slaves, and cacao . . ." The cacao bean had a dual purpose. It was—and still is—used as a beverage. But the Pochteca also acquired the cacao bean for use as money.

Of the Pochteca's travels and trade, Fray Bernardino de Sahagún wrote the following:

> "These merchants go over the entire land in pursuit of business, buying in one part and selling in another. There is no place where they do not seek something to buy or sell, no matter how hot or cold, no matter how rough the way may be. They are daring enough to go even to enemy lands, and they are very astute at dealing with strangers, learning their languages or treating them with benevolence to attract their trade. They also know where there are skins of valuable animals and where to sell them for the best price."[13]

Yes, they were daring enough to trade in enemy lands. Because of the need for trade, Coatl and other Pochteca had for years developed unwritten treaties with enemy camps which permitted them to trade in special commercial sanctuaries. These areas lay outside the battle-grounds. They were ruled by commercial princes and maintained a measure of political autonomy. Even Coatl maintained a measure of personal and political autonomy. The Pochteca had their own courts, judges, and even their own officers of administration. Their religious customs were unique to their class. They worshipped their own special god Yacatecuhtli, or Nose Lord, which involved their daily lives and their trading enterprises.

Unlike other men of rank, Coatl avoided service to the state. He avoided working in the fields that belonged to the elite and in which the commoners worked. Pochteca, as others, were required to pay tribute to the high nobility, but it was in items which they traded instead of work. "They gave clothing, feathers, jewels, and stones; or whatever they traded." And Coatl did provide the state with one other important function. As a long distance tradesman, he was also in an excellent position to spy. And spy he did. He supplied the state with valuable strategic information about its enemies; their strength, location of armies, and other vital military intelligence. Possibly this is why the unwritten alliances accorded him by enemies of the state were not always honored. Possibly this is why Coatl, and other Pochteca, traveled in groups for it was not unexpected that he might have to fight his way out of an ambush.

It sounds like Coatl lived a life of glory and privilege with only limited danger. But as the poet-king Nezahualcoyotl said, "the time will come when your vassals will be broken and destroyed, and all your things will be engulfed by oblivion . . ." This was the danger the Pochteca faced

[13]Peterson, *Ancient Mexico*, p. 173.

daily, especially as the Mexica-Azteca state became more militaristic. As time passed, the military nobles assumed a measure of authority over the Calpulli of Coatl; and jealous of his semiautonomous power, they began to restrict his actions and prerogatives. Some of the more wealthy Poch-teca were actually put to death, and their wealth was distributed among the warriors and nobles. So many like Coatl began to feign poverty and to act humble, attempting to minimize their wealth, lest they wind up with no wealth at all.

And as all things change, so did the later years of the Mexica-Azteca. The Calpulli and the merchant Pochteca's power and lustre declined while the military's increased. The Pochteca's authority as kinship leader of the Calpulli continued, but it was overshadowed by the power of royal commissars. These commissars exacted tribute from the worker-peasants of the Calpulli in order to enrich themselves and the military. But Coatl could remember the good days when he proudly walked through his splendid gardens past the rows of the sun dried brick houses of the commoners. And although his position was now somewhat lessened, he still enjoyed privileges far above the commoner, the peasant—and cer-tainly far above the slave class. Perhaps a servile class would be a more accurate name, for the slaves fell into three categories: Those who sold themselves into servitude in order to pay debts or feed their family in times of famine; those who were criminals and were making payment to the victim or the state; and prisoners of war. Prisoner of war slaves were always women and children because the men were quickly sacrificed to the waiting gods. Slaves were not chattel property in the classic sense and they had the rights of many citizens which included the right to limited contractual slavery, the right to own land, and even the right to own other slaves!

Coatl owned slaves and he still had the right to send his sons to the calmecac, a school primarily reserved for nobles and dignitaries. Ordi-nary citizens either educated their children themselves or sent them to a school called telpochcalli, where Azteca morals and ethics were taught. By attending the calmecac, his sons would have a better chance of joining the priesthood or winning a high state office. Thus, there was social mobility among the Azteca, and education was one driving force, as it is in Western civilization. Education at the calmecac was difficult and austere with little or no short term reward. Nightly, the boys went alone into the mountains to draw blood from their legs or ears with the thorns of the agave. This placated the gods. Sahaguń recorded advice given by a father to his son who was entering the calmecac. "Listen, my son, you are not going to be honoured, nor obeyed, nor esteemed. You are going to be looked down upon, humiliated and despised. Every day you will cut agave-thorns for penance, and you will draw blood from your body with these spines and you will bathe at night even when it is very cold . . . Harden your body to the cold . . . and when the time comes for fasting do not go and break your fast, but put a good face upon both fasting and penance."[14]

Education was mainly religious. But students were also taught manners, respect for authority, holy songs, Indian astrology, dream interpretations, and calendrical reckoning.

Only Coatl's sons could attend the calmecac. Unless his daughter was to be a priestess—which meant she would be consecrated to the temple— her education was entrusted to her mother. She learned to grind the maize and make tortillas. She learned to cook and sew and generally prepare for marriage and raising a family—just as her mother and grandmother before her. The codices show that, except for the priestess, women contented themselves with the domestic duties of the home.

And so Coatl's Mexica-Azteca civilization appears similar to many aspects of modern mixed capitalism. Society was stratified, but one could climb the social ladder. People at all levels carried out their functions in order to make the social order work. Yet there appeared to be deep seated contending social orders that might appear destructive. According to Eric Wolf, "it nevertheless possessed one powerful cement for social units in its doomsday ideology. The individual Mexica acquired with his very mother's milk a sense of collective mission in a world balanced upon the edge of destruction."[15]

The Azteca's myth of creation manifested this "doomsday ideology." It involved a constant struggle between two gods of good and evil; dark and light; benevolence and malevolence. Quetzalcoatl, the god of wind, agriculture, and benevolence, is constantly in battle with Texcatlipocha, the evil god of the night, of death, of the wicked and the wizards. These two gods fought and their alternating victories caused the creation and destruction of the world four successive times. Each destruction ended in a cataclysm which destroyed mankind. The destructions included the devouring of men; destruction by wind; devastation by a rain of fire; and finally drowning by a great flood. Each time the sun was destroyed. In this, the fifth sun, which the gods created by their own sacrifice, the Azteca lived under the cloud of impending doom. They believed themselves chosen by the gods to defend the fifth sun. By living a righteous life, they supported the forces of good against those of doom. The arguments vary as to why the Azteca sacrificed so many thousands of people each year. In this they were not surpassed. Perhaps it was a gift to the gods who had sacrificed their own kind to create the fifth sun. Perhaps they believed that sacrifice would maintain the balance of the heavens. Or perhaps they felt if they fed humans to the forces of good, they would

[14]Sahagun, *Florentine Codex*, Vol. I, p. 298 and Soustelle, p. 170.
[15]Wolf, *Sons of the Shaking Earth*, p. 144.

56 The People of the Fifth Sun

prevent the devastating cyclical famines. Or perhaps the religious argument was added in order to sanction the need for protein. The average Aztecan concerned himself little with the abstruse theological arguments of the priestly class. The complexities of the religion—ofttimes contradictory—and the ubiquitous nature of the gods were accepted at face value. Few questioned, fewer cared.

Perhaps it was the growing power of the military or the ever flashing sacrificial knife; but the Azteca, who lived on the edge of doom, had sealed their own. Long before the arrival of the European, the Azteca began their own decline. Perhaps they were never really a great civilization in the first place. Eric Wolf wrote:

". . . their power proved more apparent than real. There is little profit in predicting what might have happened had the Mexica been able to work out their destiny undisturbed. Perhaps they would have consolidated and integrated their vast holding more efficiently and more competently than they managed to do in their brief span of absolute domination. Yet, in essence, the Mexica remained little more than a band of pirates, sallying forth from their great city to loot and plunder and to submit vast areas to tribute payment, without altering the essential social constitution of their victims."[16]

Yet Professor Henry B. Nicholson, a scholar on Aztec civilization, has a diametrically opposite view of Aztec society and its defeat by the Spaniards. In a recent interview I had with the professor from UCLA, who is a leading scholar on Aztec civilization, he said:

"I believe there has developed a widespread misunderstanding about the role played by the people of ancient Mexico City (then called Mexico Tenochtitlan) in the cultural and political history of pre-Hispanic Middle America. They are often popularly portrayed as upstart barbarians who borrowed most of their culture from their predecessors and debased it by their bloodthirsty excesses of human sacrifice and ritual cannibalism. It is also frequently claimed that at the time of the Conquest, Mexican Indian civilization was already over the hill and sliding into a state of degeneracy and decline. In my view, their culture represents a kind of final successful synthesis of earlier achievements. The Spaniards invaded a populous and prosperous Central Mexico, which, although little fundamental except metallurgy had been added since the end of the Early Classic (about A.D. 500), was successfully maintaining its rich cultural heritage. Most of the major Middle American peoples appear to have been quite militaristic. Most of them appear to have ritually sacrificed enemies captured in battle. The Mexica and their subjects certainly engaged in the latter practice on a considerably expanded scale, but I don't believe that they were otherwise atypical. During the last century before Cortés I see no evidence of decline at all. On the contrary, the conquistadores lopped off a vigorously thriving cultural blossom, not a withering one."

[16]Wolf, p. 149.

The diminishing role of Coatl and the Pochteca might have signaled that the Azteca were unsuccessful in defending the fifth sun against the forces of destruction. In 1521 Hernan Cortes began the destruction of the fifth sun and the world of the Mexica-Azteca.

CHAPTER 7

The Spain of Cortés

Extremadura, Spain! Extrema—extreme—dura—hard—Extreme and hard. As its name implies, it is a region of southern Spain which is pressed against the borders of central Portugal. The land is baked by the sun in the summer and rocked by chilling winds in the winter. Even the foliage has been eaten by countless sheep, and survival is a constant struggle against the forces of nature. Yet the land produced men like strong steel—tempered by nature's extremes. Their names are known throughout the world—Alvarado, Pizarro, Balboa, and the legendary Hernan Cortes. Extremadura, extreme and hard!

In 1485, Hernán Cortés was born in the small town of Medellin located in Extremadura—one of the southern regions of Spain. A British writer in the London Sunday Times described the rugged landscape of Extremadura as fit for the nurturing of the Conquistador. He wrote:

"The Spanish landscape, particularly in these stretches of it whence man is almost absent, gives out an impression of endurance as does nothing else I know. One says to oneself: The well watered countries of the North have changed perpetually and are changing before our eyes to-day; the men of the North riot in experiment, triumph, failure, achievement and failure again. The desert also beyond the sea, beyond Atlas, is utterly unchanging, but unchanging after a different fashion, for no man seeks a habitation there nor thinks of it in terms of a mortal polity. But Spain—these great steppes of Spain—have something of both the changing and the unchanging, and yet resemble neither. It is land habitable enough and breeds famous races of men. From this very countryside of which I speak here came certain of the mighty Conquistadores, the like of whom was never known before their time or has been known since, riders of horses and dominators of the world. [. . .] It is everywhere a land of challenge, and, what is more, a land provoking worship of something symbolized by those wave-like mountainsides. Indeed, these sweeps of the bare Iberian land, almost treeless, almost untenanted, resemble and recall the sea, but a sea upon a scale more than titanic, a sea moved by gales such as our world never knows."[17]

Both parents of Hernan Cortes were of the lower gentry, squires in a sense; in Spain called Hidalgos. His mother was Dona Catalina Pizarro Altamirano and his father was a man of noble lineage who held the rank of captain of horsemen. He might aptly be described in the pages of Don Quixote:

"[He was] one of those hidalgos with a spear in a rack, an old leather shield, a thin horse and a swift greyhound. A stew of something more beef than mutton, meat-salad most evenings, ham and eggs on Saturdays, lentils on Fridays and perhaps a pigeon on Sundays, would account for three quarters of his revenue. The rest was spent in a broadcloth frock, velvet breeches for festivities, with slippers of the same, and on weekends he would honour himself with clothes of the finest wool."

And his home? Why Cervantes may have aptly described that too:

"[It was] spacious as village houses are; with his arms displayed, though rough hewn, on the stone above the street door; the bodega in the courtyard; the cellar off the hall, and many large earthen jars around."

The words of Cervantes likely portray most accurately the home of that hidalgo, Martín Cortés de Monróy—and his son—Hernán Cortés.

When Spain became a nation state, little changed in the daily lives of these people. Many fought the change to nation-state, including Martín Cortés de Monróy. But their resistance was more a reaction to tradition than it was a loss of status.

Unification had begun in 1469 with the marriage of the monarchs of two of the most powerful kingdoms of the Iberian peninsula. They were Ferdinand of Aragon and Isabella of Castile. The marriage provided the foundation, and the final defeat of the Moslems in the southern province of Granada was its culmination. With the fall of Granada in 1492, the Catholic monarchs, as Ferdinand and Isabella were called, were free to move against the landed aristocracy who desperately wanted to maintain their regional autonomy. The father of Cortes fought as a member of that

[17]Hilaire Belloc "A Wanderer's Note-Book: The Tagus," *The Sunday Times, London,* Aug. 13, 1939.

aristocracy. So it is no accident then, that resistance to unification was greatest in the southerly regions of Andalusia, and even Isabella's Castile.

Unification, however, was inevitable. The Catholic monarchs ruthlessly destroyed scores of castles and their noble inhabitants for rebelling against their authority. Their crushing of the centuries old Moslem regime had given them the experience in battle.

When the Alhambra was occupied by Spanish forces on January 2, 1492, it signaled the defeat of the Moslems. But the terms of capitulation were generous. The Moslems were given complete security of their persons, property, and religion. It appeared that the new state would follow the same policy of at least partial toleration practiced during the long Moslem rule. But such was not to be the case.

By 1502, the Moslems were forced to convert to Christianity or leave Spain. Many chose to convert in order to retain their property and security. Others—wisely—left the Iberian peninsula. For the Spanish Christians had little faith in the conversion of the Morisco, as they called him. And many like the Jews fell victim to the fearsome Holy Office of Inquisition. For them, security was only a word.

The Spain of Hernán Cortés was determined to make itself totally Catholic. That meant she would either convert or expel—or destroy, the "heathen" Jew. In March of 1492, the Jews were given three months to dispose of their property. Furthermore, gold, silver, or coin could not be removed from Spain. Because land and property sales were forced, they sold at a fraction of their value. In many cases, since money could not be carried out of Spain, liquidation became another word for confiscation.* Estimates of the number that left Spain differ. The most quoted is 165,000. For the exiles, there was little relief, because anti-Semitism was manifest in neighboring countries such as Portugal, Italy, and France, where executions of Jews were common. And many who fled also died during their flight.

For the Jews who remained and became baptized, called Conversos, or Marranos, assimilation into the society and the Catholic Church itself was commonplace. This was possible because most Jews, over the centuries of residency in Spain, had become hispanized anyway. It was not unusual for a former Jew to reach a position of authority in the hierarchy of the Church. But for those who stayed, there was always the fear of the Holy Office of Inquisition. A prime example was Isabella's confessor and later Archbishop, Fray Hernando de Talavera. Even this respected Archbishop was accused of apostasy and heresy by the Inquisition. It is believed that only his influence as Isabella's confessor led to his acquittal. Of all the dreaded grand inquisitors of the Holy Office, Tomas de Torquemada was

*Recent scholars believe that the proceeds from expropriated Jewish property were used to finance Columbus' voyages!

the worst. Sitting there in his red flowing robes this inquisitor of excesses in a matter of nine years sent 2,000 persons to their death and 15,000 more were condemned to lesser punishment which included the most barbaric forms of torture.

Even Jewish conversos, wishing to prove their religious commitment, on rare occasions joined in the Inquisition itself. It has been rumored (but never substantiated), that Tomas de Torquemada himself was of converso background!

The Holy Office of Inquisition, ostensibly designed to ferret out religious heretics, soon became a political weapon which attacked anyone who challenged government policy. As such, it was a hated institution, feared by the general population—since everyone became suspect. The numbers executed do not tell the full story. As has been said, many were tortured and imprisoned. And many more had their property confiscated. No one had the right to face his accuser. And no one knew who might be a secret agent of the Inquisitor.

The confiscation of land by the Spanish kings had a repressive effect on the social power of the landed gentry. The kings succeeded in removing land ownership as the most important measure of power. Instead, they encouraged respect based on loyalty and leadership—and, of course, the favor of the monarchs. To insure this they even changed the titles of the gentry from personal references to royal ones. For example, instead of *ricoshombres,* or "rich men" they substituted the title of *grandes* or grandees; instead of *conde* (or count), they added *duques* (or dukes) and *marques* (or marquis). For the lower gentry or nobility they added the title of *hijosdalgo*—literally son of something—which became hidalgo; and the title of caballero, or translated loosely—a Knight. The kings also changed the lot of the serfs. Criminal jurisdiction, which was originally in the hands of the overlord, now passed to the crown. This immensely improved an explosive situation and calmed a number of serf uprisings in the province of Aragon. By 1486, in Extremadura, freedom was granted to the serfs—subject to a ransom payment to their overlords. But the ransom to the overlords was exceedingly high and this disappointed the serf class. Yet the overlords were unhappy with the arrangement as well. However, it was the best solution to a difficult problem, and in time served the state well. Some of the emancipated serfs became small proprietors while others rented the land upon which they had been bound.

Spain, during the time of Cortes, also brought the military and political forces under the control of the crown. Prior to the unification of Aragon and Castile, the military was dominated by various military orders. Each was a semi-autonomous unit whose leader was, in a sense, a war lord.

The monarchs entirely reformed the military establishment. One out of every twelve males between the ages of twelve and forty-five was subject to conscription in the royal army. Spain equipped her army well and taught them new tactics. They developed an infantry square with pikemen on the outside and swordsmen on the inside. The artillery and cavalry would soften the enemy and the infantry square would complete the job. Unquestionably the reforms in the Spanish army were very effective, and it came to be regarded with respect and awe throughout continental Europe.

Undoubtedly, the father of Hernán Cortés was converted from a rank of personal nobility to one under the auspices of the crown. And in fact, all new titles of nobility were initiated and confirmed by the Catholic sovereigns. Power which had belonged formerly to the municipalities (and thus to the middle class) fell into the hands of the crown. It was the wish, the very purpose of the sovereigns—to maintain absolute control over all systems of government—and in this they succeeded. The cortes or court, which had formerly debated and passed on legislative matters of the kingdom, degenerated into a forum for endless debating. And it met infrequently. In the twenty-five years from 1475 to 1503, the cortes was convoked only nine times, and in the most critical period from 1492 to 1498, when matters of great importance were being decided, it met not once. The defeat of Granada, the discovery of the New World, the zeal of the Inquisition, and the expulsion of the Jews, passed without one meeting of the cortes.

Instead of the elective cortes, the monarchs looked to the Royal Council of Castile, which was dominated by lawyers appointed by the crown. Other royal councils were also established as insurance for royal control. There were royal councils of the Inquisition; of the military; of justice; and of the Indies—which administered the governing of the New World. Both combined kingdoms of Castile and Aragon placed the regulation of justice under royal control. But the monarchs did not wish to tamper with the local autonomy of the judicial courts. Rather they wished to set minimal royal standards which would eliminate incompetence and corruption.

Of major difficulty to Isabella was the problem of jurisdiction of Civil and Church courts. Despite her Catholic piety, Isabella was determined to prevent Church intervention in what she regarded civil matters. However, her success in this area was limited. She wished, as did Fernando, to create what she considered to be a moral and law abiding society. In keeping with this, the medieval *plieto* or judicial duel was abolished. In order to enforce the law and prevent crimes, a mounted militia of citizens was maintained. In light of many similar controversies we have today, it might be interesting to note that the use of firearms was prohibited, especially in the settlement of disputes.

As the bureaucracy expanded, so did the royal debt. By 1509, the debt had expanded to 180,000,000 *maravedis*, an excessive sum in those days. In order to maintain the government, and the program of foreign conquest, a stamp tax was initiated.

This was similar to the one used later by the British, which caused such a massive dissent prior to the American revolution. In addition, the hated *alcabala* or sales tax of ten percent was levied on all items sold in the kingdoms. Still those taxes, plus customs duties, could not pay the costs of government. Finally, the tithe or *diezmo,* and the sale of indulgences were collected by the crown. Indulgences had been collected by the Church in order to reduce one's time in Purgatory. Prior to the fall of Granada, these moneys were used to fight the Moslems. Now, with the demise of Moslem rule, the Catholic monarchs demanded the right—and got it—to continue the collection of the tithe and use it for state purposes. And yet with all of these revenues the sovereigns could not balance their budget. This gives us some idea of the expansion of the state and its attendant bureaucracies.

Compounding state budgetary problems were those of agriculture, commerce, and industry. Constant droughts in the meseta or high plains of Castile caused poor grain harvests. This, plus the importation of wheat, led to inflated prices and a flow of gold from Castile. When a bumper crop was harvested in 1509, it drove the price of wheat so low that the farmers suffered. And as with most emerging modern nations, there was a mass exodus of farmers from the dry meseta into the cities, where the jobs were. The exodus was encouraged by the new laws, which granted the serf his freedom and his right to travel.

Industrially, Spain fared a little better. Imports were discouraged and exports encouraged, especially salt, olive oil, wine, leather, and iron. Incentives were provided for skilled labor to immigrate to Castile but few came. "Seville manufactured ceramics, tiles, arms, silver work, leather, silks, and velvet; Toledo produced silks, ceramics, hats, and arms; Saragossa, Valencia, and Barcelona made glass; Granada was a center of silk; and inferior textiles were produced in many centers."

Because men such as Hernan Cortes had not yet conquered foreign lands and extracted gold and silver from them, Spain experienced a sharp decline in commercial enterprises. Most foreign commerce was handled by the Italians and Portuguese because Spain had never given much attention to her merchant marine. In fact, of all the positions of low respect in Spain, sailors held one of the lowest. The imperial status that Cortes and other conquistadores were soon to bring to Spain changed the complexion of commerce significantly. Much of Spain's commerce and banking had been in the hands of Moslems and Jews. Even after their expulsion in 1492, these enterprises were treated with much suspicion.

Since banking was so necessary for Spain's economic well-being, the vacuum was filled by German, French, Flemish, Genoese, and Florentine bankers and merchants. A reaction soon developed against these foreigners, however, and restrictions were eventually placed on them.

The expulsion of the Moslem and Jew affected the intellectual climate of Spain as well as its economy. While the loss was great, Spanish scholarship did not come to an abrupt halt. Probably the most brilliant scholar of the period was Antonio de Nebrija who lived from 1441 to 1522. Nebrija studied first at the University of Salamanca but after a short time he moved to Italy, where at Bologna and other institutions of repute he studied philology, or the structure and origin of language; and humanism, a philosophy which is concerned with the achievements and direction of man. After ten years in Italy, Nebrija returned to Spain in 1473 and acquired the Latin chair at Seville. He later transferred to his alma mater, Salamanca, until Cardinal Ximinez de Cisneros asked him to join the staff at Alacala. Here he directed the translation of the polyglot Bible into Latin and Greek and completed his *Introductiones Latinae* which was a major Latin grammar. In addition Nebrija wrote a Latin-Spanish and Spanish-Latin dictionary which were outstanding for the period. Nebrija also wrote on theology, law, archaeology, pedagogy, rhetoric, and Latin poetry. But by far his work of greatest impact was his grammar of the Spanish language. His *Arte* or *Gramatica sobre la lengua castellana,* written in 1492, was the first grammar ever composed of any modern language. This work was extremely important to the Hispanization of the New World. Nebrija correctly assessed language as an important tool for conquest and imperialism. Spanish, taught as a common language among the conquered, solidified Spain's hold on the New World. It also meant that precepts of Spanish civilization could more easily be introduced into Spain's new empire.

The records are incomplete on the number of *conversos* or Jewish Catholics who were also contributing intellectuals. It is probable that universities and other centers of learning had a number of *conversos* teaching and studying there.* Poets, novelists, artists, and architects, composers, and historians all contributed to a minor intellectual renaissance. Spain encouraged the importation and printing of books and many entered the country. Medicine too experienced a resurgence, but this and other classical fields always faced the scrutiny of the Holy Office of Inquisition. Antipathy toward natural science and medicine was not limited to Spain. Most Catholic countries saw medicine as part of religious mysticism. Illness and disease were thought to be the work of the devil, or

---

*The contributions of Spanish Jews to the intellectual development of Spain before the expulsion were enormous.

believed to be the result of the poisoning of wells by the Jews, or the punishment of social sins by God. Their cure lay with the saints, or at least with God's intermediaries, the priests.

Ah, but the binding tie of Cortés's Spain unquestionably was Catholicism. Not only were the monarchs Fernando and Isabella called los Reyes Catolicos, but they were in a sense the Catholic Church. Castile and Aragon had powerful influence over the hierarchy of the Catholic Church. Cardinal Pedro Gonzalez de Mendoza, archbishop of Toledo, was called "the Third King of Spain." His influence in creating a state church or at least state dominated Catholicism was immense. In addition, Pope Alexander VI was formerly Cardinal Rodrigo Borgia, a member of a prominent and powerful Aragonese family, who supported Spain's Church policy. And that policy revolved around the Patronato Real, or royal patronage. The patronage consisted of a number of rights nominally belonging to the Church but given to the Spanish monarchs in return for the promotion and establishment of Catholicism. The collection of the diezmo or tithe—which is a tenth of what one earns—is a right that Spain gained early. The sovereigns also had the right to nominate for Church benefices or vacant offices in the hierarchy if confirmed by the Pope. These and other benefits fell into the hands of the Spanish crown—and were extended through the establishment of a colonial empire.

This then was the Spain in which Hernan Cortes was born and reared. A man from a rugged country, accustomed to hardship and the need for endurance, he saw himself as not just a representative of Spain but Spain itself. The Catholic faith was first and foremost to him and he would have given his life in its defense. Yet as the noted historian William Hickling Prescott wrote, "His character is marked with the most opposite traits. . . . He was avaricious, yet liberal; bold to desperation, yet cautious and calculating in his plans; magnanimous, yet very cunning; courteous and affable in his deportment, yet inexorably stern; lax in his notions of morality, yet a sad bigot."

"The great feature in his character was constancy of purpose; a constancy not to be daunted by danger, nor baffled by disappointment, nor wearied out by impediments and delays.

"He was a knight-errant, in the literal sense of the word." It is in this description that we find the true story of Spain. A land of paradox, of dichotomy, and yet constancy of purpose. Spain's history did not begin with Hernan Cortes, nor with the Catholic sovereigns Fernando and Isabella, nor even with the defeat of the Moslem. In fact, the unification of Spain under Los Reyes Catolicos was as much an end as it was a beginning.

CHAPTER 8

The Birth of the Nation State—
Spain

You might expect the people living on a single peninsula that is connected by just a narrow neck to the European continent would have much in common. They might share the same language and culture. They should resemble one another with modest variations. They ought to have a history of working together to solve common problems. You might expect all of these conditions, but when you examine the Spanish peninsula of Western Europe none of them is present.

Iberia is isolated from the rest of Europe by the Pyrenees mountains, which guard the peninsula from France. Except for the relatively flat grasslands of the north, the peninsula is a massive central tableland or meseta, intersected by rugged mountains. It is generally a dry land, and both the climate and geography have led to cultural fragmentation. The mountains divide the peninsula and, consequently, its peoples into four major regions—with a number of subregions. The rugged character of the land has led to isolation and individualism. The land has isolated groups to such an extent that society has developed regionally and has produced a conservatism in these isolated areas.

The geography of Spain has worked in concert with the divergent peoples that occupied the peninsula over the many centuries. Probably the two most important occupiers in Spain's long history were the Romans and the Moslems. But they too built on the traditions and heritage of Iberia's other visitors which began around 30,000 B.C.

Cro-Magnon man lived in areas of the peninsula from 30,000 B.C. to about 10,000 B.C. His weapons of roughhewn stone made him paleolithic. And he might have even learned how to count and keep records, as evidenced by notches on his artifacts. He certainly knew how to draw; and in the caves at Altamira there are paintings of a native mountain goat, great bisons, a magnificent deer over seven feet long, horses, and bulls. At cueva del Castillo near Altamira, he left not only drawings of animals—he left imprints of himself. There are forty-four life size hands, thirty-five from the left and nine from the right. In addition, there are a series of dots and rectangles which may symbolize early man's attempt to write. In the centuries that followed, these paleolithic people were succeeded by neolithic man and by the men of the ages of copper, bronze, and iron.

Little is known of the Iberian peoples, whose origins remain a matter of controversy. Many writers believe they were somehow related to the ancient Chaldeans and Assyrians who migrated from Asia into northern Africa—and then after coming into contact with the Egyptian civilization, entered Spain. Others believe they may have been part of an early civilization, a greater Iberia, which covered all of present day Spain and northern Africa. From where they came, and how long ago is still not known.

And the controversy does not end with the Iberians. Sometime between the twelfth and fifth century B.C., three other civilizations intruded into the Iberian peninsula. They were the Phoenicians, the Celts, and the Greeks. The Greeks may be treated with a bit more certainty; but no one is certain when the previous two groups made their presence known.

The Phoenicians, who appear to be the first Semites to enter Iberia, left an indelible mark on the cultural patterns of the Spanish people. Writing, mining, and commerce have been attributed to these early Phoenicians, as well as art forms, jewelry, and sculpture all imported with a middle eastern flavor. There is also little doubt that the Jewish presence in Spain started during the Phoenician period.

The major incursion of the Celts appears to be around the 7th century B.C. There is little evidence of Celtic artifacts that can be dated before the 8th century B.C. The blonde, blue-eyed invaders from western Europe crossed the Pyrenees and settled in the northwestern regions of present day Spain. There is little physical evidence of Celtic occupation in present day Spain. However, their circular huts of stone, capped with thatched roofs, have been reproduced in Asturias which is located in northwestern Spain. And some of the original stone houses, built by the Celts more than 2,500 years ago, still remain at Monte de Santa Tecla. Aside from the obvious contribution of the bagpipe, the rather light complexion of the Galician Spaniard may be residual evidence of their presence. The Celtiberian civilization which they formed was politically tribal and based on familial ties. There was no real sense of nationality.

Around 600 B.C., there was a major Greek migration into Iberia; this was a logical extension of their expansion into the western Mediterranean. The Greeks strongly influenced the Celitberian trade patterns by introducing the first coinage money to Iberia. In addition, they are noted for importing two of the most important commodities to the peninsula. Both grapes and olives have had a profound effect on the economy, not to mention the eating and drinking habits of Spain and the world. Spanish wine and Spanish olive oil from vineyards and olive trees such as these here in southern Spain still rank among the best in the world today. Much of the viticulture in the Western Hemisphere was imported from Spain. The same is true for American olive trees.

The Greek expansion southward in the peninsula was blocked by the presence of the Phoenecians, who were reinforced by their African based cousins, the Carthaginians. By the third century, B.C., the Carthaginians had established a foothold in Iberia. While their main purpose was silver mining, they were not above exacting tribute in the form of money and soldiers from the native tribes. Eventually Carthage came into conflict with the rising power of Rome. The first showdown was the First Punic War. Carthage and Rome battled against each other with Sicily as the prize. Carthage lost in 242 B.C. Thus, having lost her foothold in Italy, she attempted to consolidate her control over the Iberian peninsula. A new army was sent to Iberia under the great Hamilcar Barca in 236 B.C. And he was successful. With help from friendly native tribes, they quickly moved into central Iberia. Two beautiful cities still reflect this period of Carthaginian control. Barcelona, named after the Barca family, and the exquisite city of Cartagena—the former New Carthage. The Carthaginian control over Iberia came to an end with the defeat of Hannibal at Zama, near Carthage, in 202 B.C. Their actual control in Spain had lasted over two hundred years. During that time they built a substantial cultural and social system which served as a basic foundation for certainly the most important occupiers of Iberia, the Romans.

The Roman legions moved into Iberia with the intention of occupying the whole peninsula. But tenacious resistance mounted by independent tribes continued to harass the Roman occupiers for several centuries.

By the first century A.D. Iberia experienced a measure of internal peace. After considerable slaughter by Rome, especially by armies under Pompey and Caesar, the tribal uprisings became few and relatively insignificant.

For six hundred years, the Romanization of Spain continued its inexorable process. Not only were more legionnaires sent to the peninsula, but laborers as well. Farmers and miners were sent to apply the more advanced Roman methods of agriculture and silver mining. Attempts were made by Julius Caesar and then Augustus Caesar to extend civil and political rights enjoyed by Romans to Hispania. The two Caesars wished to peacefully assimilate the native Spanish tribesmen into Roman society and to perpetuate the higher Roman culture. And since most Roman men came without wives and their familes, this resulted in intermarriage and thus speeded up the process of Romanization. It also facilitated the cultural and linguistic assimilation of the people. Another important factor in facilitating this transformation was the creation of the Roman town or *municipia*. This creation was really more a transformation of established cities into those that would freely accept Roman domination. Some resisted—and they remained in a lesser classification. Those that accepted, such as the city of Italica near Seville, were given the status of "free cities" and they were accorded limited autonomy and self-government. In time, there was an almost complete acceptance of the Roman civilization—and hegemony by Rome was complete.

Roman contributions to Spain were not only enormous but also lasting. Leading the list would be "law and administration." These permitted society to evolve peacefully with a measure of agricultural prosperity. Gradually, as the Roman legionnaire intermarried with native women and as native men were conscripted into the Roman legions, a general acceptance of Roman ideas ensued. Effective law and administration meant an end also to intertribal warfare and an upsurge in agriculture. Roman law was conceived by Romans, but some could claim a Spanish heritage. The emperiors Trajan, Hadrian, and possibly Theodosius were all born near Seville. And all were great contributors to Roman law. The philosopher Emperor Marcus Aurelius could also claim Spanish descent.

Commerce was another area of important Roman contributions. Because commerce was such an integral part of Italy, naturally it was transported to Hispania. For commerce to succeed, roads and travel facilities are needed. The roads built for military purposes could be used to move commercial goods. And the Romans, who also had maritime experience, developed rivers for navigation—and built excellent ports.

The cities began to assume the style of those of Rome. The city was constructed to accommodate political and social activity. The central plaza or square, which was so common to Rome, became common to the cities of Spain—and eventually common to the cities of the New Spain. Massive public buildings were constructed, as were theatres and coliseums. To improve the flow of water in a semi-arid country, great aqueducts were built. These aqueducts, with their beautiful, high arches, are as common to Spain as they are to provincial France and Italy. In fact, the only aqueduct still in use from the Roman period is in Segovia, Spain, built by the Emperior Trajan in 100 A.D. Aqueducts such as this on the edge of the city of Merida, Spain, may be seen throughout Mexico today.

Education was also important to the perpetuation of Romanization. Education was highly prized in Rome. This one of social mores, coupled with its utilitarian value, furthered its advancement. Education served as a vehicle by which the Latin language could be disseminated. The result is obvious. Aside from Christianity, the most lasting and pervasive influence of Rome was language. Spanish, a derivation of Latin, comprises one of the major languages spoken in the world today. Like the Roman emperors born in Spain, many great educators and intellectuals were influenced by the Spanish countryside and Spanish traditions. One of the most important was the son of the rhetorician, Annaeus Seneca, a scholar born in Cordoba. Lucius Annaeus Seneca is considered a major literary figure. He lived from the year one to sixty-five A.D. During that time he wrote verse and prose and became a major Stoic philosopher. He also acted as a major advisor to Emperor Nero. The nephew of Lucius Annaeus Seneca, Marcus Annaeus Lucanus, was also a noted poet, philosopher, and political scientist.

Two distinct social classes developed in Romanized Spain. They were the freemen and the slaves. The freemen consisted of the wealthy aristocracy and what could be considered an emerging middle class. The middle class included some professionals, minor bureaucrats, merchants, soldiers, sailors, farmers, tax collectors, and a host of manual laborers. While slavery existed, and while slaves were treated cruelly, slavery did have legal limitations. And slaves did not comprise the major portion of the population. Incidentially, that population figure increased from some six million at the dawn of Christianity to more than nine million by the year 400 A.D.

Christianity became one of the most important contributions of Rome to Spain—and by logical extension, to the New World. But it was not without conflict that Christianity took hold in Spain. It was during Rome's decline that it emerged as a major religious force. The Roman gods, which had been brought to Spain as a perfunctory, patriotic duty, had never received much homage. Christianity in Iberia developed as a Spanish Church and after the 9th century it claimed apostolic origin.

It is claimed that the martyrdom of James the Apostle and the discovery of his body at Santiago de Compostela accords to Spain that dignity of apostolic origin.

Even though the Catholic church was granted legal status in 312, conflict continued, and unique Spanish doctrines of the Church were practiced despite reproofs from Rome. One of these doctrines ultimately became part of Catholic dogma. It came from the Council of Iliberis in

306 and prohibited the marriage of priests. This was probably the introduction of clerical celibacy to the Catholic Church.

Unquestionably Catholicism became the binding tie of the various peoples that occupied Iberia. And it was through Romanization that Catholicism was inadvertantly introduced, in the twilight of the Roman Empire. But six hundred years of Rome's domination of Iberia made a lasting impression beyond Catholicism. For one, Latin became Spain's national language. Certainly, a common language had a mitigating effect on the social fragmentation of Spain. Furthermore, in response to a question from Queen Isabel, Nebrija (a student and later Professor here at the U. of Salamanca) indicated what usefulness a common language would have. His answer was almost prophetic for Spain's future: "siempre la lengua fué compañera del imperio" "Always language was the companion of empire." Roman occupation also had a premanent effect on governmental administration, law, commerce, agriculture, architecture, education, and the very life styles of Iberia.

Nonetheless, Iberia was Hispania, a colony of Rome. And as such, it was an integral part of the ebb and flow of Roman politics, of Roman civilization, and of Roman foreign policy. It was all of these things which led to the collapse of the Roman Empire and the loss of Hispania by Rome. Internal decadence had been enfeebling an otherwise developing Roman society. The same was true in Iberia. As people turned more toward leisure and luxury, they became more flaccid and vapid. Into this power vacuum moved the Germanic tribes from the north and east. In the year 409, two groups of Vandals along with the Alans and Suevians entered Spain after devastating France. The invaders occupied and divided up portions of the Iberian peninsula. Many of the Hispano-Romans were able to escape to the larger and better protected cities which remained independent of the invaders.

The most important of the Germanic tribes were the Visigoths. These tall blonde and militant peoples had probably originated in the region of present day Sweden. After migrating to the Balkan area near the Danube river, they came into contact with the powerful Huns. Retreating from the Huns, the Visigoths crossed into Roman territory in the latter part of the fourth century A.D. The strength of religion was manifest, for the Visigoths were soon converted to Arian Christianity.

Indeed, the Visigoths came into Iberia as mercenaries of the Roman Empire. They had contracted with Rome to challenge the Alans, Vandals, and Suevians who had occupied portions of Iberia. The alliance was at best tenuous. In 410 A.D. the Visigoths, as the result of a dispute with the Roman emperor, captured and sacked the city of Rome. It was thereafter that the Visigoths made peace with Rome and crossed the Pyrenees into Iberia.

They then made their agreement with Rome to throw out the previous Germanic invaders. They succeeded in ejecting the Alans, Vandals, and Suevians. But the shaky alliance of the Visigoths and Romans came to an end with the fall of the Western Roman Empire in 456 A.D.

Rome made several futile attempts to eject their former allies. By 624, however, Visigothic rule over Iberia was a *fait accompli*. And it continued until the major Moslem invasions in the year 711.

While the Visigoths offered little toward the cultural advancement of Iberia, they had a profound influence on Spain's future development. Germanic energy, vitality, and willingness to work energized the luxury loving Iberians. In a reaction against the Visigoths, Romanism became firmly entrenched. This was manifested throughout the religious and legal processes.

The Visigoths by their dress, their appearance, their living habits, their language and their religion set themselves apart from the Hispano-Roman peoples who were there before them. They preferred to live in their rural castles away from the Roman towns. They wore extravagant clothing, gaudy jewelry, and long flowing hair which was the sign of their manhood. Unlike the Romans who came before, these Germanic tribes entered as family groups with women and children, thereby slowing down linguistic and cultural assimilation. One of the major sources of conflict between them and the Hispano Romans was religion, for the Visigoths were Arians. The earliest form of Christianity in Spain was the so-called Arian type—or that form common among the Visigoths. It generally denied the trinity, a concept basic to present day Catholicism. Increasing pressures upon the Visigoths to convert to Orthodox Christianity were great; for in the northern area of Gaul were the Franks, who were also Orthodox Christians. Arian Christianity was pervasive in Spain until 589 A.D. when a Visigothic king, Reccared, converted to Catholic Christianity. Interestingly enough, Jewish persecution was unknown while Arian Christianity was prevalent. Not until King Reccared converted did persecution of the Jews become commonplace. Jewish persecution continued until the latter part of the seventh century when most of the Jews left Spain for North Africa, not to return until the Moslem Conquest in the eighth century A.D.

There were other collateral contributions born out of the Visigothic occupation. Bullfighting gained in popularity—a sport which would be transported to the New World. It is believed that Julius Caesar, as early as 45 B.C., brought bullfighting to Rome after his contacts with Iberia. In addition, the Visigoths introduced high respect for leadership, especially military; and personal and family fidelity.

In spite of the power of the Visigoths and their successful spread of

Catholic dogma, they were never able to fuse the Germanic with the Iberian-Roman civilizations. The results were multifold: A sense of insecurity developed across the land which tended to increase the distinctions between the classes. Free cultivators, who were peasant farmers that owned land, gave up their rights in order to gain protection. This expanded the already immense serf class and increased the burden of state costs on the lower elements of society. The privileged classes—king, nobility, high clergy, and military—grew richer while the serf-farmer grew poorer. The culture became more and more agricultural, and there was a consequential decline in industry and commerce. In order to support their high position, the privileged classes exacted greater tribute from the impoverished serfs, using oppressive methods.

One of the major causes of social instability was the Visigothic inability to establish clear lines of succession to Kingship. Heredity played only a part. Succeeding kings were elected by the nobles from any male member of the family. A constant jockeying for power by hereditary heirs, compounded by the intrigue of the nobles, made governmental stability impossible. In time all of this would lead to a general breakdown in society, which ultimately left Iberia ripe for conquest by Moslem invaders pouring in from North Africa.

In the year 711, a Berber army of no more than twelve thousand crossed the straits of Gibraltar. The swiftness with which this small force of Moslems conquered the southern tip of Spain must have left them emboldened with confidence. Visigothic resistance was weak, and their leader Roderic was killed in battle. The Moslems, under Tariq, the commander of Tangier, soon overran Cordoba. With the aid of dissident Hispanic tribesmen, the Moslems occupied the Visigothic capital, Toledo.

The following year 18,000 more Moslem warriors entered the peninsula. Their zeal and their tactics led to the conquest of the Visigothic kingdom within three years. They did not attempt to extend their conquest throughout the entire peninsula. They did, however, make expeditions across the Pyrenees into France in an attempt to extend the Holy War and spread the Muslim religion. In France they met with resistance and failure. But such was not the case in Spain, for internal dissension had left Visigothic resistance weak and divided. For the rest of the population, there was such antipathy toward the Visigoths that resistance was nonexistent.

The Moslems called their newly conquered land Al-Andalus. And so began the second most important era of Spain's early history, an era that was to last a remarkable eight hundred years. The Al-Andalus kingdom lasted until the eleventh century as the dominant force of Moslem Hispania. But the Moslems never had complete control of Iberia nor did they achieve even a homogeneous society. During this period there were increasing waves of invasions from the North African Berber tribesmen. The Arabs of Hispania never really accepted the Berbers and they attempted to guard their higher status jealously, without success. This was just one indication of the political and social fragmentation Al-Andalus was experiencing.

Often historians speak with a feeing of praise for the Moslem as a result of the religious toleration they practiced. Clearly, there was a measure of religious and social toleration, but only a measure. Christians and Jews were permitted to maintain their religious affiliations—but they were not totally free. They were never free to debate or dispute the merits or demerits of the Muslim religion. There were periods of persecution against the Christian majority. At times Christian leaders were put to death in order to reduce the influence of the Church. Many Christians who feared similar treatment fled to the north. This resulted in a dwindling number of Catholics—and hence by the end of the 9th century the Christian majority became a minority.

By the tenth century A.D., the Moslems had developed a cultural florescence higher than that of Western Europe. The Moslem intellectual elite turned their attention to history, philosophy, astronomy, mathematics, botany, medicine, and other technological advances which made possible great architectural masterpieces, such as a beautiful example of buildings known as the Alhambra located in Granada.

The cultural florescence of this era was in a sense a Renaissance. Irrigation projects which had been destroyed during the Visigothic era were restored and improved. Agricultural production improved in productivity and diversity. Land tenure changed and rented family farms as well as small privately owned Moslem farms appeared.

The greatest change appeared in the cities. Silk and textile production rose dramatically to be exported beyond the peninsula. The Moslem artisans excelled in ceramics and tile work, and they set a world standard. Armaments and other products of fine steel were highly sought after in Western Europe. The cities themselves became show places of progress and architectural splendor. One of the most beautiful was the city of Granada. It was a triumph of architectural, economic, and cultural progress.

The Roman Christian culture also had an effect on the Moslem occupier. But the influence of Moslem culture was in the final analysis far more dominant. Moslem social customs and mores were firmly implanted during their eight century rule. An ofttimes quoted example is the seclusion and restrictions placed on women, particularly in regards to premarital chastity. Concubinage permitted a Moslem man to have up to four wives. However, the first wife enjoyed the privilege of veto over the next three.

But Moslem Spain did not control all of the Peninsula. Several Christian areas co-existed alongside the Moslem. During the first three centuries of Moslem rule the most important was the mountainous northern kingdom of Asturias. Legend tells us it was during the reign of the Catholic king Alfonso II that the tomb and body of one of the apostles, Saint James, or Santiago, was found. Located in northwestern Galicia, the site is called Santiago de Compostela. It became a site for great Christian pilgrimages. And Santiago became the Spanish protector in the great battles against the Moslems—which ultimately led to the so-called Spanish Reconquest.

It appears that this Christian Reconquest began shortly after the Moslem take-over. By 800, the major cities of Catalonia had fallen to the Spanish Christians. The political dissension and bickering among the Arabs did not allow them to present a unified front against the Christians, who were themselves by no means fully united. Toledo was recaptured in 1085 and, by the year twelve hundred, Leon, Castilla, Navarre, and Aragon had been "liberated." The Moslem administration began to disintegrate, and by 1230 only Granada remained in the hands of the Moslem occupiers. Granada resisted for more than 150 years, but it was destined to fall before the zealous Spanish Christian armies. The year was 1492. The same year that the first Spanish Grammar was published. And the year that Spain, with the aid of an Italian-Portuguese mariner, named Columbus, purchased a far-flung empire for somewhere around $13,000.

CHAPTER 9

Search for Cipangu

The New World was discovered by a Genoese-Portuguese map maker who was searching for the Grand Khan on the beaches of the Caribbean. In a ship of less than 100 tons, he made his journey across the uncharted Atlantic ocean. It would take a man of great courage today to sail this course with only the aid of a compass and an astrolabe. In 1492 Christopher Columbus was such a man. In the harbor of Barcelona there is a scale replica of the Santa Maria. It was the great city of Barcelona to which Christopher Columbus returned in triumph to meet with Queen Isabella and King Ferdinand.

Portugal has always shown a certain contempt toward Spain because of Spain's claim to American discovery. The Portuguese have contended for many years that it was they and not Spain that really happened upon this undiscovered land. Although there is no direct evidence to support this claim, it is possible. In an age where national secrecy was commonplace, it is entirely possible that Portuguese mariners might have found America by sheer accident.

Portuguese maritime experience began with the third son of King John the First, otherwise known as Prince Henry the Navigator. Prince Henry, who was born in 1394, spent much of his 66 years in maritime discovery. In 1420, at the age of twenty-six, he established a school for the study of seafaring and oceanography at Sagres, Portugal, located on the most southwest tip of continental Europe. In that same year Portugal began the settlement of the island of Madeira. Under the auspices of royal sanction, and the direct sponsorship of Prince Henry, Madeira was cleared and planted with a new product that soon found great demand in Western Europe: sugar.

In time sugar became so important that Portugal had to expand her maritime fleet in order to handle the trade resulting from this product. The Madeira Islands held another importance for Portugal, they served as a base for exploration and discovery to the south. Within twenty years Portuguese ships sailed south along the coast of Africa to Cape Bogador. The Azores were settled and an agricultural stock-raising community was established in these uninhabited islands. By 1460, the year of Henry's death, ships under his command had sailed to and claimed the Cape Verde Islands along the coast of Africa.

Prince Henry did not live to see his ships round the tip of Africa, but he was certain that it could be done. Under his auspices, Portuguese ships contacted the Guinea coast of Africa and brought home gold. But gold was not Portugal's major interest. Sugar was even more important in Portuguese commerce with Africa. Also ivory, pepper, and grain were increasingly in demand by Europe. But by 1441-1443, the Portuguese found that one of the most profitable exports from Africa was the African. In those years, Portuguese ships began to transport their human cargo to Europe for sale. So Portuguese maritime commerce continued to expand.

In 1488, Bartholomeu Dias, another Portuguese mariner, sailed the coast of Africa past the Cape of Good Hope believing that a new trade route to the Far East could be established. Thus, before Christopher Columbus made his famous voyage to the west, Portugal had gained a complete knowledge of Africa's entire Atlantic coast; and she had established a profitable trade in African products. Lisbon was the trading post of Western Europe, and the Portuguese merchant fleet had expanded to accommodate the growing demand. In addition, Portuguese marine technology developed the lighter and more versatile three-masted caravel, which was capable of sailing against the wind. It appeared that the logical nation to discover the New World was Portugal—but it was not to be.

The Italian city states also helped set the stage for exploration and discovery. Early in the fourteenth century, Genoese and Venetian merchants settled in Spanish and Portuguese trading ports and directed merchant vessels that handled the trade between southwestern Europe and the Far East. Exotic goods were carried by swaying camel from Asia to Constantinople, where they were purchased by Italian merchants and shipped for sale in Lisbon and Seville. Even after passing through many hands, the profits of this trade were great enough to motivate men of foresight to look for new trade routes. New sea routes could circumvent the middle men, particularly the Moslems, and increase the merchants, profits. But for all of Italy's culture, Italians lacked the technological know how for sailing the open sea. Other factors also eliminated Italy from competing for the riches of the New World. "Italy" was not yet a unified nation and the Italian city states lacked the unity and national resources required for exploration. In addition, Italy's geographical location placed her farther east by a considerable distance from the Atlantic sea lanes. Given the fact that all provisions had to be carried on small ships, distance in those days was critical.

But Italians did impart their mercantile experience to the Portuguese as traders and residents of Portugal. To a great extent, it was this combined knowledge of Italy and Portugal that provided the land-locked state of Castile with the key that would unlock the riches of the New World.

If anyone, the man Christopher Columbus carried that key. In effect he distilled the knowledge of seafaring he had learned from his experiences in both Italy and Portugal. The story of this remarkable man is noteworthy. Prior to his arrival in Portugal, there is little we can say about him with great certainty. Columbus appeared to be reluctant to reveal the details of his early life, so we must rely heavily on the biography written by his learned son Fernando Colon. Because a number of statements written by Fernando are out and out lies, the accuracy of the body of his account is clouded. Nonetheless, despite various assertions, it is clear that he was Genoese; that he was born in the fall of 1451; that his father Domenico was a woolenweaver; that his grandfather Geovanni was a woolenweaver; that his mother Suzanne was the daughter of a woolenweaver; and that he was named Cristoforo Colombo.* He was the eldest of five children and it was his brother Bartolomeo with whom he maintained his closest friendship. There is scant knowledge of his educational background; however, it is almost certain that he did not attend the University of Pavia, as both he and his son Fernando maintained. It is more probable that this man of great intelligence was self educated. It is certain that he had a speaking knowledge of Genoese, a good knowledge of Latin, and a writing and speaking knowledge of Portuguese and Spanish. Whether Columbus acquired his linguistic skills in his seaport city of Genoa, or whether he learned these languages as he emigrated to Portugal or to Spain is speculative. And Columbus' own words don't help us any. In fact, historians have faced the problem that the words of Columbus and his biographer-son Fernando lead one to believe that our

---

*Many reputable scholars believe that Columbus was the son of Converso or Marrano parents who fled from Spain to Italy when Columbus was a child of about twelve.

great navigator/explorer either engaged in fantasy or outright false-hoods. Let us look at a few examples.

According to his own words, there are at least three separate and distinct times that he began sailing: 1461, 1465, or from 1469 to 1470. In addition, Antonio Gallo, a Genoese chronicler and friend of the Colum-bus family, wrote that Columbus entered upon the sea somewhere be-tween 1465 and 1470. To what do we attribute this? Fantasy? A poor memory? Or was it periodic desires to curry favor by saying or writing that which would be most acceptable?

In another instance, Fernando, in his *Life of Columbus*, cites an impossible quotation from his father, Christopher:

> "In the month of February, 1477, I sailed one hundred leagues beyond the island of Thule (Iceland), the north part of which lies at a latitude of 73 degrees north, and not 63 degrees as some affirm. Nor does it lie on the meridian where Ptolemy says the West begins, but much further west. And to this island, which is as large as England, the English come with their wares, from Bristol in particular. When I was there, the sea was not frozen, but the tides were so great that in some places the water rose twenty-six fathoms, and fell to the same extent."[18]

According to Bjorn Landstrom, in his work on Columbus:

> "If these are Columbus' own words, he was a liar. He cannot possibly have been 'beyond Thule' in February. In those days no one sailed to Iceland in the depths of winter. If he really told that story, he could only have been repeating what he heard, and believed, from mariners in Bristol."[19]

While Columbus' early life is obscure, it becomes clearer as he moves to Portugal. There is a question as to what brought him to Portugal in the first place. He tells us of a sea battle and shipwreck off the coast of Portugal that is almost impossible to accept. But we do know that his brother Bartolomeo had already settled in Portugal as a map maker. Now it might have been that Columbus decided to live with his brother. Or it could have been that he was in the service of a trading firm, entered Portugal, and once there, was persuaded to remain by his brother.

It appears most likely that he went to work for the Genoese trading firm of Centurione and that he entered into the African and Madeira Island sugar trade in 1478. In the following year, Columbus met and married Felipa Moniz de Perestrello, the daughter of a former governor of Porto Santo, a Portuguese island. His father-in-law, Bartolomeu Peres-trello, a man of Italian descent, must have been in a position to offer

[18]Björn Landström, *Columbus* © Bokförlaget Forum AB. (Allen & Unwin, 1967), pp. 23-24. Also in Samuel Eliot Horison, *Admiral of the Ocean Sea*. (Boston: Little Brown, 1942) p. 24.
[19]Landström, pp. 23-24.

Christopher a certain amount of influence and assistance. In any event, Christopher spent the next few years with his brother Bartolomeo, engaged in map making. It was here, from dreams, from tales, from hopes for fame, and from other's journals, that Christopher Columbus hit upon the idea of sailing west in order to reach the lands of the Far East. In this respect, Columbus was a representative of the transition taking place in Europe from Medieval myth to a modern search for truth. Undoubtedly, sailor's lore played a heavy role in Columbus' thinking and excitement about sailing west; his own words tell us that. His knowledge of maps and charts certainly influenced him to search for a new route west. But of prime importance were two journals, one of Pierre d'Ailly, entitled *Imago Mundi* printed in 1480; and the other of Marco Polo, probably written in 1312. His copies contain copious notes and underlines, which prove that Columbus was heavily reliant on the theories and discoveries of these explorer-journalists. In fact, much of what Columbus wrote about sailing west are abridgements of d'Ailly's *Imago Mundi*.

Armed with his experience, his dreams, and his knowledge of Marco Polo and Pierre d'Ailly, he undertook a scheme that he felt would open a new trade route to the Far East. He felt it feasible because he estimated the size of Asia to be much wider than it was, in addition he miscalculated the breadth of the Atlantic by almost half. Therefore, the route was there and all he needed was to convince the authorities of that fact, and he would gain royal sanction.

Because the evidence indicates that he was in the employ of the Portuguese maritime service, he turned first to Portugal to gain royal sanction. Sometime around 1481, when his son Diego was born, and his wife died, Columbus made his presentation to John II, king of Portugal. King John referred the project to a royal commission of very learned men, including an astronomer, a cosmographer, and a physician-scientist. After studying his proposal, they rejected it on the ground that his calculations were far too conservative and that he had made serious errors in distance. As for the island of Cipangu, which was Columbus' destination, and which Marco Polo described—it might not even exist! A Portuguese chronicler, Barros, described Columbus' proposal:

> "He came to the conclusion that it was possible to sail across the western ocean to the island of Cipangu and other unknown lands. For since the time of Prince Henry, when the Azores were discovered, it was held that there must be other islands and lands to the west, for Nature could not have set things on earth so out of proportion that there should be more water than land, which was intended for life and the creation of souls. With these fantastic ideas that he had obtained on his continual voyages, and from talks with men who were versed in such matters and in this kingdom had great knowledge of past discoveries, he came to King John II, asking him for ships that he might sail away and discover the island of Cipangu in the western

Ocean. . . . When the King found that this Cristavao Colom was very proud and boastful in presenting his talents, and more fanciful and full of imagination than accurate when speaking of his island of Cipangu, he had little faith in him. But as he would not be put off, the King sent him to Dom Diogo Ortiz, the Bishop of Ceuta, and to Master Rodrigo and Master Josepe, who dealt with such questions of cosmography and discoveries; and all of them found that Cristovao Colom's words were empty, for they were based on fantasy, or on such things as Marco Polo's island of Cipangu."[20]

But Columbus was neither to be discouraged nor deterred. Since the king had not provided him with ships and since he was deeply in debt and could not finance the project himself, he decided to try elsewhere. In 1484 he and his son Diego left for Castile.

For the next seven years, with great tenacity, this Genoese-Portuguese mariner-cartographer, fought to have his plan accepted by someone—anyone of royal lineage—who would listen to, and finance his plan. For at least four of those seven years, Columbus worked as an itinerant book seller and he was usually penniless. In 1488 he fathered a son by a commoner named Beatriz Enriques de Harana. Although his second son, Fernando, was born to her, he never took her as his wife—and this brought him pangs of guilt for years to come.

It was also in 1488 that a royal commission was set up by Ferdinand and Isabella to study Columbus' proposal. The Spanish commission's recommendations were exactly the same as those of the Portuguese commission. And still Columbus, who now called himself Cristobal Colon, was not deterred. That same year he wrote again to John II of Portugal hoping that he would change his mind. John answered showing renewed interest in the project and guaranteeing Columbus freedom of passage and freedom from arrest and debtors' prison if he would return at once and again present his plan. No one knows if the trip was made. Meanwhile, brother Bartolomeo went to England and negotiated with Henry VII, where again his ideas were rejected. By 1490, while Columbus was apparently having intermittent meetings with Ferdinand outside the beleaguered city of Granada, Bartolomeo was attempting to negotiate with Charles VIII of France. Early in 1491, Christopher Columbus decided to travel to France and present his ideas in person to Charles VIII. This was to be a most fortuitous trip. Together with his ten year old son, Diego, he began his journey. On the way, they stopped at the La Rabida monastery near the town of Palos, on the Atlantic coast. Here Columbus met Father Juan Pérez, who purportedly was one of Isabella's former confessors. It is believed that Father Juan Pérez was a converso, or converted Jew, who had risen to a position of rank in the Catholic heirarchy. Nearby, at the town of Palos, lived the Yañez Pinzon brothers, also conversos, who

[20]Landström, p. 31.

became deeply interested in the project to the extent that they later financed part of the expenses for the journey—and, of course, captained the two smaller ships the Niña and the Pinta.

Father Juan Pérez convinced Columbus to wait while he intervened with the Queen. Within a short time, Isabella sent Columbus funds for proper court attire and a horse upon which to travel. Columbus probably arrived at Santa Fe, near Granada, just in time to witness the fall of the city in November of 1491. In January of 1492, Granada was formally occupied by the Spaniards and Columbus was now in a position to personally present his ideas. He did so, and they were seconded by the king's treasurer, and Columbus' friend, Luis de Santangel, also a converso. Back at Santa Fe, a commission of the sovereigns listened carefully to his proposals, and promptly rejected them. With that, Columbus rode off to Cordova only to be overtaken by the Queen's horsemen and ordered to return. Luis de Santangel had convinced the Queen that the risk was low for such possible high gain.

Apparently half the journey was funded by Queen Isabella, and the rest through Santangel and his wealthy friends who lent the money directly to Christopher Columbus.* On April 17, 1492, a formal agreement was signed by the Catholic kings which gave Columbus certain rights and privileges to what he might discover. He was to have the title of Admiral of all he discovered. He was to be Viceroy and Governor-General over all islands and mainlands he discovered. He would keep one tenth of all gold, silver, spices, and other riches he might acquire—free of taxes. He would have the title of Don, and certain other minor privileges.

Together with this document and another spelling out the charting and equipping of the vessels, Columbus arrived at the tiny town of Palos on the southwestern coast of Spain. From the church, he could see the uncharted Atlantic, across which lay his dream of reaching India. So here he outfitted the three vessels obtained for the expedition. The two smaller vessels, both caravels, the Niña and the Pinta, were captained by the Pinzon brothers, Martin Alonso Pinzon and Vicente Yañez Pinzon. The flagship was the 100 ton Santa Maria, captained by Admiral Columbus. Ninety men and boys were contracted for the voyage, and except for four, all were of Spanish extraction. Luis de Torres, another converso, was the interpreter. He knew Hebrew, Aramaic, and Arabic.

On August 3, 1492, Columbus' three tiny ships began their memorable journey. With the aid of a compass and an astrolabe or quadrant which could take a reckoning by measuring the distance of a polestar above the horizon, Columbus set sail for the Canary Islands. After taking

---

*Some scholars believe that contrary to popular legend, the Queen did not sell her jewels in order to finance Columbus, rather she used funds confiscated "illegally" from the Jews of Spain.

on water and provisions, they sailed due west on September 8, 1492—
their goal was Cipangu.

After a relatively uneventful voyage of thirty-three days, they arrived at a small coral reef which today is part of the British Bahamas. It is
scarcely thirteen miles long and six miles wide and today it is called
Watlings Island. Columbus named it San Salvador for the Patron Saint of
the day on which they landed. Samuel Eliot Morison, in his monumental
work on Christopher Columbus, entitled *Admiral of the Ocean Sea,* gives the
following description of the landing. It is a composite of two contemporary journals:

> "Presently they saw naked people, and the Admiral went ashore in the
> armed ship's boat with the royal standard displayed. So did the captains of
> Pinta and Nina, Martin Alonso Pinzon and Vicente Yanez his brother, in
> their boats, with the banners of the Expedition, on which were depicted a
> green cross with an F on one arm and a Y on the other, and over each his or
> her crown. And, all having rendered thanks to Our Lord kneeling on the
> ground, embracing it with tears of joy for the immeasurable mercy of
> having reached it, the Admiral arose and gave this island the name of San
> Salvador. . . ."[21]

As the curious natives approached, Columbus offered them small
items of "little value" for trade. Thus he began what has been termed
America's trinket trade. Columbus eloquently described the trinkets and
the Indians with whom he came into contact:

> "In order that we might win good friendship, because I knew that they were
> a people who could better be freed and converted to our Holy Faith by love
> than by force, I gave to some of them red caps and to some glass beads,
> which they hung on their necks, and many other things of slight value, in
> which they took much pleasure; they remained so much our friends that it
> was a marvel; and later they came swimming to the ships' boats in which we
> were, and brought us parrots and cotton thread in skeins and darts and
> many other things, and we swopped them for other things that we gave
> them, such as little glass beads and hawks' bells. Finally they swopped and
> gave everything they had, with good will; but it appeared to us that these
> people were very poor in everything. They go quite naked as their mothers
> bore them; and also the women, although I didn't see more than one really
> young girl. All that I saw were young men, none of them more than 30 years
> old, very well made, of very handsome bodies and very good faces; the hair
> coarse almost as the hair of a horse's tail and short; the hair they wear over
> their eyebrows, except for a hank behind that they wear long and never cut.
> Some of them paint themselves black (and they are of the color of the
> Canary Islanders, neither black nor white), and some paint themselves
> white, and others red, and others with what they have. Some paint their
> faces, others the whole body, others the eyes only, others only the nose.
> They bear no arms, nor know thereof; for I showed them swords and they

[21]Morison, *Admiral of the Ocean Sea,* pp. 228-29.

grasped them by the blade and cut themselves through ignorance; they have
no iron. Their darts are a kind of rod without iron, and some have at the end
a fish's tooth and others, other things. They are generally fairly tall and
good looking, well made. I saw some who had marks of wounds on their
bodies, and made signs to them to ask what it was, and they showed me how
people of other islands which are near came there and wished to capture
them, and they defended themselves. And I believed and now believe that
people do come here from the mainland to take them as slaves. They ought
to be good servants and of good skill, for I see that they repeat very quickly
all that is said to them; and I believe that they would easily be made
Christians, because it seemed to me that they belonged to no religion. I,
please Our Lord, will carry off six of them at my departure to Your
Highnesses, so that they may learn to speak. I saw no beast of any kind
except parrots in this island."[22]

In sign language, he asked the natives what the wounds were on
their bodies. They answered that people from the mainland came and
took them as prisoners. Columbus assumed that he was on an island off
the coast of India, and that the people from the mainland, the Indians, came and took these people as slaves. He concluded, therefore,
that he had somehow reached India or at least territory allied with India.
And he believed he was in fact endowed by God to find that land and these
people, whom he incorrectly called Indians. The error has been per-
petuated throughout history and been the cause of great confusion. Even
years later, when the Spaniards found they were not in India, but a new
land—they called the area the West Indies, and the people the West
Indians.

From San Salvador, Columbus sailed to Cuba where he believed he
had reached the mainland of either China or Japan. Cuba or Colba, as he
heard the natives say, contained more simple huts and natives who
seemed primitive to Columbus and his crew. But he found no Grand
Khan as described by Marco Polo. Columbus described the natives as ripe
for conversion, but was disappointed at not finding the fabled cities about
which he had read.

From Cuba he went to Hispaniola, the island which the Dominican
Republic and Haiti presently share. Here again he searched for the Grand
Khan without success. On Christmas morning, the Santa Maria was
caught upon a reef, and as the tide rolled out, her seams opened and she
was lost. The crew of the Santa Maria formed the first permanent colony
in the Americas, La Navidad. It was so named because it was founded on
the day of the Nativity, or Christmas.

Columbus' return voyage was stormy—and took him off course—so
that he landed in Lisbon, Portugal. Some in the Portuguese Court wanted
the disloyal Admiral jailed or even killed. But King John II, concerned

[22]Morison, pp. 229-30.

about reprisals from Castile, permitted Columbus to return to Spain. He arrived in the tiny town of Palos on March 15, 1493, amidst the greatest amount of glory that could be accorded one individual. It was indeed his moment of triumph. He made three more journeys to the New World, each with growing resentment from his adversaries, and from the crown itself. He maintained to the end that he had found a new route to the Far East, and persisted that with other voyages, his vision could be fulfilled. It was not fulfilled, nor was his dream of fame and stature. Instead, at age fifty-five, he died—with certain claims against the crown, but with his dreams unfulfilled and with the social disdain accorded to a failure.

His voyage, of course, did have great meaning. At the time, Portugal and Spain were vying for supremacy over trade routes to Asia and for the rights to the islands and lands which they might discover. So a line was drawn around the world in 1493, dividing the world in half. It was set forth in the form of a Papal Bull issued by Pope Alexander VI. Everything discovered west of a line 100 leagues west of the Azores and the Cape Verde Islands was to go to Spain. All to the East would go to Portugal. The following year, in the treaty of Tordesillas the line was moved to 370 leagues west of the Cape Verde Islands, placing the still to be discovered Brazil squarely in the Portuguese sphere. These treaties indicated the confidence exuded by these two Peninsular powers.

And that confidence was manifested in the singular symbol of one man, Christopher Columbus. He was the symbol, the forerunner of European commercial expansion or Europeanization of the New World. It was only by chance that Spain made the discovery. Luckily, Queen Isabella changed her mind and granted Columbus the commission he so desperately wanted. She had no way of knowing that his voyage would give most of the New World to Spain at so little cost—and that the culture of Iberia would be transplanted to the Caribbean and thence to Mexico and the Americas. The conquest of Mexico is ascribed to one man, Hernán Cortés. But like Columbus, he is a symbol of European and Spanish expansion, and the forces that expansion had set in motion.

CHAPTER 10

The Conquest

It has become known as "Noche Triste," or Night of Sadness. On the night of July 1, 1520, the celebrated conquistador Hernán Cortés wept and mourned the loss of so many of his men. In his flight from Mexico City, 450 Spaniards died along with four thousand of their Indian friends and allies. Many others were wounded and forty-six horses were lost in battle. Cortés' personal secretary Fray Francisco Lopez de Gómara later wrote: "Who, indeed, would not weep at the death and ruin of those who had entered in such triumph, pomp, and rejoicing?"

To a lesser warrior, the struggle for Mexico would have ended on "Noche Triste." But for Hernán Cortés it was only a setback; a time for regrouping; a temporary disruption in his inevitable accomplishment—The Conquest of Mexico!

Spanish conquest of Mexico did not begin in 1519 with the landing of Hernán Cortés. It started almost as soon as the Caribbean was settled. In fact, the conquest was much more than a military action—it was mercantile as well. It was inevitable that Mexico would fall prey to the Spanish sword; but it was not inevitable that the sword would belong to Hernán Cortés. As important as he was, Cortés was one of many conquistadores who looked to conquest as a means to expand the Empire and wealth of Spain—and of themselves. In effect, each area into which the Spaniards ventured may be viewed as a conquest—the fame of it determined by the size of the prize and the resistance offered by the natives. Since most of the Caribbean lacked the concentrated populations and wealth of Mexico—and their technological advancements—the islands, conquest was neither flashy nor dramatic. But the Spaniards did meet with resistance in Hispaniola—and they subdued it. They also met with resistance in Cuba—and they subdued it. And now, they faced a mainland population—diverse but organized into highly developed agricultural-military states. Still, it is fascinating how a relatively small handful of Spaniards conquered Mexico in a dramatically short amount of time. How was this possible? And why was it inevitable?

The story must begin with the man, Hernán Cortés. He was born in 1495 at the small town of Medellín in the region of Extremadura, in the semi-arid, mountainous region of southern Spain. He was only fourteen when his parents sent him to the famous University of Salamanca. They knew that without an education, he would be nothing but a poor squire. As a lawyer, he would have status, respect, and a profession. But after two years he gave up his studies and returned home, much to the consternation of his parents. Yet Cortés' years at Salamanca were not lost, for at the university he had learned Greek, Latin, Logic, and the basic skills to become a notary or local attorney. This, coupled with his excellent native intelligence was to serve him well in the future.

His first opportunity for fame and fortune came in the person of Nicolas de Ovando. In 1501, when Cortés was just sixteen, Ovando had been commissioned to lead a colonizing expedition to the Indies with thirty ships carrying three thousand five hundred colonists. This was to be one of the greatest colonizing ventures in history. And Cortés had been invited to accompany Ovando, who was to become Governor of the Indies. But fate, and Cortés' amorous desires, would have it otherwise. Cortés' personal secretary and biographer Fray Francisco López de Gómara wrote about the incident: "Cortés went to a house one night to visit a woman and, as he was walking along the badly cemented wall of the garden, it gave way beneath him. At the noise made by the falling wall, and by the clatter of the arms and shield, a young husband jealous of his wife ran out and tried to kill him, but was prevented from doing so by his old mother-in-law. Cortés was injured by the fall, and besides was stricken by a quartan fever which kept him in bed for a long time; so he was unable to go with Governor Ovando."[23]

Fray Francisco López de Gómara tells that he wandered idly about for a year before he expressed a desire to depart for the Indies. With

[23]Francisco López de Gómara, *Cortés: The Life of the Conquistador by His Secretary,* translated and edited by Lesley Byrd Simpson (Berkeley: University of California, 1964), pp. 8-9.

money and blessings from his parents, he sailed with a supply expedition to the Indies in 1504 at the age of nineteen.

After arriving at Santo Domingo, he was appointed notary to the council of a small town that Ovando had founded. It is here that his education at Salamanca became so important. Under the Spanish system, a notary does more than witness signatures. He is in effect a local attorney with some administrative authority. Since politicians commonly used their office for their own economic betterment, Cortés for the next five or six years was engaged in trade and building his fortune and reputation. When Diego Velázquez was commissioned to conquer and settle Cuba, Hernán Cortés went with him as "clerk of the treasurer." Over the next six years, Cortés became a wealthy rancher, distributor of slaves, and notary to Santiago de Cuba. After all, Hernán Cortés was a friend and confidant of the powerful Governor, Diego de Valázquez.

Through a series of events which began with Francisco Hernández de Córdoba in 1517, Hernán Cortés was to become one of the most amazing men in the history of the New World. Hernández de Córdoba had sailed to the island of Cozumel off the coast of the Yucatan peninsula. He was met with a shower of arrows from hostile Indians who inhabited part of the island. Wounded, he returned to Cuba, but only lived long enough to tell of the magnificent civilization he had seen. It was probably one of the Mayan cultures. Velázquez, in keeping with the tradition of the conquistador, saw the conquest of this area as an opportunity for wealth and fame.

The following year Gov. Velázquez sent his cousin, a prudent man named Juan de Grijalva, to make contact with the native civilizations there. Grijalva sailed past Cozumel, past the Yucatan to the present site of Veracruz. Here at this Aztecan port city he was welcomed and presented with more than 350 gifts of value. They included gold idols, gold nuggets, gold vessels, gold necklaces, forty axes of gold and copper, gold fish-hooks, gold earrings, gold pendants, jewelry of stones, masks, skins, featherwork, cotton mantles, perfumes, chili, and fruits.

The return of Grijalva to Cuba was met with both great enthusiasm and anxiety. If there was this much gold to be given in tribute, then why not more!

And why had Grijalva not planted a colony so that the Indians could be exploited for their labor and wealth. Velázquez was ready to pay for a new expedition himself, but he preferred to have someone privately fund the trip thereby keeping what state money he controlled. Cortés was not his first choice—but in his eagerness, he turned to the 34 year old cavalier. Cortés was quick to see the opportunity to gain fame and riches. So with the aid of several wealthy backers he hurriedly presented a written agreement to Velázquez.

But no sooner had he started on the project, when Velázquez

showed signs of regretting his sanction to Cortés. Furthermore, Cortés had many enemies and they too advised the Governor to retract his agreement.

Cortés of course was angry, but he also realized the exigency of the moment. While soothing the anxious governor, he hurriedly recruited 300 men in Santiago de Cuba. Eventually he gathered eleven ships and stuffed them with live pigs, turkeys, salt pork, corn bread, wine, and a host of other foodstuffs. He also bought thirty-two crossbows, thirteen muskets, ten brass guns, and four falconets or small cannon. There was armour, lances, and—oh yes—sixteen horses, horses that the Indians had never seen, horses that were to evoke the fear which, more often than not, accompanies the unknown.

Late one evening less than four weeks after the agreement was signed, he ordered his men on board the ships. The next morning he invited Velázquez to the harbor to join him in a mass, and to give blessings to his men. And then he sailed. But hardly had the ships left the harbor when Velázquez sent an order to Trinidad to detain and arrest the arrogant captain. But, at Trinidad, and again at Havana the orders were ignored for the commanders of these areas pleaded fear of Cortés. Many not only granted Cortés and his men sanctuary, but also gave them aid and comfort. By the time he sailed from Cuba, his ranks had swelled to 550 men. At the moment of embarkation, Cortés addressed his men in a speech charged with emotion, clothed in confidence, and filled with the blessings of God.

> "Certain it is, my friends and companions, that every good man of spirit desires and strives, by his own effort, to make himself the equal of the excellent men of his day and even those of the past. And so it is that I am embarking upon a great and beautiful enterprise, which will be famous in times to come, because I know in my heart that we shall take vast and wealthy lands, peoples such as have never before been seen, and kingdoms greater than those of our monarchs. Certain it is also that the lust for glory extends beyond this mortal life, and that taking a whole world will hardly satisfy it, much less one or two kingdoms.
>
> I have assembled ships, arms, horses, and the other materials of war, a great stock of provisions, and everything else commonly needed and profitable in conquests. I have spent large sums, for which I have put in pawn my own estate and those of my friends, for it seems to me that the less I retain of it the greater will be my honor. Small things must be given up when great things present themselves. As I hope in God, more profit will come to our King and nation from our expedition than from those of all the others. I hardly need mention how pleasing it will be to God Our Lord, for love of whom I have willingly offered my toil and my estate; nor shall I speak of the danger to life and honor to which I have exposed myself getting this fleet together, because I would have you know that I do not seek gain from it so much as honor, for good men hold honor dearer than riches.
>
> We are engaging in a just and good war which will bring us fame. Almighty God, in whose name and faith it will be waged, will give us victory,

and time will see the accomplishment that always follows upon whatever is done and guided by intelligence and good counsel. We must, therefore, employ a different way, a different reasoning, and a different skill from those of Cordoba and Grijalba. I shall not pursue the matter further because of the pressure of time, which urges us onward. There we shall do as we shall see fit, and here I offer you great rewards, although they will be wrapped about with great hardships. Valor loves not idleness, and so, therefore, if you will take hope for valor, or valor for hope, and if you do not abandon me, as I shall not abandon you, I shall make you in a very short time the richest of all men who have crossed the seas, and of all the armies that have here made war. You are few, I see, but such is your spirit that no effort or force of Indians will prevail against you, for we have seen by experience how God has favored the Spanish nation in these parts, and how we have never lacked courage or strength, and never shall. Go your way now content and happy, and make the outcome equal to the beginning."[24]

On the first night out of Cuba, a violent storm drove the expedition to the Island of Cozumel. There while they repaired his ships Cortés explored the island. He made contact with the natives who were fearful of him. He received some gifts and heard a story of the arrival of bearded men. When the ships were repaired they departed, only to have a ship spring a leak. Upon returning to Cozumel they encountered an astonishing person. He arrived in a canoe with three Indians, and spoke Spanish, "Gentlemen, are you Christians?" When they said they were Spaniards, he broke into tears, and offered a prayer of thanks to God.

"Sir, I am Jerónimo de Aguilar, of Ecija, and I was cast away as I shall relate: I was in Darien, involved in the wars and quarrels . . . in 1511. (I) set sail . . . for Santo Domingo in a small caravel to acquaint the Admiral Governor with what was going on in Darien; also, to make an accounting of the men and supplies, and to bring 20,000 ducats belonging to the King. We had got as far as Jamaica when the caravel struck on the shoals called Las Viboras, and twenty of us barely escaped in the ship's boat, without sails, without water, without bread, and with only one miserable pair of oars. We drifted in this fashion for thirteen or fourteen days, when we were caught in the current that runs very fast and strong to the west, and were cast ashore in a province called Maya. Seven of us had died, or as I believe, eight. A rascally cacique, into whose power we had fallen, sacrificed Valdivia and four others to his idols, and then ate them, making a fiesta of it and offering a share to his friends. I and six others were placed in cages to be fattened for the next banquet, and to avoid such an abominable death we broke out of our prison and fled to the woods. And it was God's will that we should meet another cacique, a mortal enemy of the first, a humane man, . . . who sheltered us and spared our lives, although he kept us in servitude. . . ."[25]

[24]López de Gómara, pp. 24-25.
[25]López de Gómara, pp. 9-10.

Although Aguilar's story caused "astonishment" and "fear," he nonetheless was an excellent person for Cortés to encounter. His eight years among the Maya had forced him to learn the language—thus Cortés added a translator to his complement. And what about that complement. What kind of men shipped with Cortés? It is commonly believed that Mexico was conquered by conquistadores, military men; but remember that Cortés himself was not a regular soldier. He was a rancher, and notary—or quasi attorney. True, he had the rank of captain, but after all, there was only one military rank, and that *was* captain. Contrary to popular belief, the majority of Cortés' men were not professional soldiers; rather they were hidalgos, men of high rank such as squires. Some were artisans who had been involved in metal and glass working; and others were tailors, carpenters, and shipbuilders.

The conquerors had no real organization; they had no real military training; no pay; and no rank. Then how did this handful of people, motivated only by a civil calling, achieve their ends? How in heaven's name did they conquer the powerful and militaristic Azteca? Looking back on the conquest and attempting to analyze it beyond its romantic aspects it appears that the main advantage of the Spaniards was technological. They possessed steel. Steel armour, steel lances, and steel swords gave the Spaniards tremendous superiority over the wooden swords of the Indian. Upon striking the Spanish shield, these wooden swords literally disintegrated.

Horses were another advantage to the Spaniards. Armored horses could be used as tanks, and in "V" formation they could drive a wedge through Indian ranks and create panic. The horse gave them speed and mobility. Also the Indians were generally afraid of the horse. They had never seen this animal, and some believed the horse and rider were one. Hernán Cortés played upon this fear of the horse. On a number of occasions, when he had cowed a group of Indians, he ordered his horsemen to ride at great speeds, rear their horses, and fire their arms. These firearms were mainly used for noise and fright since they took several minutes to reload, and were terribly inaccurate. Before rifling, or the grooving of the barrel of a weapon, was invented, firearms had limited accuracy. But to some Indians the firing of these weapons meant that the Spaniards had control of the gods of lightning and thunder—and therefore the invaders' power was divinely established. Furthermore, problems among the Indians themselves aided the conquering Spaniard. The Indians were divided and constantly at war for sacrificial prisoners, political hegemony, and economic supremacy. Several of these enemies of the Aztecs, to avoid tribute and to reestablish their independence from the Aztec, joined the Spaniards as Indian allies. Finally, Indian military tactics were not able to cope with those of the Spaniards. The Indians saw warfare as a means of capturing prisoners; they were not oriented toward killing their adversaries to win territory. Because darkness had certain ominous religious connotations, they were reluctant to engage in night fighting. To the Spaniards, the cover of darkness was an advantage to fighting. Spanish battle plans were devised to meet the needs of the moment while the Indians fought a formalized conventional warfare, constrained by rules and tradition. And the Indians knew neither how to resist nor to employ one of the most powerful of all European weapons, the seige.

There were still other non-technical factors which weighed against the Indians achieving victory. The Europeans brought diseases with them to which the Indians had never been exposed; diseases which killed thousands of natives. Some of these reached epidemic proportions and were disastrous to the Indian populations both friendly and hostile. The two most devastating diseases were smallpox and measles.

Then there were the psychological factors. The Indians were truly surprised and shocked at the power of the Spanish; their firearms, their horses. And finally, there was the myth of the feathered serpent, Quetzalcoatl; the legend of a man-god who left his people vowing to return one day from the East as "a light man with a beard." Hernán Cortés landed at Veracruz on the day of Ce Acatl—the birthdate of this man-god, the legendary Ce Acatl, Topilizn Quetzalcoatl.

Cortés and his entourage had a strong belief in themselves—a superiority complex—in terms of both their culture and their religion. Thus they saw the Indians as barbarians who deserved whatever punishments were meted out. But this was far from being a decisive factor. It was the weaknesses of the Indians, primarily technological ones, that made the ultimate difference.

Before leaving Cozumel, Cortés ceremoniously destroyed the gods and idols of the Indians and delivered a touching sermon on the evils of paganism and the benefits of Christianity; it was a ceremony which he repeated in each town and village he conquered. From Cozumel, they sailed slowly along the coast toward their destination. At the mouth of the Grijalva river they were relieved to be able to drop anchor, for many had contracted a sickness which they called el vomito. Their relief was quickly changed to consternation since they were greeted by hundreds of Indian warriors waiting in full battle regalia. Cortés attempted to mollify them—to no avail. In the three pitched battles that ensued, many men were lost on both sides. Unquestionably, in these as in future battles, the Indians fought very bravely, even in the face of the supernatural horses and gunpowder. Bernal Díaz del Castillo, a soldier in Cortés' army, described the battle of Cintla, "The Tabascan squadrons, as they approached us, were so numerous that they covered the whole savannah. . . . All the men wore great feather crests, they carried drums and trumpets, their faces were painted black and white, they were armed with large bows and arrows, spears and shields, swords like our two-handed swords, and slings, and stones and fire-toughened darts, and all wore quilted cotton armour. They rushed on us like mad dogs, and completely surrounded us, discharging such a rain of arrows, darts and stones upon us that more than seventy of our men were wounded at the first attack."[26]

But the Indian bravery was for naught. Again, European technology prevailed and the forces of Cortés were triumphant.

Having lost the battle, the Tabascans pledged their fealty to Cortés and gave him presents of gold and twenty beautiful maidens, Cortés distributed the females among his captains. One of the most beautiful, bright and coquettish, was given to Cortés' close friend, Hernándo Alonso Puertocarrero. The Spaniards called her Doña Marina. Her name was Malinche or Malitizin or Malinulli, and she soon became a mistress to Cortés and his indispensable friend and interpreter. Although her parents were Azteca aristocrats, her life had been unhappy for her father died when she was a child, and her mother, in order to preserve the family fortune for her son, sold Malinche into slavery to the Tabascans. Having little allegiance to anyone she grew attached to Cortés, and even bore him a son. Later, Cortés married her to one of his high ranking soldiers, Juan Jaramillo. Although the marriage brought her wealth, fame, and power, she always remained loyal to the father of her first son, Hernán Cortés.

With the arrival of Malinche, Cortés now had two interpreters, Aguilar who interpreted from Spanish to Mayan, and Malinche, who interpreted from Mayan to Azteca. And soon, Malinche's intelligence brought her the knowledge of Spanish—so she became a direct interpreter. From Tabasco, they sailed toward Veracruz, and on Good Friday, 1519, they landed on a sandy beach in a river inlet called La Antigua just twenty miles north of the present city of Veracruz. Because they landed on Good Friday and because the area was so beautiful, Cortés named it La Villa Rica de Vera Cruz—or the rich villa of the true cross. In an attempt to sever his relations with Velázquez and assume direct authority under the king, Cortés ceremoniously resigned his commission; and knowing Castilian law, he formed a town council or cabildo, to which he was elected Governor, Captain General, and Justice. He was now ready to begin his march to the Azteca capital of Tenochtitlan. Emissaries from this capital had been bringing Cortés and his men gifts for days, hoping these would placate the Spaniards and cause them to sail away. But it only strengthened their resolution to acquire even more. "Sailing away" became an impossibility since Cortés removed all temptation of desertion by

[26]Diaz del Castillo, *Bernál: The True History of the Conquest of Mexico*, translated by Maurice Keatinge, esq. (London: Hohn Dean, 1800), p. 45.

scuttling his ships. Cortés marched to Zempoala, where he gained the support of the chiefs. He then moved further inland to the present state of Tlaxcala, where he met his stiffest resistance. The Tlaxcalans, who had never been conquered by the Azteca, proved to be valiant foes on the battle field, and Cortés was almost overrun. But again he prevailed, and the Tlaxcalans became Cortés' chief allies. Now accompanied by a large Indian army he moved ever closer to the Azteca capital. At Cholula, a plot was devised to assassinate Cortés. But Malinche warned Cortés, who punished the Cholulans by massacring several thousand of their warriors.

After several days of marching and fighting, Cortés and his allies reached the Anahuac valley, and Lake Texcoco, the Island of Tenochtit-lan lay within his grasp.

When they arrived in the city, Moctezuma, the ruler of the Azteca, welcomed them. But Cortés, believing that a trap was being prepared for him, arrested Moctezuma, and made him a prisoner in his own palace. Looting and plundering of gold and silver began in haste and was only interrupted by the arrival of news that a fleet of eighteen ships under the command of Pánfilo de Narváez had been sent by Governor Velázquez to capture, arrest, and return one Hernán Cortés to Cuba. With a small detachment of troops Cortés quickly marched to Veracruz where he surprised Narváez, captured him, and gained the allegiance of eight hundred more Spanish soldiers. Unfortunately, when Cortés returned to Tenochtitlan, he found Indians struggling to expel the foreigners. His Captain, Pedro de Alvarado, had acted hastily and killed a number of nobles and priests who were gathered in a religious ceremony, which caused the Aztecs to rebel. Even Moctezuma could not control his people, and was killed either by the Azteca themselves or by Cortés, who no longer found him useful.

On June 30, 1520, Cortés retreated after suffering a humiliating defeat. He and his men were almost captured as they crossed Lake Texcoco; and many drowned while attempting to carry gold away from the island city. Legend says that on the following night Cortés sat under a tree and cried for the loss of his men and the loss of the city. This event is commonly known as *noche triste* or night of sadness.

But Cortés' losses were temporary. He would not accept defeat. With the lumber from his scuttled ships, he prepared landing craft for the recapture of Tenochtitlan. On December 26, 1520, Cortés began his march from Tlaxcala for the final conquest. On December 31, he reached Texcoco, and spent three months in preparation for the assault. The battle raged for more than four months, and casualties were heavy on both sides. Many of the Spaniards were captured and put to the sacrificial knife on the great pyramid at Tenochtitlan. But on August 13, 1521, Cuauhtemoc, the last of the Azteca Emperors, was captured and the battle was won. The city of Tenochtitlan, which Cortés called the most beautiful city in the world, was virtually destroyed. The conquest was complete. The last major fighting took place at Tlatelolco, Mexico City where there is a commemorative plaque at the Plaza of the Three Cultures. Its words constitute Mexico's national attitude toward the conquest. It reads: "In 1521 Tlatelolco, heroically defended by Cauhtemoc, fell under the power of Hernán Cortés. It was neither a victory nor a defeat, but the painful beginning of the mestizo people, which is Mexico today."

CHAPTER 11

The Administrative System
of New Spain

The plaza of Merida is located in the state of Yucatan, Mexico. This plaza, like hundreds of others throughout Spanish America, represents the transference of the complex culture of Iberia to the New World. The plaza was the center of activity in Spain, and became equally important in Mexico. In fact, much of the fascination and lustre of the plaza is still with us today.

Much of what we find in Spanish Colonial America were adaptations of cultural and political institutions found in Spain. Even structural and architectural styles found in Spain were transferred to the New World. Little was new, and if it appeared to be different, it was only because the institution or the style was modified to meet the differences of geography, climate, and population. The plaza in Merida, Spain, as the one in Merida, Mexico, has a church, public buildings, and the houses of the wealthy residents constructed around the plaza; and the plaza was usually the center of the city.

The best example of the cultural transference from Spain was the establishment of the Mexican city. Spain was an urban oriented society; and under Roman, Visigothic, and Moslem influence, the city became the center of activity. In the Spanish provinces, there was at least one large urban center and several secondary centers. Since Spain's largest provinces were land-locked, the major cities were located inland; this was true

96

for important trading centers as well. A good example is Seville. Located inland, on the Gaudliquivir River, its geographic disadvantages outweigh the advantage of being safe from piracy. Yet it remained the predominant commercial center of Spain for several centuries.

Looking at a map of Mexico, one can see that the predominant urban centers of Mexico are also located inland: Mexico City, Guadalajara, Monterrey, Chihuahua, Oaxaca, and Puebla are all inland population centers. And the advantages for the Spaniard settling inland were also native to Mexico. Mexico City, or the Anahuac Valley, had two basic prerequisites to support a major city. The first was the Valley's large sedentary population; and the second was the natural resources the area had to offer—an agreeable climate, and a good agricultural base.

So Hernán Cortés established the city of Mexico where the Azteca had built the great center of Tenochtitlan. Here the city grew to become the most important metropolis of the entire colonial period, and today it is Mexico's most important city. Mexico City was designed around the same plan found in any city in Spain. The pattern was to lay out a central plaza around which would be constructed the important buildings. There would be a church, or if the city were important enough, a cathedral. In Mexico City, the great cathedral, with its imposing architecture of Gothic and Romanesque styles, dominates the massive plaza or zocalo. And it is built where the Aztecas major pyramids once stood—a testament to the superiority of the Spanish God. The government buildings in Mexico also display the massive Romanesque architecture, especially the National Palace, which is well over 300 years old, and is still being used as the seat of Mexican government. During the colonial period, over sixty-two viceroys resided in the National Palace. Finally, the homes of the wealthy completed the plan of construction around the plaza. The large building on the southeast corner of Mexico's zocalo was once the home of Hernán Cortés. It now houses the national pawnshop, El Monte de Piedad, or literally, mountain of pity.

In 1625 an English priest, Thomas Gage, described the activity in the center of Mexico City:

"The gallants of this city shew themselves daily, some on horseback, and most in coaches, about four of the clock in the afternoon in a pleasant shady field called *la Alameda*, full of trees and walks, somewhat like unto our Moorfields, where do meet as constantly as the merchants upon our exchange about two thousand coaches, full of gallants, ladies, and citizens, to see and to be seen, to court and to be courted, the gentlemen having their train of blackamoor slaves some a dozen, some half a dozen waiting on them, in brave and gallant liveries, heavy with gold and silver lace, with silk stockings on their black legs, and roses on their feet, and swords by their sides; the ladies also carry their train by their coach's side of such jetlike damsels as before have been mentioned for their light apparel, who with their bravery and white mantles over them seem to be, as the Spaniard saith, *mosca en leche,* a fly in milk. But the train of the Viceroy who often goeth to this place is wonderful stately, which some say is as great as the train of his master the King of Spain. At this meeting are carried about many sorts of sweetmeats and papers of comfits to be sold, for to relish a cup of cool water, which is carried about in curious glasses, to cool the blood of those love-hot gallants. But many times these their meetings sweetened with conserves and comfits have sour sauce at the end, for jealousy will not suffer a lady to be courted, no nor sometimes to be spoken to, but puts fury into the violent hand to draw a sword or dagger and to stab or murder whom he was jealous of, and when one sword is drawn thousands are presently drawn, some to right the party wounded or murdered; others to defend the party murdering, whose friends will not permit him to be apprehended, but will guard him with drawn swords until they have conveyed him to the sanctuary of some church, from whence the Viceroy his power is not able to take him for a legal trial."*

During the colonial period, a number of secondary centers arose throughout the valley. Some such as Santo Domingo still remain, dominated by a church and the homes of the wealthy. But no center ever supplanted the importance and grandeur of the Zocalo of Mexico City.

The rather loose administrative system which developed for the New World was also similar to the system introduced in Spain by the Catholic monarchs. Many governmental positions and titles were given to individuals as rewards for their loyalty to the crown. Persons of influence might also be given a title or position in order to further their social and economic status. This became true in Mexico as well. So power, which is the test of any governmental position, depended not on the office as much as it did on the individual. To say that a governor is more powerful than a mayor might be erroneous. Much depended on the administrative district of each officeholder and his own ability to enforce his authority. (For example, if he were an encomendero, he could augment his power with an Indian army.)

This constant shifting and searching for legitimacy and power continued throughout the entire colonial period, and to some extent it still prevails today. It is still of great importance to have a title of status. This is something which the state guarantees, and that guarantee was one of the main functions of the Spanish crown during the colonial period. With guaranteed title and rank, it was almost certain that one's economic and social status would be enhanced. (This remains true today.)

The administration of New Spain began not in Mexico, but in Spain. It was the sovereigns' desire to maintain final control and authority over the colonies. In 1503, an office known as the *Casa de Contratación* was established in Seville in order to put into effect that desire. The *Casa de Contratación* or house or trade—which met in Archives of the Indies, or *Lanja*—was to administrate all political and economic affairs in Spain's

*Thomas Gage, *The English American,* pp. 91-92.

colonial empire. In 1524 a second administrative body was founded—*El Real y Supremo Consejo de las Indias*—The Royal Supreme Council of the Indies—which also met in the *Lanja,* was designed primarily as an advisory body for the crown. But soon it took over all administrative, judicial, and fiscal authority for the crown and ultimately administered the *Patronato Real* or Royal Patronage as well. This patronage gave to the crown and its subordinates certain political authority over the structure and operation of the Catholic Church!

Originally, the *Casa de Contratación* was formed to handle all sailings, customs, and immigration to the colonies. But as gold and silver were discovered, the *Casa de Contratación* introduced a scheme known as the Fleet, Flota, Fair system. The great convoys which sailed to the colonies departed from the harbor of Seville. The idea was to convoy the silver across the Atlantic and thereby reduce the threat of piracy. Each convoy consisted of forty to sixty ships protected by twenty to thirty warships. Two convoys sailed from Seville each year. The larger of the two, known as the fleet, sailed to the ports of Cartagena and Portobello. Cartagena is located on the coast of present day Colombia, while Portobello is on the coast of the modern nation of Panama. The small fleet, or *flota* sailed from Seville to Veracruz. At each of these ports a fair was held where silver and gold collected from all parts of the colonies were traded for goods from Spain. In this way, Spain could effectively maintain control over the flow of gold and silver while at the same time hold monopolies on manufactured goods from Spain and Europe. The system had many defects, and timing was the major one. For the fair to be economically successful the fleets and the merchants had to arrive simultaneously, a feat not always possible given the poor methods of communications. Merchants sometimes arrived early, or late, and in either case the cost was disastrously expensive. Furthermore, the fairs themselves were crowded and ineffectual. Towns which were built to house a small number of people were suddenly invaded by a host of ships and thousands of sailors, each bringing his share of disease. Ships brought rats, and the lack of sanitation facilities spread disease. Sailors carried venereal diseases which became endemic in the small port cities. And the cities themselves harbored their own brands of malaria, yellow fever, and dysentery.

In the 1730's two youthful Spanish scientist-naval officers, Jorge Juan and Antonio Ulloa, visited the fair at Portobello. Their description is typical for other fairs throughout Spanish Colonial America:

> "The town of Porto Bello, so thinly inhabited, by reason of its noxious air, the scarcity of provisions, and the soil, becomes, at the time of the galleons, one of the most populous places in all South America. . . .
> . . . The concourse of people, on this occasion, is such, as to raise the rent of lodging to an excessive degree; a middling chamber, with a closet,

lets, during the fair, for a thousand crowns, and some large houses for four, five, or six thousand.

. . . The land is covered with droves of mules from Panama, each drove consisting of above an hundred, loaded with chests of gold and silver, on account of the merchants of Peru. Some unload them at the exchange, others in the middle of the square; yet, amidst the hurry and confusion of such crowds, no theft, loss or disturbance, is ever known. He who has seen this place during the *tiempo muerto,* or dead time, solitary, poor, and a perpetual silence reigning everywhere; the harbour quite empty, and every place wearing a melancholy aspect; must be filled with astonishment at the sudden change, to see the bustling multitudes, every house crowded, the square and streets encumbered with bales and chests of gold and silver of all kinds; the harbour full of ships and vessels, . . . bringing . . . cacao, quinquina, or Jesuit's bark, Vicuna wool, and bezoar stones. Others . . . loaded with provisions. . . . And thus a spot, at all other times detested for its deleterious qualities, becomes the staple of the riches of the old and new world, and the scene of one of the most considerable branches of commerce in the whole earth. . . .

Formerly this fair was limited to no particular time; but as a long stay, in such a sickly place, extremely affected the health of the traders, his Catholic majesty transmitted an order, that the fair should not last above forty days, reckoning from that in which the ships came to an anchor in the harbour. . . ."[27]

But the system could never supply enough goods for the colonists in New Spain and so smuggling of European goods and commodities became rampant. So accepted was smuggling, that even officials of the *Casa de Contratacion* participated in it! There was one more trading system permitted by the Spanish crown, the so-called Manila Galleon. For sometime after the Philippines were acquired by the Spanish crown, ships would sail between Acapulco and Manila on a seven thousand mile round trip journey. The profits from the silks, jade, ivorys, and spices were so great that the crew actually slept on the top deck, in order to protect the valuable cargo below. As the profits of the Galleon soared, the crown became worried about the excess of power associated with the system and attempted to limit the sailings and the size of the Manila Galleon. The result was more smuggling, and systematic payoffs to customs officials, a practice which became almost traditional throughout colonial and national Latin America.

The second of the two governmental agencies which operated as a direct arm of the Crown, was the Royal Supreme Council of the Indies. The Council acted as the intermediary between the Crown and the colonies. From its headquarters in Seville, the Council or *Consejo* ultimately took over most of the political functions of the House of Trade, and

[27]Borzoi, ed. Intro by Irving A. Leonard (New York: Knopf, 1964) pp. 55-56 . . . ; also appears in George Juan and Antonio de Ulloa, *A Voyage to South America* (London: 1772), pp. 103-105.

introduced a few more. At the head of the Consejo was a High Chancellor whose power was unique since he presented laws to the Crown for his signature. The High Chancellor had executive authority because he would also administer the laws which he had created. And since the Council could act as a Supreme Court for all judicial matters arising in the New World, he had judicial authority as well! The High Chancellor was assisted by eight lawyer counsellors, an attorney, and a host of secretaries, historians, cosmographers, treasurers, and clerks. In addition, there was a chaplain, advocate for the poor, and a sheriff. The size and complexity of the Council depended upon the king and the times in which the Council functioned. Generally, throughout the colonial history of Spain, the Council became larger, more corrupt and power hungry. However, under the rule of Charles III, in the late eighteenth century, all aspects of colonial administration went through stages of reform, and this included the Royal Supreme Council of the Indies.

Probably the most glaring example of transference of the Spanish system to the New World was the office of the viceroyalty. In Spanish, Viceroy is *Virrey* or assistant king; and he was a king in almost every sense of the word. He had his own realm, his own palace, his own royal guard, a moderate salary, and in addition to wearing royal robes, he was accorded the royal salute of the bow or courtsey. On the surface, it appeared as if the viceroy was as omnipotent in the New World as was the king of Spain. But this was far from the truth. There were many checks placed upon the authority of the viceroy, including those of the Catholic hierarchy and the powerful merchant guilds. Furthermore, the power and authority of the viceroy shifted with the changing fortunes of the mother country—Spain and with the personality of the viceroy. In the sixteenth century, those chosen for this important position were persons whom society had considered the fittest to rule. They were members of the nobility, often the grandees. They often exerted great influence over the Church, wealthy encomenderos, and merchant guilds. The earlier viceroys appear to have been in command of their advisors. As Spanish fortunes declined in the seventeenth century, so did the quality of the viceroys. Men of rank sought the office in order to improve their social and economic position in Spain. Their main motivation became that of acquiring high office in order to enhance the fortunes of themselves, their families, and their clients. And in some instances, the motivation was to contract for a handsome retirement and a life of ease in Spain. It is no wonder then, that men of this calibre employed trickery and bribery in order to solve problems rather than their moral influence or skill. The viceroys literally became captives of the system they came to administer, and the payoff— or *mordida* as it is called today—was the major weapon in a viceroy's arsenal of enforcement. In 1716 the Viceroy of Mexico, Duque de Linares, wrote to his successor, "Justice is sold like goods in a market-place where he who has money in his pocket buys what he wants. In this market-place, mystery and secrecy rule. . . . Furthermore, judgements are revealed before they are signed, and interested parties are prepared to elude them or to prevent appeals by the injured. . . . Such justice is like a worm consuming the wealth of the Kingdom."[28]

On the surface it appeared that the advisory body to the viceregal court was free from bribery and corruption—but it was not. The *audiencia*, which was the most powerful group below the viceroy, functioned much the same as the Royal Supreme Council of the Indies did in Spain. In fact, it was considerably more than an advisory body. Like the council or *consejo* it had certain executive, legislative, and judicial authority. Like the *consejo* it was made up of attorneys, called *oidores* or listeners, and a host of support personnel. Also like the *consejo*, it could draw up local laws for the viceroy's signature; it could advise on appointments; it could act as court of review; and in the case of the death or transfer of the viceroy, it would act in his stead. The continuity of personnel of this advisory body should have insulated it against the petty struggles of local interest groups, but it did not. In time, these offices went up for sale in Spain to those who wished to better their status. While the New World was ultimately divided into four viceroyalties; New Spain, Peru, New Granada, and Argentina or Rio de la Plata—there were twelve audiencias, which made positions on these bodies more available. For the most part, they were located in centers of population and mineral or trading wealth. If there were no viceroy in the locality of an audiencia, then the president of the audiencia acted in his behalf.

Below the viceroy and audiencia were a series of offices which appeared to give local control of the government structure. But effectiveness depended upon the individual's ability to enforce his authority rather than the inherent authority vested in the office itself. Individuals in New Spain, not unlike other New World European colonists, used whatever methods were most likely to work—bribery, trickery, and economic favors seemed to be the favorites. The most important local organization was the town council. Sometimes called the *Cabildo* and at other times the *Ayuntamiento* its function was to give local representation for the citizens of a community. At times it did just that. But it also served as a vehicle for those who wished to rise in society. In addition to the town councils, locals swelled the ranks of the official bureaucracy. Governors, mayors, and the intermediate office of *corregidores*, all seriously burdened an already overgrown bureaucracy. There was never enough tax money to adequately pay all the governmental officials, and the taxes were burdensome.

[28]Stanley J. Stein and Barbara H. Stein, *The Colonial Heritage of Latin America*, (New York: Oxford University Press, 1970), p. 68.

The Crown collected 20 percent or one fifth of all treasure that was acquired by anyone. This was called the qunito real or royal fifth and probably constituted the lion's share of royal revenue. But it was never enough. There was also an Indian head tax of several dollars per year assessed on encomenderos. This provided the crown with additional monies but it also had a constraining effect on the power of the encomendero, for he kept only enough Indians on his hacienda necessary for efficient and optimum farming.

In addition, there were the alcabala, a hated sales tax of from two to six percent; a fifteen percent import duty; and a two percent cargo-convoy tax. The crown also augmented its revenues through its government-owned monopolies on salt, gun powder and quicksilver; and through the sale of governmental offices and religious indulgences; indulgences which could shorten one's time in purgatory for the commission of earthly sins.

But with all of this, there was never enough money. The office and the title meant much more than the wages one received. Therefore, it became common practice that one needed to have some way to augment his governmental salary in order to maintain a lifestyle commensurate with his position. As a result practically every officeholder used his political position to enrich his outside business connections. Many of these were connected to Spain, with clients who wished to gain an economic foothold in the colonies. In this way, the activities of a government official might provide a vital link between regions in the colonies and the economy of Spain.

In any case, the whole system, almost out of necessity, became accepted—and yes, even expected. For the average citizen not engaged in government service, the system was unjust—but to the bureaucrats there was no need for reform and constraint—for them the system worked well. From time to time the crown saw the possibility of a challenge to royal authority, especially with the higher ranking officeholders.

So from time to time, the monarch would introduce more bureaucrats designed to check the authority of viceroys and other high ranking officials. One such office was the *residencia* or resident. It was usually composed of a number of judges appointed by the Crown, and empowered to review an official's conduct during his time in office. The judges of the *residencia* were to review the acts of lower politicians, such as corregidores and alcaldes. But they were soon empowered to hear and pass judgement upon the conduct of governors, presidents, and even the Viceroy! Another major check on the colonial bureaucracy was the *Visitador General,* or inspector general. This person was vested with immense authority by the Crown. He could literally make heads roll, and at times he did! Probably the most noted Visitador General was sent to the colonies under the authority of the reformer king, Charles III. José de Gálvez came to New Spain in the 1760's in order to reform the colonial administration and to effect fiscal reformation. He was moderately successful at both. Gálvez came from petty nobility and a very poor family. Able and ambitious, he had been privately sponsored in his educational pursuits. He was typical of many capable men who saw civil service as a means to success. With the aid of his second wife, he rose to prominence in governmental service and ultimately was appointed to Inspector General when only forty years old. An example of his power is in the legacy of change and expansion he left in America. Not only was he responsible for revamping the frontier administration of New Spain, but it was Gálvez who effected Spain's incursion and settlement of present day California. Even after Gálvez experienced an extended mental illness, he returned to Spain to become Minister of the Indies in the Royal Supreme Council of the Indies.

Gálvez is an example of an individual using his political authority, which was guaranteed by the crown, to advance his social and economic position. He is also an example of how the crown constantly attempted to limit the power of any one office or individual by placing checks on them—even upon his own personal representative in America, the viceroy.

CHAPTER 12

The Encomienda of
Juan de Cuevas

The encomienda of Cuitlahuac was first owned by Juan de Cuevas. He acquired it from the viceroy sometime before 1544. When he died in 1560, his son Alonso de Cuevas inherited the grant. For more than one hundred and twenty five years his descendants continued to collect labor and tribute from the Indian population in the area of Cuitlahuac near Mexico City. There were many attempts to abolish the encomienda, but the length of ownership of Cuitlahuac attests to the durability of Spain's "benevolent" labor system, the *encomienda*.

Juan de Cuevas was different from many of the early encomenderos since he had not performed military service in the conquest, for most of the first encomenderos in Mexico had participated in the actual conquest. After all, wasn't military service to the crown the road to wealth and fame? Juan de Cuevas, however, was typical of the later holders of encomiendas in that their political and economic connections made them favored candidates for grants. The encomienda, one of the most important institutions in the New World, has commonly been regarded as a grant of land; but it was really a grant of Indians—that is, the use of Indians for their labor and tribute. Any grants of land that an encomendero might receive came as a totally separate transaction and from a different office of the bureaucracy—and those who received an encomienda in all likelihood already possessed land.

The encomienda was a carry-over from feudalistic Iberia. It was first introduced into Spanish America through the West Indies, when the landowners of Hispaniola demanded of the governor, Diego Columbus, that they be given the right to use Indian labor on their farms. These first Indian labor grants bore the name of *repartimiento.* The main difference between repartimiento and the encomienda lay in the set of laws and customs attached to the newer encomienda. The purpose of these laws was to make the institution benign and responsive to the needs of the Indians—both features which were missing from the earlier repartimiento.

In New Spain, the conquering Spaniards thought little of the tribal and regional differences of the Indians they conquered. Of far greater importance to them was the concentration of Indian populations in established urban centers. And here again, Spain transferred its institutions to the New World. The urban centers of greatest population became known as *ciudades,* or cities, of which there were four in the valley of Mexico. The Spaniards used the term *villa* for medium sized urban centers and *pueblos* for the smaller centers. And where there were a number of interconnecting urban centers, one in particular would be singled out as the main center or *cabeza* or head. The word eventually changed to *cabecera.* Sometimes, an encomienda grant would cover four to five *cabeceras* and a whole series of *villas, peublas,* and their diminutives of *villitas* and *pueblitas.* The numbers of encomienda Indians that would be granted could range from several hundred to more than ten thousand. The following is a reconstruction of events surrounding an actual encomienda grant called Cuitlahuac, granted to one Juan de Cuevas.

Cuevas was well qualified to receive a grant from the viceroy of New Spain. He held the title of *escribano mayor de minas,* or a major notary for the treasury of the viceroyalty. It is inconceivable that he would have received that high position without political and family connections in Spain itself. Furthermore, the grant was given to Cuevas by the viceroy in the form of "an exchange," which is evidence that services to the crown in the New World were given in exchange for political, social, and economic betterment to the individual offering his services. While legally the encomienda was granted for meritorious service to the crown, in practice the grant was given to those few Spaniards who had seniority in the conquest and to friends and relatives of those in power. No doubt, Cuevas had friends in high places.

As encomendero, Juan de Cuevas was legally required to fulfill certain obligations. Some he grudgingly fulfilled and others he overfulfilled, particularly if they would enhance his social standing in the community. Unlike the country squire in Anglo North America, the encomendero did not reside on his sprawling estate. In fact, he was required to maintain a residence in the city as well as in the countryside; and he was obliged to live in the city to which his encomienda was attached. In order to prove his lordly status, Juan de Cuevas built a palatial residence on a plaza in Mexico City. This home was known as the *casa poblada,* or the populated house. It was much the same as the sixteenth century mansions seen throughout Mexico's large urban centers. The larger the home, the greater the proof of wealth and lordly existence. But his ostentatiousness did not end with an imposing mansion, for it was merely a vehicle with which he exhibited his high social standing. Juan de Cuevas, like other encomenderos, made certain that his wife was Spanish and that his children were raised with all the accoutrements of Spanish high society. His house, or casa poblada, was usually filled with guests, some of whom were relatives, and others who were mere transients with no roots at all. Cuevas also had as many black slaves as he could afford, for the ownership of Blacks constituted an obvious measure of one's wealth. So important were they, that the encomendero might be seen walking through the Alameda park in the center of Mexico City with his black slaves trailing behind him. Of course, Cuevas also had a number of Hispanized and semi-Hispanized Indian servants which formed a permanent part of the casa poblada. And a mansion of this size must have fine furniture and works of art, so Cuevas supported a number of skilled workers and talented artisans through his many purchases. In addition to his city residence, he was expected to maintain a country home located in the area of the encomienda. So he did, although he rarely if ever lived outside of the city.

In addition, Cuevas was required to keep a horse and arms for the defense of the encomienda. Since the ownership of these items implied wealth and status, Cuevas kept a stable full of horses and many weapons, whether he needed them or not.

Political office holding was not part of a professional career but merely an indicator of social and economic wealth. All encomenderos sought political office—to sit on city councils, or to be members of the viceroy's advisory body. Thus, Cuevas' position in the treasury of the viceroy served his social needs.

The encomienda was *not* designed solely to serve the social standing of the encomendero. In fact, the encomienda was an economically profitable enterprise; and it was also the major link between the city and countryside—and between the Spanish and Indian populations. Obviously a city needed a certain amount of food in order to survive. The Spanish very early realized that they did not like the Indian foods, so there was a demand for Spanish foodstuffs; and as the Hispanized Indians and Spanish populations grew in the cities, the demand for Spanish goods and products increased dramatically. The encomendero, with his massive assets of Indian labor, built his enterprise around the needs of the city population.

As the demand increased, the encomendero became aware of his diverse economic opportunities. With his basic asset—the legal right to the use of Indian labor and tribute—he exploited these opportunities to his economic advantage.

In order to improve his credit, and his economic position, he sought private ownership of land. This would permit him to use fully his Indian labor to increase his profits. Of course, the encomienda had nothing to do with land ownership; but as a private individual the encomendero could and did acquire land. He could receive land either from the town council—of which he was usually a member—or from the governor of the province in which he resided. And because the encomendero had the Indian labor with which to exploit his holdings, he usually became the owner of the largest parcels of land. These grants were called *estancias* and varied widely in size and number. Like the land patterns in Spain, it was not necessary that they be contiguous. The primary use of the *estancia* was for raising Spanish agricultural products and livestock, both of which were alien to Pre-Columbian America.

While the encomienda of Juan de Cuevas was not one of the largest in the Valley of Mexico, it had less than one thousand Indians, it was still of major size. And since Juan de Cuevas rarely left the city, it was necessary for him to have a management structure that would run the encomienda efficiently. The structure which Cuevas used had been established by encomenderos before him, and was institutionalized in New Spain.

This organization had three levels. At the top was the manager. On smaller estates, the manager might even be the owner himself. But Cuevas was able to hire an estate manager who was called a *mayordomo*. Under the mayordomo were the skilled overseers. These were in a sense straw bosses and were called *estancieros*. The labor force, which was the third level, was Indians.

The mayordomo who ran the estate in the name of the encomendero was the most important figure of the encomienda. Because of his responsibilities, he had to be a literate man. Since he kept accounts for Juan de Cuevas he needed to have basic skills in math and accounting. And he had to be trustworthy! In addition, he also performed the most important duty of selling the estate's products, which certainly required he have at least a feeling for the laws of supply and demand. And a major feature of his duties was to watch over the estate's labor force; he supervised Indian activities—which included construction, and the planting and harvesting of crops, and the production of a variety of handicrafts by Indian artisans. But despite these critical responsibilities there was a wide social and economic gulf between him and the encomendero. *Mayordomos* were usually Spaniards of humble origin who did not qualify for social standing equal to their bosses.

As with most straw bosses, the *estancieros* were far from well-loved—in fact—they were more often hated. This disdain increased because of their relatively low social standing. They were the most marginal members of Spanish and Hispanic society. They were always Spanish speaking, but they were from such groups as foreigners, sailors, and sometimes Blacks; so they commanded little respect even though they were teachers of European culture to the Indian.

While the vast majority of labor on the encomienda consisted of tribute Indians, Juan de Cuevas, and his mayordomo, some were able to recruit free labor as well. This was especially desirable during the harvest season when extra labor was needed. Maintaining an excessive number of encomienda Indians throughout the entire year was often unprofitable especially since the crown attempted to restrict the size and power of the encomienda by placing a head tax on the Indian. This forced the encomendero to restirct his Indian charges to a number which would give him the most efficient year round operation. Added to this was the proclivity of the Indian to leave the estate and "strike out on his own", hence the formation of a transient free labor force, available for hire.

Juan de Cuevas had certain legal obligations designed for the welfare of his encomienda Indians. As the colonial period developed, the crown, under pressure from the clergy, increased those obligations in order to protect the rights of the Indians. While the encomienda system has often been likened to slavery, nothing could be further from the truth for slavery in its legal sense denoted chattel ownership. That is, the slave is owned by the master as one would own a horse or a building, a concept absent in Mexico. Slaves, especially in Anglo North America, were never citizens, had few rights and no recourse to the established legal system and were chattel property. None of this was true for the encomienda Indian. He was never chattel property; rather it was his labor and tribute to which the encomendero was entitled. And even that entitlement had its limits. Furthermore, the encomienda Indian always had the Catholic Church through which he could offer some protest at times with powerful effect. And finally, he had some status as a citizen with the right to recourse in the courts.

So what were the legal obligations of Juan de Cuevas? And did he observe them to the letter of the law? The main thrust of the laws was to integrate the Indian into Spanish society—in the process of which the Indians' rights were to be protected. One must always remember that Spain was a Catholic nation, with the Church and state as one. In fact, Spain was often referred to as the "Defender of the Faith;" and it is this ideal that needs to be considered along with the laws of the state. The Catholic Church saw the Indian as a child of God, to be protected and taught the ways of the Church and the society into which he must be integrated. Here stands the first general charge and obligation of Juan de

Cuevas. He was responsible for employing clergy on the encomienda as a means of educating his Indian charges. In addition, he was responsible for making certain that his Indian charges were properly fed, housed, and clothed.

There were other laws designed to prevent the exploitation and abuse of the encomienda Indian. For example, only the padres could inflict punishment on the Indians; Indian produced goods could be sold only on market day, and then only at the designated marketplace; and there were a series of rules which were designed to prevent the Indians from being overworked. These laws and obligations were not always fulfilled by the encomendero and Juan de Cuevas and his subordinates often found ways to circumvent them. Nevertheless, their promulgation gives us some indication of the goals and efforts of the Church and the crown to effect a certain amount of justice for the conquered Indian civilizations.

During the colonial period Mexico's countryside was not just a series of uninterrupted encomiendas. In fact, there were two distinct economies functioning—that of the Indians and that of the Spanish. The Spaniards were primarily concerned with the concentration of Indian populations located in established urban centers. Therefore, it stands to reason that it was the urbanized centers with the most people which became Hispanized most rapidly. But the degree of this so-called Hispanization is questionable. For it was not always the Spaniard asserting his cultural, economic, and religious patterns over the Indian; at times it was the other way around. Hispanization may be generally viewed as the outcome—but this often means the merging of both Indian and Spanish cultures. Probably the best examples lie in religion and in trade patterns. Even today, much of Catholic Mexico is really heterodoxy where Indian rituals find formal expression through the Catholic Church. A good example is the Virgin Mary, who in Mexico becomes the Mestiza Virgin of Guadalupe. We must view the mixing of cultures more as an accommodation; for in many areas of Mexico, the Indians kept their language, their clothing, and their local political organization.

And what about these two economies that exist side by side? Well, as we move more into the countryside or the areas of less concentrated population, the impact of Hispanization decreases. It is primarily in these areas that we find the Indians functioning economically side by side with the emerging Spanish economy. In the colonial period, a sizable Indian population remained intact. This population continued to consume Indian foodstuffs of corn, fruits, and vegetables. Many of the pre-conquest trade patterns remained almost uninterrupted and Indian markets continued to trade only Indian goods. In some of these more prominent market places, the Spaniard began to encroach—and Spanish goods found their way into the Hispanized and semi-Hispanized Indian homes. But not all Indians wanted to accept the Spanish culture and religion. For them, there was a constant emigration into the countryside. It was clearly an attempt to protect their own Pre-Columbian cultural patterns and structure. This was not a static society of docile Indians accepting Hispanization, but an evolving pattern of social and cultural change. Add to this the movement from the countryside to the city and a picture emerges of a changing Mexico, and that change continues today.

The common link in this chain of movement between the Indian population and the Spaniards was the encomienda. And the most frequent form of contact between these two communities was through the collection of tribute. In Mexico, tribute from the Indians was often not in the form of money or goods, but in the form of services. The outlying encomienda Indians would migrate to the edge of the city where they would reside temporarily so they could be available to work for the encomendero. This practice exposed the country Indian to Spanish culture. Thus, the slow but inevitable process of Hispanization continued.

But even the Hispanized Indian maintained his contact with friends, relatives, and economic sources. In fact, some Hispanized Indians found themselves in a position to profit from Juan de Cuevas as well. Since they spoke Spanish, they could move freely within Spanish society. And their Indian heritage gave them a sort of dual nationality. With these resources, they found themselves as middle men selling surplus products to the outlying Indians. And where did they get the surplus? Well, sometimes it came from their own plots of land, and at other times they merely stole it from the encomienda.

Gradually, this institution of granting Indians to an individual diminished and finally died out; that is, it died out as a legitimate government-sanctioned-enterprise. But the basic precepts and tenants of the institution were merely transformed from government sanctioned to private ownership. The loss of government grants of Indians led the encomendero to search for other sources of labor to work his massive estate. The *encomienda* became the great estate—or more commonly called the *hacienda;* and this represented a major cultural and economic shift. During the encomienda period, the chief economic asset consisted of Indians—during the hacienda period, the major asset was privately owned land. So did the descendants of Juan de Cuevas lose their land and status because of the gradual death of the encomienda? Probably not; more than likely, Cuevas' descendants had been acquiring more land for some time. And so had others. So while the number of encomenderos remained relatively few, the hacendado class grew significantly. This had no small effect on the internal development of the economy of New Spain. With the additions to the upper class—the landed gentry—the demand for labor and products of ostentation increased. The Indians freed from the encomienda were thrown into a free labor force that had little stability. For some it was an improvement—for others merely a change in overseers. The demand for domestic labor also increased, as did products produced by artisans. While economic and social patterns were changing, the basic structure of colonial social patterns endured. Nevertheless, changes were inevitable. And many of those changes took place within the encomienda system and with men like the *escribano mayor de minas,* and *encomendero,* Juan de Cuevas of Cuitlahuac.

CHAPTER 13

"The End of the Line"

The legal nomenclature for blood mixtures in New Spain may have exceeded one hundred names. Probably the most common was the mixture of Spaniard and Indian which resulted in a *mestizo*. A Spanish woman and a *mestizo* begat a *castizo;* a *castizo* woman and a Spaniard begat—of all things—a Spaniard, which indicates the system was not rigidly racist. A *morisco* woman and a Spaniard begat an *albino*, but a Spaniard together with an *albino* begat a *torna atras*, or "a throwback." But the most interesting mixture was that of a *coyote mestizo* and a mulatto woman which begat an *ahí te estás*, translated loosely, "well that'll hold you," or "it's the end of the line."

Blood lines were only one way of determining status in New Spain. As in Anglo North America, the determinants were complex and varied. Americans certainly take pride in discovering that their ancestors were linked to those who came over on the Mayflower, or to the first settlers in Jamestown. This was true for New Spain as well where one's ancestors were not just a matter of pride but of legal standing and certification as well. The final determining factor of social standing was, as it is in North America, wealth. However, one's ability to acquire wealth could be influenced, if not controlled, by other factors of social standing, again, not unlike the United States. Actually, it was a complex of ethnic and cultural backgrounds; of birth and education; of profession and wealth—that finally established social status.

For years, writers have put a great deal of emphasis on ethnic origin as the major factor of social status. It was believed that an Indian would be eternally delegated to menial tasks, that his chances of sharing in the higher levels of society were totally non-existent. While there was a tendency for certain ethnic groups to follow established paths, there was a significant amount of movement up and down the socio-economic ladder.

New Spain was a complex, multidimensional, multiracial, constantly changing society.

Historians believe that race mixture, or blood lines, may not have been as important as once thought. Nonetheless, these bloodline classifications did have legal status, and at times carried with them certificates legitimizing and confirming one's legal racial title.

The highest racial position belonged to the Spaniard who was born on the Iberian peninsula—in other words in Spain. He was called a *peninsular*—or in later years *gachupin,* a pejorative term which means "one who wears spurs." In the late colonial period the term *gachupin* was used by the *peninsular* themselves to indicate high social standing. Generally, below the *peninsular* were the creoles or *criollos.* These persons were not at all like the creoles of Louisiana, who are multiracial; or the creoles of Brazil who were blacks born in the New World. The *criollo* of New Spain was a Spaniard who was born in the New World as opposed to those Spaniards born on the Iberian peninsula. Aside from the social snobbery associated with being a *peninsular,* there were some who maintained that the air in America was not conducive to clear thinking—and that even *peninsulares* ought to return to Iberia occasionally for a mental cleansing.

The peninsulares and criollos generally occupied the upper echelons of society, although they were not the dominant ethnic group. By the mid-colonial period, the majority of the population consisted of the mestizo. This term derives from a Latin word which means mixed—and they were just that, but a mixture of a particular blend. Only Spanish and Indian begat a mestizo. Since many Spaniards took Indian wives and Indian mistresses, this sector of society grew the fastest. Mexico today considers itself a mestizo nation—and it is proud of it. However, the pride of the mestizo did not emerge until long after Mexico had achieved its independence. During the greater portion of the colonial period, there was a great deal of prejudice against the mestizo. Why this prejudice was so strong against the offspring of the higher cast Spaniard might have been a result of the illegitimacy of the children—even though recognized by their fathers. Illegitimate mestizo children, raised by Indian mothers, provided the white hierarchy with a scape-goat for the sins of the status conscious white Spaniard. "To them mestizo became almost synonymous with illegitimate."[29] Added to this was the Spanish pride of lineage for

[29]Magnus Mörner, *Race Mixture in the History of Latin America* (Boston: Little, Brown, 1967) p. 55.

every Spanish cavalier wished to see himself as related to some Old Christian family of at least squire ranking. Spain permitted only loyal Spaniards of Christian descent to migrate to the New World. No one known to be of Moorish or Jewish descent would receive permission. Therefore, Spanish emigrants to New Spain viewed themselves as an elite, legitimized by the very crown of Spain. Thus, the prejudice, both social and racial against the mestizo was immense. And this prejudice extended to all levels of non-white New Spain; Indians, mulattoes, negroes, and their mixtures, met with the same disdain as the mestizo.

Bartolomé de Góngora living and writing in New Spain in the mid seventeenth century, tells an amusing and illustrative story about this prejudice: "One day, Don Juan Pareja, well known in Mexico for his great quality, canon of the Holy Church there and illustrious for his sayings and actions, was touring the streets of the city. Then he met an old, well dressed and white haired mulatto. Having brought the coach to a stop he asked the pardo to approach and asked him: "What is your name?" The pardo told him, whereupon the canon exclaimed: "In all my readings I have never come across a mulatto Saint and mulattoes cannot become Saints. God bless you, I am going to canonize you because a mulatto who seems to be honorable and who has grown as much white hair without being hanged or stabbed to death, must be a Saint.""[30]

Well, there is no record that the brown-skinned Pardo ever reached the stage of canonization. But records are replete with examples of racial discrimination. The basic names which were used and understood everywhere were Spaniard, mestizo, mulatto (a word which has its roots in the Latin *mulo,* which is mule or hybrid), Indian, *Negro,* and *zambo.* Zambo was a mixture of either mulatto and Black, or Indian and Black. There were also a number of social distinctions invented by artists and intellectuals who wished to minutely define various observable genetic prototypes. Most of these were not commonly used and should be viewed from the prejudices of their authors. But there were other distinctions, which although they had no legal standings, did have social acceptance. In addition to the mestizo there was a *castizo,* a mixture of *mestizo* and Spanish woman—the term *castizo* meaning pure-blooded or correct. There were mixtures which were called *albinos, lobos* or wolves, *zambaigos* or half Chinese, *cambujo* which is a reddish-black donkey, *albarazado* which is streaked with black, *chamiso* or half-burned tree, and a *"no te entiendo,"* or "I don't understand you."

In spite of all of these classifications, basic usage oftentimes referred to only three categories—"Spaniards," *"castas de mezcla"* or mixed casts, and "Indians." In addition there were relatively few legal categories such as Spaniard; Indians; mestizos; Free Negroes, mulattoes and zamboes

---

[30]Mörner, pp. 56-57; as quoted from: Bartolomé Góngora, *El Cerragidor Sagaz,* Madrid, 1960, pg. 235.

lumped together, and finally slaves. The social status of these groups did not always correspond to their legal status. Although Indians occupied second position legally, they were certainly the most inferior socially.

Coupled with these social-racial titles were titles of rank. The highest was *"don"* or for a woman *"doña."* These were purportedly reserved for the true high nobility whose lineage could be traced to the *duques and condes*—that is the dukes and counts—in Spain. But descendants of *conquistadores*, high civil officials, and wealthy creoles also formed part of the aristocracy which was granted the title of *don* or *doña*. While they were never very numerous, they held a monopoly on the legal profession, the high clergy, the militia command, and high political offices. They were often referred to as the *gente decente*, and they always wore the finest clothes of silk and ruffles so they could be discerned from the lower classes.

Under the *dons* were the *hidalgos*, a term for lower gentry which was a contraction of the Spanish *hijo de algo*, or son of something. One might expect these titles were closely guarded by those who granted them—the sovereigns—but such was not the case. Castilian law permitted anyone— above the rank of peasant—to turn his property into a *mayorazgo*, which is the same as the English entail—or estate which could not be divided and would be inherited in its entirety by legal family heirs. The formation of the *mayorazgo* is an indication of the importance of property as a determinant of wealth and status. Anyone who could form a *mayorazgo* was entitled to the privileges of the *hidalguia*, with the title of a *don*. One could also gain the privileges of rank by purchasing it from the crown. In otherwords, even a *mestizo* could gain a new lineage—and the commensurate title—through a legal purchase from the crown. Philip II, in 1557, sold one thousand *hildalguias* to anyone in the colonies, "without question of defect of lineage" in order to meet his pressing financial obligations; his successors followed his example. Many in the New World who were clearly mestizos created detailed genealogies to prove a heritage which they never really had.

But the true leaders of society—the effective nobility—were the *encomenderos*, or persons who were given *encomienda* grants. And many of the *encomenderos* were men of humble birth in Spain who had participated in the conquest—hoping to improve their social and economic status. And many did just that! Wealth and land ownership were important determinants of status. Some encomienda grants even went to Indian nobles, such as the sons and daughters of the emperor Moctezuma—and since they were economically and socially wealthy, they too were granted the titles of *don* and *doña*! Although the crown originally forbade the use of these titles to anyone who was engaged in commerce or industry, as the colonial period matured even these people moved up the socio-economic ladder and used the coveted titles.

Profession and occupation were also part of one's ethnic origins and legal title. At the upper levels of New Spain's society were the professions such as the clergy, physicians, lawyers, and the all important notaries. Most of these people held the title of *hidalgo*, and could be considered as upper-middle class. The most prevalent of all these professions were members of the clergy. They were found virtually everywhere throughout New Spain, even in the outlying provinces and the mining regions—and so were the notaries.

Because the Spanish had such respect for the written word and knowledge of the law, the notary was a vital person to Spanish society. Notaries oftentimes held important governmental posts such as constables, clerks, and accountants. Their access to important records and documents gave them a certain amount of "privileged" information which enhanced the respect accorded them.

Lawyers and physicians migrated primarily to the urban centers which could afford their services. Their presence or absence accorded or denied a city a certain amount of prestige and importance.

Merchants were exceedingly important and also occupied a relatively high status in colonial society—because they maintained a flow of gold and silver to Spain, and European commodities to New Spain. However, they were neither trusted nor liked by the colonial population. Frequently the parent company was based in Seville so the merchants' loyalties were directed toward Spain, and not New Spain. Sons and junior partners stationed in Mexico City merely waited to earn enough capital so they could return to Spain to form their own trading network. This was another reason to be suspected and disliked. The higher levels of the merchant class did not include local merchants. This small dealer or *tratante*, whose operation was local and very humble, never held the position of respect and rank accorded the long distance merchant.

Because crafts were necessary and profitable enterprises, a rather large and growing artisan class existed from the very moment of conquest. In fact, many of the conquistadores themselves were trained artisans. The colonists of New Spain wished to emulate life in the mother country and the demand for European type goods was immense. Artisans, who numbered individuals of all ethnic groups, also included members of most all trades such as tailors, blacksmiths, leather workers, carpenters, cloth makers, and glass blowers. The tradition of glass blowing was brought to Spain from Italy, particularly Venetia. And in several cities in Mexico that tradition is carried on today.

Many Mexican glass blowers are descendants of families that have been working with glass for many generations; and there are some who say that the product they produce cannot be distinguished from the finest Murano glass of Italy.

Most of the early artisans were Spaniards of humble origins, but after one generation Hispanized Indians were also becoming apprentices in the various trades. Far more important to the early artisans were the freed Blacks, many of whom had skills and experience they had acquired in Spain.

Blacks had been a part of Spanish society long before the conquest. Some Blacks arrived during the conquest and served primarily as military auxiliaries. Service in the military was a socially leveling device and prejudice diminished significantly. Here Blacks were called *morenos* and *mulattoes* were termed *pardos*. Many Blacks had worked as laborers and domestics in Spain and acquired Spanish language and cultural traits. Even those who were later brought over from Africa were more easily assimilated into Spanish society than were the Indians, because they were removed entirely from their previous cultural patterns. Since Blacks came from Spain as freedmen, and from Africa as slaves, both existed side by side.

Because of their Spanish heritage, Blacks learned Spanish ways and techniques faster than Indians, and because their ownership was a sign of wealth and prestige, Blacks were in great demand among the higher levels of society. This, of course, forced the cost of Blacks up even higher, and made them valuable commodities indeed. Thus, only a few wealthy Spaniards held Blacks, and their ownership became a matter of great ostentation. But the arrival, ownership, and miscegenation of Blacks in New Spain is a matter of great complexity, and not at all similar to chattel slavery in Anglo North America; and it is really that one point that makes the big difference—chattel property. While Blacks could be owned as slaves, they did have rights as citizens. They, like the encomienda Indian, could avail themselves, at least in theory, of the structure of society to prevent abuses against them. In other words, a Black was considered a Spanish citizen; an attitude that was reflected in the occupational patterns of Blacks and mulattoes, and their social and cultural position.

Because Blacks were quickly assimilated into Spanish culture, the distinctions between Blacks and Spaniards became blurred and inconsistent. This was particularly true for mulattoes who were quickly absorbed into Spanish society.

Those Blacks who were in the slave category were usually personal servants, skilled worker-artisans, and farmers in agricultural operations located near the urban centers. In fact, Blacks really constituted the main labor force in the artisan shops of the Spaniards. While they occupied the position of apprentices, there were no closed guilds which prevented them from entering the production market on their own; and free Blacks did just that. According to Baron Alexander von Humboldt, the astute German geographer who traveled through Spanish America from 1799 to 1804, New Spain's Blacks were mostly freedmen. And within another twenty years after the visit of von Humboldt, slavery died out as an institution in Mexico. Blacks could obtain their freedom for a number of complex reasons. Many were manumitted upon the death of the owner; and there are some records showing manumission as a compulsory punishment to slave holders who had mistreated their charges! Others bought their freedom or were set free by grateful masters.

Blacks who became free generally served as intermediaries between the Spanish and Indian societies. It is here that a mutual disdain of Blacks and Indians developed. Blacks were often put in charge of Indian labor, particularly on the encomiendas and later on the great estates, where freed Blacks became *estancieros* or straw bosses in these agricultural operations. In addition, renegade Blacks sometimes went into the frontier and intimidated the Indians, forcing them to work for them. The Blacks, as well as the Spaniards saw the Indian as inferior; and thus a mutual antipathy developed.

Every society has troublesome transients, and New Spain was no exception. Many Spaniards arrived in the New World with little possibility of achieving economic independence. Society viewed these transients as social troublemakers. Since many were relatives of encomenderos and because an encomendero's prestige was enhanced by the number of his guests, many transients became house guests at the encomendero's palacial residence known as the *casa poblada*. Some became permanent guests of the encomenderos! And some actually sued for wages! Of course there were other ways of ridding the society of unwanted troublesome elements.

Because there were always expeditions, or entradas as they were called, into the frontier areas to subdue the recalcitrant Indians, there was always need for personnel to do the fighting. Here was an opportunity for an unwanted transient to gain eternal glory—and for Spanish society to gain eternal freedom from a few uninvited guests.

It is impossible to view the complete Spanish society without examining the role of women. Many historians view women as a separate entity. This is almost impossible since women occupied an integral part of the socio-economic structure of New Spain. Indeed, women were active members of the Spanish society; and even in this male dominated world, women often carried on in the absence of the male authority. There was a large and significant minority of Spanish women who immigrated to the New World. From 1509 to 1559 there are records of 15,480 licenses for emigrants from Spain to the New World, but it is possible that flow may have reached 100,000. Records for the thirty years from 1509 to 1539 indicate that ten percent of the licenses went to women. As the colonial period matured, it may have been that almost fifty percent of the arrivals to the New World were women.

It was always more prestigeous to marry a Spanish woman than an Indian, particularly if one could find a mate with good ethnic lineage. Since Spanish women often raised their own children alongside the illegitimate mestizo children of their husbands, they were true purveyors of Spanish culture.

Women, and that includes Spanish, Indian, and mestizo, also ran many successful enterprises. Some were artisans, others were involved in low level trade, and some were even noted scholars. It was most common for women to run the *encomienda* or *estancia* in the event their husbands died or were absent. And there is even the case where the wife of Governor Pedro de Alvarado became governor of Guatemala, a part of New Spain, for a brief period in 1541. The case of Doña Béatrize de la Cueva de Alvarado is a fascinating early example of the woman as political chief. Another such person was Anna de la Zarza. Anna was the wife of a prosperous, petty merchant, Antonio de la Zarza. Antonio ran a family operated enterprise which traded cacao, cloth, and mules. While his main base of operations was in Texcoco, the major amount of trading and sales took place in Mexico City. Since the sale of his goods was most important, Antonio spent most of his time negotiating in Mexico City while the operations in Texcoco were managed by his wife Anna. She also owned and rented property located within the Indian neighborhoods or barrios. Each day Anna received incoming products and then shipped them to Mexico City with her sons acting as carriers. By 1580 Antonio died and Anna literally took over the business. She continued to oversee the operations in both Texcoco and Mexico City—and under her tutelage, the trading and managing operations not only continued but prospered and expanded.

Although Anna was Spanish, women of other ethnic origins also participated in the economic and political structure of New Spain. Mulatto women played a very significant role in the local market places of Mexico City—and even mestizo and Indian women acted as foremen in their own homes where small textile or craft operations were established. So are women passive forces in Latin society as the myth would have us believe? Not on your life. They were not inactive then, nor are they cast in that role today. Women continue to play a significant role in the development and operation of all of Mexican society.

CHAPTER 14

A Mission to Christianize

The Cathedral of Curenavaca is attached together with the Capilla del Tercer Orden—or the Chapel of the Third Order. It was founded by the Franciscan fathers of the Catholic Church under the direction of the conquistador, Hernán Cortés. The gardens and the sculptures were executed by Indian artists; and the outside altar accommodated the Indians who were more comfortable worshiping in an outdoor setting. The paintings inside this cathedral are also done by Indian artists and are of great significance to the development of the Catholic church in Mexico.

Cathedrals and churches like the one in Cuernavaca are all over Mexico. By 1570, scarcely fifty years after conquest, the three major orders of the Catholic Church, the Franciscans, the Dominicans, and the Augustinians, had already built more than one hundred and fifty convents, churches, cathedrals, and missions throughout New Spain. One town, Cholula, has as many as three hundred and sixty-five churches, attesting to the zeal of the Spanish and Mexican church fathers.

The Catholic church in Mexico as in the rest of Spanish America was inextricably woven into the very fabric of society; Catholicism was part of the daily lives of the people socially, economically, and politically. To a great extent, the existence of the State depended heavily upon the function of the Catholic church.

Spain's relationship to the Roman Catholic church has been described in many different ways. It has been called a partnership; a theocracy; while some have even called Spanish America a "papal colony." But all of these terms are inadequate for they carry with them the impression that the Church and state were separate and distinct; or even that there was a conspiracy on the part of the Church to subvert the power of the state. Nothing could be further from the truth. In most cases it was impossible to separate the Church and state—spiritually, and in many ways intellectually, the Church was the state and the state was the Church.

Even before the defeat of the Moslems in Spain, the Spanish monarchs were accorded certain rights which normally belonged to the Catholic Church. These rights, known as the *Patronato Real* or Royal Patronage, were defined as powers or acts of distributing governmental positions—or of a patron supporting someone or something. During the reconquest, that is, during the period prior to 1492 in which Spain fought the Moslems, the Catholic Church gave to the Spanish monarchs the right to collect the *diezmo,* or tenth—commonly called the tithe; and tithing was manditory. In order to support the wars against the Moslems, the monarchs were permitted to use the tithe as they saw fit. The crown also received the authority to sell indulgences—which were remissions for sins. This money also could be used against the Moslems. So far reaching were these powers that they virtually wed the Catholic church to the crown; the Church and state became as one.

The *Patronato Real* also granted the crown and its subordinates the right to nominate a cleric to a benefice, which is an office of dignity in the Catholic Church. Benefices included Monsignors, bishops, archbishops, and cardinals. And in most cases, nomination really meant appointment—for the Church's role in confirmation was often perfunctory. But of course the patron, who made the nomination, also had an obligation to support and defend the benefice of his choice, which often meant that the patron would spend large sums to assure his benefice a life commensurate with his position of social standing. And the patron's reward? He was given special seating in church; had special prayers said for him and his family; and he was insured of an honored burial site within the church compound. In an upper class society given to display and ostentation, this attraction for wealthy patrons was great.

Actually, patronage in the New World began with a Papal Bull, *Inter Caetera,* published on May 4, 1493 and issued by Pope Alexander VI. This document divided the unexplored world neatly into two halves in order to prevent conflict between Catholic Spain and Catholic Portugal. Everything discovered west of an imaginary line of demarcation running through the Atlantic at one hundred leagues west of the Cape Verde Islands would belong to Spain, and everything to the east, to Portugal. As part of this document, Pope Alexander VI gave the Spanish kings the duty to missionize and Christianize the population of the New World.

Some eight years later the Papal Bull *Eximae Devotionis* extended to the New World Spain's right to collect the tithes. Clearly, control of the purse strings gave the state literal control of the Church. However, this gift did not come without certain conditions. The state was charged with the responsibility to economically support the development and operation of the Church in the New World. Often, the state spent more than it collected from the mandatory tithe; but in exchange for control, it was more than willing to spend the extra money.

But the development of the *Patronato* did not end with the papal bull of 1501. There were others issued over the years which accorded still more rights to the government of the New World. Ultimately, the state acquired the right to construct all church edifices. *Fueros Eclesiasticos* gave it control over clerical courts. The right of the *Pase,* or to pass on papal documents, permitted the crown to censor all papal documents to be published in the New World. Finally, the Church even granted the crown the control and operation of the Holy Office of Inquisition. It is no wonder that so many of the indictments issued by the Holy Office in the New World were for political and not religious violations.

But because the objectives of the Church and the State were not always identical, conflict arose. Armed with the power of the *Patronato Real,* the state was in a position to inflict great pressure on the Church for failure to cooperate. But the Church was not without its power as well. The moral force of the Church was immense—and the fear of heavenly retribution was especially strong among the converts in New Spain. The Church fathers did not hesitate to exert their influence upon the Indians; an influence that was exerted through the power of the Church fathers themselves—their holy status—their words. In addition, the Church exerted its influence through the weapons of excommunication and interdiction. Interdiction did not affect just one person, it could actually affect thousands. By placing a decree of interdict on a city, a province, or even a viceroyalty, the Church could withhold the issuing of small or all of the holy sacraments. The effect is comparable to excommunication *en masse.* Without the sacrament of marriage, those who lived together did so in sin; and without the sacrament of extreme unction, the dead could not be interred.

Nevertheless, the Church was composed of men, Church fathers, who were not first saints and then priests. If they became saints, or even saintly, it happened because of their experience within the structure of the Church. Many of the religious entered the Church because of the prestige it offered and not because they were devoted to carrying out good works. In fact, many of the later priests were citizens who were appointed to a benefice or office of dignity in order to—well—increase their own dignity!

In New Spain, as in the rest of the New World, there were two basic branches of the Catholic Clergy, the regular and the secular. And like everything else related to the Catholic church, it is difficult to completely separate the activities of one from the other. Furthermore, in many cases one branch of the clergy acted in lieu or at least in tandem with the other. It is the secular clergy with which most Catholics come into contact, for they are the parish priests—and the general hierarchy of the Church which includes the Monsignors, the bishops, the archbishops, and the cardinals. The primary function of this branch of the clergy is to carry out the day to day functions of the church and to repeat the mass.

According to Catholicism, there are seven sacraments or sacred ceremonies which were introduced by Jesus Christ. They are baptism, holy eucharist, penance, confirmation, holy matrimony, holy orders, and extreme unction, which has been renamed "the sacrament of the sick and the dying." The secular clergy may give all of the seven sacraments, although two of them, confirmation and holy orders are reserved for bishops or higher. And they are important ones too. For without confirmation, no one could be completely and finally accepted into the Catholic faith; and without the sacrament of holy orders, no new priest could be added to the Church. When a priest took his vows or holy orders, he vowed to remain chaste, to accept poverty, and to obey the hierarchy of the Church and the word of God. That meant, at least on the earthly level, that all members of the clergy in the New World should give a measure of obedience to the bishop or whatever other benefice of the secular clergy may be in charge.

(And that was the start of the problems between the secular and regular clergy.) The regular clergy consisted primarily of the monasterial orders, which in New Spain, during the early colonial period, was dominated by three mendicant orders.

(Mendicant is from the Latin *mendicare,* which means to beg and thus a mendicant was a beggar; and since the founders of these early orders gave up their wealth to become beggars, the orders were called mendicant.) The three mendicant orders which dominated the early colonial period were the Franciscans, the Dominicans and the Augustinians.

The Franciscan order was founded by Saint Francis of Assisi who lived from 1182 to 1226. Saint Francis was devoted to the brotherhood of man. He believed in poverty, simplicity, and the sustenance of man, animals, and nature. The brotherhood which he founded was dedicated to these ideals. During the same period, the Dominican order was founded by a Spaniard, Domingo de Guzman, who became known as Saint Dominic. The Dominicans were dedicated to preaching and teaching, and their influence on education was immense. The third order followed the teachings of Saint Augustine, Bishop of Hippo, in North Africa. Saint Augustine believed in the kingdom of God on earth; that is of creating on earth God's kingdom; his righteousness—a sort of Catholic fundamentalism.

As the regulars arrived in the New World, their dedication to the specific ideals of their orders became blurred because their mission was the Christianization of the Indians. And while the orders operated legally under the hierarchy of the Church and the direction of the state, they often acted on their own, particularly on the frontier areas.

The first twelve Franciscans to arrive in New Spain, May 15, 1524 became known as the "Twelve Apostles." Since the main function of the regular friars, known as "religious" was the saving of souls, they and those of the orders who arrived later moved into the Indian villages on the frontier to achieve their goals. Many friars became part of the encomienda system which also acted as a christianizing element. The encomienda granted to its owner, the encomendero, the right of the labor and tribute of a certain number of Indians, but he was also charged with the responsibility of Christianizing and Hispanizing his encomienda Indians. The laws of Spain placed the friars in charge of the Indian villages in order to protect and defend these "children of God." The mendicant orders took these charges seriously, and their role as intermediaries became indispensable for although the friars were required to teach the catechism in "the rich Spanish language," they saw fit to learn Nahuatl from the Indians and teach the catechism in Nahuatl instead. As a result, Nahuatl became the second major language in Mexico and raised a barrier between the Spaniard and the Indian. The paternalistic mendicant fathers were not dissatisfied with this, since their knowledge of Nahuatl made them even more indispensable.

But the work of the mendicant fathers was not limited to the saving of souls. Within twenty-five years of their arrival they had constructed a number of rather large, sumptuous buildings. In this first quarter century, the Franciscans built more than eighty convents while the Dominicans and Augustinians built over forty convents apiece.

The Catholic church has been severely criticized for constructing such grandiose edifices. But in defense of the early fathers, it should be remembered that even the most self-abnegating and pious persons believed these religious structures to be good expressions of piety and religious dedication.

Also, since the friars believed they were competing with the established Indian religions, they felt that they had to outdo the Indians in the magnificence of their religious structures, in order to prove the superiority of their God, and of their religion. As with all structured organizations, internal rivalry existed; the various religious orders were highly competitive, always attempting to outdo each other.

Some buildings were constructed in response to an apparent mira-

cle; a heavenly request; a place for religious pilgrimage. One such building is the most Holy Shrine of Guadalupe. While there are a number of
conflicting accounts of the miracle of Guadalupe, one of the most pervasive was told by Luis Lazo de la Vega. It begins with a humble Indian
called Juan Diego. In December of 1531, while on his way to worship he
heard the singing of many birds at the hill of Tepeyacac. Suddenly the
singing stopped and the voice of a lady called from the top of the hill:
"Juan." He was filled with joy and delight. As he climbed to the top of the
hill, he saw . . . "a lady who was standing there . . . he was struck with
wonder at the radiance of her exceeding great beauty, her garments
shining like the sun; and the stones of the hill, and the caves, reflecting the
brightness of her light were like precious gold; and he saw how the
rainbow clothed the land so that the cactus and other things that grew
there seemed like celestial plants, their leaves and thorns shining like gold
in her presence."

She spoke to him and said "You must know, and be very certain in
your heart, my son, that I am truly the eternal Virgin, holy mother of the
True God, through whose favor we live, the Creator, Lord of Heaven,
and the Lord of the earth. I very much desire that they build me a church
here, so that in it I may show and may make known and give all my love,
my mercy and my help and my protection. I am in truth your merciful
mother—to you and to all the other people dear to me who call upon me,
who search for me, who confide in me; here I will hear their sorrow, their
words, so that I may make perfect and cure their illnesses, their labors,
and their calamities . . . go now to the episcopal palace of the Bishop of
Mexico and tell him that I send you to tell him how much I desire to have a
church built here . . . Now hear my words, my dear son, and go and do
everything carefully and quickly."

Juan Diego went immediately to the Bishop of Mexico, Don Fray
Juan de Zumarraga, a religious of Saint Francis. While the Bishop was
cordial and friendly, his response left Juan Diego full of sorrow. "My son,
come again another time when we can be more leisurely; and I will hear
more from you about the origin of this; I will look into this about which
you have come, your will, your desire."

On that same day, Juan Diego returned to the hill, knelt, and prayed
to the Holy Mother. He said that a more worthy person should convey her
message for he was only a poor man and not worthy of her sending him.
The Virgin Mother answered that while she did not lack in important
emissaries, that it was with him that she wished to entrust her message.
She then exhorted him to return to the Bishop and again make her desire
known on the following day. And so Juan Diego returned to see the Lord
Bishop. After much questioning, Bishop Zumarraga asked for a sign to be
given which would verify this miracle.

After several days had passed, Juan Diego returned to the hill and was commanded by the Holy Mother to "Climb up to the top of the hill . . . and there you will find many flowers; pluck them and gather them together, and then bring them down here to my presence."

And he did so. He picked the beautiful flowers and wrapped them in a mantle. When the Virgin had seen them, she gathered them together again, and placed them in the cloak of Juan Diego and told him to take them to the Bishop. Again he returned to the Bishop only to be prodded and jostled by his servants. They saw and smelled the fragrant flowers, but as they tried to pick them from the cloak, they could not. For the flowers had turned to embroidery. The Lord Bishop, having heard this, ordered that Juan Diego be brought to him. After some discussion, Juan Diego opened his cloak in which he had been carrying the flowers. And as the roses dropped to the floor, "suddenly there appeared the most pure image of the most noble Virgin Mary, Mother of God, just exactly as it is, even now, in Her holy house, in Her church which is named Guadalupe; and the Lord Bishop, having seen this, and all those who were with him knelt down and gazed with wonder; and then they grew sad, and were sorrowful, and were aghast, and the Lord Bishop with tenderness and weeping begged Her forgiveness for not having done Her bidding at once."[31]

That cloak of the poor Indian Juan Diego is in a glass case on the main altar in the New Basilica of the most holy Shrine of Our Lady of Guadalupe. Catholics from all over the world make pilgrimages here, as they have done for years. And each day, the pious may be seen struggling forward on their knees, to make their request; their peace; and their homage, to the Virgin of Guadalupe.

The Shrine of Guadalupe is, in a sense, a Mexican adaptation of the Virgin Mary. While she is an Indian maiden, she is that same Virgin Mary—and with all due respect to the veracity of the miracle, she is representative of Mexican Catholicism. And much of Roman Catholicism became Mexican; not the basic dogma of the religion, but many of the outward expressions. Religious processions, music, dances, and plays, assumed a distinctive Mexican flavor. There was a religious dance, one with a story of conflict and resolve; of courage and strength, which resembles the present-day *corrido*, or story in song. There is also a dance-play called the *Danzas de Moros y Christianos,* which is built on a theme of mock combat between the Christians and the Moslems. Of course, the Christians always win. The masks, the costumes, and the music is distinctively Mexican.

[31]Sister Simone Watson, O.S.B. *Cult of Our Lady Guadalupe,* (Collegeville, Minnesota: The Liturgical Press, copyright by The Order of St. Benedict, Inc., 1964), pp. 75-82.

The lasting quality of Catholicism in Mexico would have been impossible without the heroism of many individual friars. Probably the most well known, particularly for his defense of the Indian and his rights, was Father Bartolomé de Las Casas. Las Casas, who, like Cortés, studied lat at the University of Salamanca, was an early conquistador. At age thirty-six he became a Dominican friar, and spent the rest of his life writing and defending the Indian's cause. His most famous work was entitled the *Very Brief Recital of the Destruction of the Indies*, and was published in 1552. In it he wrote that:

> "The Christians, with their horses and swords and lances, began to slaughter and practise strange cruelty among [the Indians]. . . . They penetrated into the country and spared neither children nor the aged, nor pregnant women, nor those in child labour, all of whom they ran through the body and lacerated, as though they were assaulting so many lambs herded in their sheepfold.
>
> They made bets as to who would slit a man in two or cut off his head at one blow; or they opened up his bowels. They tore the babes from their mothers' breast by the feet, and dashed their heads against the rocks. Others they seized by the shoulders and threw into the rivers, laughing and joking, and when they fell into the water they exclaimed: 'boil body of so and so!' They spitted the bodies of other babes, together with their mothers and all who were before them, on their swords.
>
> They made a gallows just high enough for the feet to nearly touch the ground, and by thirteens, in honour and reverence of our Redeemer and the twelve Apostles, they put wood underneath and, with fire, they burned the Indians alive.
>
> They wrapped the bodies of others entirely in dry straw, binding them in it and setting fire to it; and so they burned them. They cut off the hands of all they wished to take alive, made them carry them fastened on to them, and said: 'Go and carry letters': that is; take the news to those who have fled to the mountains."

These and other cruelties described by Las Casas were quickly translated and used by the Spanish adversaries, particularly the English, to prove the deviltry of the Iberians. Las Casas' writings have been generally termed the basis of the so-called *Leyenda Negra*, Black Legend. Many subsequent writers have felt that he grossly exaggerated in order to draw attention to the Indian's cause; or that he was going through a mental ablution for his own sins as a conquistador. Others feel that his writings have a measure of truth and that the events he described did take place. In the National Palace, the renowned muralist Diego Rivera gave lasting credence to Las Casas' description of how a prisoner's hands were cut off and as Las Casas wrote, "fastened to them."

Not all clergymen wrote of the cruelties perpetrated against the Indians. . . . Their devotion lies in the way they dedicated their lives to record the history, the language, and the lives of those they came to convert. Often they wrote in order to impress the crown with their achievements in Christianizing the "barbaric" Indian. But sometimes they wrote because they had to; because that was their calling. These Church fathers were the chroniclers and the leading Catholic chronicler was Fray Bernardino de Sahagun. He arrived in Mexico in 1529 and spent the next thirty years of his life interviewing descendants of the conquered Azteca. His interviews were in Nahuatl, and he wrote in Nahuatl. While much of his work is composed of myths and stories of the Azteca civilization, often greatly distorted, it does not detract from the value of his Chronicles. Thirteen volumes cover virtually every aspect of Azteca life and history. He called his work, "a synthesis of all I have learned." Today they provide the most valuable record of Indian mythology and they establish a foundation for the understanding of pre-conquest society. His contribution to the knowledge of Pre-Columbian Mexico is monumental.

By 1572, the Jesuits or Society of Jesus arrived and expanded on the work begun by the early mendicant friars. Not all was benevolent, and as Catholicism became firmly entrenched, the religious orders and the secular and regular clergy began bickering and vying for the control of the most lucrative and prestigious areas—those with productive Indian populations and those close to the major populated cities. But it was during this early period that Catholicism supplanted the Indian religions as the central faith of Mexico.

CHAPTER 15

Brotherhood of the Cloth:
The Relationship of
the Church and Friars
to the People of New Spain

They came to missionize—to Christianize, these men of the cloth. There were seculars wearing the cassock of Sunday mass; there were the brown robed Franciscans; the grey robed Dominicans; the Augustinians with their black tunics; and the black robed Jesuits. They came from Spain, and they came from America. They came to Christianize—but what they accomplished was far more. They built; they invested; they institutionalized a whole nation; they wove the Catholic church into the very fabric of society.

When discussing Catholicism and the Catholic Church in New Spain, there is a tendency to look at the structure of the Church and to evaluate its operations only in terms of that structure. However, the Church in the New World did not always function according to patterns established in Spain. For one thing, the Church fathers in New Spain were not always Spaniards and for another, they were not always operating exclusively in a religious context. And most important, the Church in New Spain was intricately tied to the social, economic, and political activities of the local community. This did not diminish the religious activities of the Church; quite the contrary is true, as conversion of the Indian population was the first order of business, and extensive missionary activity was carried on. However, as the colonial period developed, the Church was influenced by the society which it served. Generally during the seventeenth century, a large proportion of the Catholic Clergy in New Spain was creole—that is they were born of their own parishioners. They were, in many cases, the sons, nephews, brothers, and other relatives of the encomendero. Because of the principle of "Primogeniture in perpetuity," that is, "the first son inherits everything for ever and ever," there was always a need for the other brothers and sisters to find prestigious positions that would offer economic security. Hence the choice of the clergy. The pattern was that the second son or daughter would be channeled into the Catholic Church so that by the seventeenth century the Church became an extension of the dominant social groups in New Spain.

Yet this did not prevent the development of a schism between the regular and secular clergy. Similarity of social background of the clergy notwithstanding, the basic differences of regular and secular branches created a basic social difference. While the children of the encomendero became attached to both the secular and regular clergies, they did not always maintain an allegiance to the family from which they came. The secular clergy acted on their own initiative and therefore they relied on their own ingenuity for financing themselves and their diocese. Because of this, they could benefit from both their own abilities and their family's political and social contacts. Since the secular clergy took only the vows of chastity and obedience—not poverty—they were free to engage in local businesses, and they did! In fact, so extensive were their economic activities, they were indistinguishable from those of other non-church creoles.

But the same did not apply to the regular clergy, the monasterial orders. The regular clergy was intricately tied into the structure of their order. Furthermore, they did take the vow of poverty, in addition to chastity and obedience. While many of the regular clergy also came from the families of the encomendero, they soon found their allegiance was to the Church and the order to which they belonged, and not family ties. And while the orders did engage in business, they did so in the name of the order, not of the individual priest.

Business activities of both the regular and secular clergy were prominent in the purchase and rental of urban properties, the ownership of grain mills, and the ownership of certain textile industries. Both branches of the clergy even owned and rented rural farm and grazing land. A major source of wealth for the clergy was the so-called *capellania*. The capellania was a tax-free donation deposited in favor of the church diocese. If a member of the family who deposited the capellania entered the priesthood, he could draw on the interest from the fund in order to support himself. The family of the cleric could also use the capital for further investment—and the capital remained tax free. Since the interest accrued to the clergy—the Catholic Church—and since the fund was tax-free to the donor, both sides benefited. And it is in this mutual benefit that the *capellania* was so important. In effect it did not increase the wealth of the Church, for it was always available to the donor from which he could draw; and because the money was tax-free, it was an established socially prestigious and economically rational mechanism for the wealthy families of New Spain. The religious orders of the Catholic church soon adopted the same mechanicism as they too saw interest accruing from the loan of capital. Through this mechanism of placing capital in interest, the regular orders and even individual priests became the major lenders and lending institutions in New Spain.

While capital loaned to individuals—primarily wealthy creoles—was used for the purchase of private property, the operation of that property was not in the control of the clergy. The loan then acted as a mortgage without strings of control. If the mortgagee defaulted on the loan, the clergy, in its benevolence, would merely acquire the property at the death of the mortgagee. In some cases, other members of the community would take over the defaulted mortgage. Foreclosure by the lending clergy was rare.

The clergy then, had very diversified holdings based upon working capital. The key to the success of the church as a banking institution lay with its willingness to plow liquid capital back into the community. And now a new picture of the Catholic Church in New Spain begins to emerge. It is not the traditional one of an inflexible institution, highly structured, and controlled from Spain; rather, it is a picture of a flexible institution which is an integral part of the social, political, and particularly the economic society in which it functions. And since there weren't any private banks—the church as a banking institution was indispensable.

The church also acquired some private property. Property was occasionally foreclosed; and a considerable amount was willed to the Church by wealthy parishioners. But these properties were immediately rented, and the profits were turned into new investments.

There were other ways in which the clergy acquired capital. Sons of encomenderos, who were usually secular clergy acting on their own initiative, used their encomienda connection. Remember the encomendero was required to maintain a priest in the Indian villages. The most frequent pattern was that the priest-son of the encomendero would occupy that position. His religious duties often found expression in the labor of the Indians he served. In other words, the priest wore two hats—the one as the teacher/priest—and the other as a quasi-*estanciero*, or labor boss.

Because the priest was an authority figure, he was in a good position to recruit needed Indian labor for the encomienda.

Many priest's activities as labor recruiters did not end with the termination of the encomienda. It is true that during the encomienda period they gathered tribute-labor that belonged to the encomendero. But as the encomienda was replaced with the great estate, the priest became a recruiter for the new free labor force. Thus, he occupied a very powerful position as the middle man between the estate owner and the Indian community. He was paid by both the estate owner and the Indian villages. The goods he received from the Indians he could either sell or use himself. In this way, the priest, in the name of clerical duties, could actually make a fair and reasonable living.

In addition to its economic role, the Church also fulfilled a vital social function within the Spanish community. Not only did the Church act as an economic outlet for upwardly mobile families, but it was an acceptable social outlet as well. In other words, it provided a prestigious occupational opportunity for families of excessive size; for sons and daughters of these families who otherwise would have nowhere to turn.

The Church engaged in other significant social activities as well. One of the most vital links between the clergy and the people was the hospital. These were located in the major urban centers as well as in the countryside. The great majority of the early hospitals were built and operated by the Franciscan order of the Church.

In addition to ministering to the ill, the hospital also served as a way station for travelers. Besides the main buildings which were reserved for the ill, there were auxiliary buildings which served a multitude of social needs. There were dwellings for the staff and for travelers who wished to remain overnight; there were workshops, storehouses, orientation rooms; all surrounding a central patio with a church for the purpose of issuing the sacraments.

The storehouses were usually filled with foodstuffs; grains and *maize,* collected by the fathers in the form of tithes or tribute stored for future needs. In this way, the Church could distribute food to the community in the event of a drought or other disaster. Here again the Church became inextricably woven into the very fabric of society; and it became the major charitable institution.

Another vital link between the Church and the Spanish urban society was education. Less than a block from the National Palace in Mexico City are the original buildings of the Royal Pontifical University of Mexico, founded in 1551, by order of King Charles I, of Spain. Instruction began there in 1553, and it was primarily religious in nature. In fact, throughout the entire colonial period, the faculty was dominated by the clergy, even though the University's charter was given by the Crown—another example of the marriage of the Church and state. While theology was the major subject area, instruction was not limited to religion alone. Law occupied an important part of the University's curriculum, as did philosophy, medicine, anatomy, rhetoric, and even astrology.

The faculty of the university was not professional; that is, they did not derive their income solely from their teaching position. Both clerical and lay members of the faculty were actively involved in diverse economic and social activities. What the university did offer them was a position of prestige; and the prestigious aspect of the university is still prevalent in Mexico today. Much of the faculty which staffs the ultra modern and avante-garde National University of Mexico today are successful in fields outside of education.

The clergy was also in complete control of primary and secondary education. The earliest primary schools were initiated by the Franciscan order. In Texcoco, a port of Mexico City, the first primary school in Mexico was founded by Fray Pedro de Gante, in 1523. This school, which is attached to the Cathedral of Mexico, was founded even before there was a true missionary organization in Mexico. The school was not only a place for the teaching of children, but it served as an orphanage as well, and they received orphans from both Spanish and Indian families. This primary school, as well as others, was mainly concerned with the education of the young boys. Girls were taught reading and writing along with household responsibilities. But the primary schools for girls were separate and different and fewer in number.

In spite of these educational limitations, opportunities for self education and creativity remained within the Church. Convents gave women the opportunity to find self expression as a by-product of their theological studies. Although the greatest amount of history and literature was written by the friars, nuns also made a significant and lasting contribution . . . especially in the light of the attitudes toward women in the early colonial period. Clearly, New Spain was male dominated—and this was true for the religious sector as well. While the monasteries were well run, the nunneries were insipid little communities filled with petty scheming and intrigue. The monasteries of Spanish America produced many Saints and Venerables. The convents found none. However, one woman distinguished herself in Mexican society in the seventeenth century. Before entering the convent at age sixteen, Sor Juana Inez de la Cruz was known as the "Tenth Muse of Mexico." She composed poetry for birthdays, weddings, and in honor of notables such as the viceroy, and the bishop. She also wrote theological treatises which openly took issue with the arrogant Jesuit Father Antonio Vieira. She called for humility and reminded him of the need for meekness in Christianity. For a woman of the Church to argue theological questions was unheard of. Nor did she limit her commentary to religious matters. In her poem, *Redondillas,* (or "Quatrains with Rhymes") she commented on a male dominated society.

The bond between the clergy and the general population, both Spanish and Indian, was best expressed through the building of churches, cathedrals, and other religious edifices. One measure of the piety of a community was to have one or more impressive religious

Stupid men, quick to condemn
Women wrongly for their flaws,
Never seeing you're the cause
Of all that you blame in them!

If you flatter them along,
Earn their scorn, their love incite,
Why expect them to do right
When you urge them to do wrong?

You combat their opposition,
And then gravely when you're done,
Say the whole thing was in fun
And you did not seek submission.

You expect from action shady
That some magic will be done
To turn courted courtesan
Quickly into virtuous lady.

Can you think of wit more drear
Than for one with lack of brain
To smear a mirror, then complain
Since it is not crystal clear?

Yet with favor and disdain
You the same results have had,
Angered if we treat you bad,
Mocking if we've loved in vain.

She who's modest cannot hold
Man's esteem. We're all thought naughty.
If we don't accept, we're haughty;
If we welcome you, we're bold.

Since there's only scorn or pain
Lurking in the love that burns you,
Luckiest is the one who spurns you.
Just go on, then, and complain!

Which will have the greater blame
In a passion, erring, faded:
She who falls, by man persuaded
Or he whose begging brings the shame?

Do not look surprised or rave
When guilt's placed at your own gate!
Love the girls your whims create
Or create the sort you crave

Tempt us not to acquiesce,
Then with justice can you censure
Any girl who dares to venture
Near you, seeking your caress.

Women need be strong, I find,
To stay safe and keep unharmed
Since the arrogant male comes armed
With Devil, flesh, and world combined.

buildings. It became a tradition for Spanish members of the community to donate excess funds for the construction of these buildings. The more impressive the structure, the more prestige that flowed to the community. A rivalry developed between the urban centers for the magnificence and opulence of these churches. This competition really augmented the rivalry that existed between the various orders and between the secular and regular clergy as well.

And let us not forget that the more impressive the Church, the more awe-filled the Indian would be by the power of Christianity; and frequently it was Indian labor which built the church. In the colonial period much of the art work which adorns Mexico's religious structures was executed by Indian artists. Many of the church interiors have an Indian appearance. At Cholula, just six miles outside of the town of Puebla, is the chapel of Tonanzintla. The interior is a mass of baroque carvings, practically all executed by Indian artists. Some people call this the "eighth wonder of the world."

The pillars appear to be intertwined with a serpent's body—possibly the god Quetzalcoatl—and the faces are far from European looking, although many are of European saints. Many are adorned with feathered headdress reminiscent of the Aztec codices. While this chapel is unique, it is representative of the magnificence and opulence of religious buildings throughout Mexico.

[32]*Spanish American Literature in Translation,* edited by Willis Knapp Jones, Vol. I, (New York: Fredericks Under Publishing Co. 1966), pp. 208-209.

It was natural that this magnificent structure would become not only the focal point of the community, but the focal point of the family within the community, for each family and each community had its own patron saint. This is where Catholicism and the Indian spiritual needs really merged. It is common that the religious sanctuaries that existed prior to the conquest re-emerged as Catholic religious centers of great importance with patron saints whose miracles are often connected with the area. The Church of Los Remedios in Mexico is a good example. It is built atop the Cerro de Toltepec where once stood a Pre-Columbian pyramid. Legend says that on the night that Cortés retreated from Mexico City—that night of Noche Triste—the Virgin Mary appeared atop this hill. There with one hand she shone a bright light which gave the Spaniards the way of escape while with the other she shone a bright light which dazzled the pursuing Indians. She was thus considered the patron saint of the Spaniards and was called by the Indians, La Gachupina. The Church of the Virgin of Los Remedios ranks today alongside the Chapel of the Virgin of Guadalupe as a shrine of pilgrimage, as a religious sanctuary.

Another example is in the little village of Otatitlan. Not more than three hundred and fifty people reside in the village, which is located in the tropical area along the Papaloapan River. Yet the village of Otatitlan is laid out according to the traditional plan used throughout Mexico during the Colonial period. On one side of the plaza is the home of the encomendero, the estate owner. It is now occupied by his heirs, the family of Rutilo Parroquin. While the massive estate no longer remains, the Parroquin family still farms and markets mangos, sugar cane, bananas, and a variety of other agricultural products. But it is with the church—also built on the plaza—that one finds great interest. Inside is the life-size statue of *El Cristo Negro,* or the Black Christ. It is sometimes called the *Santo Negro,* or the Black Saint. Around the inside of the church are oil paintings of events which surrounded this miraculous image. It includes its theft, destruction, and miraculous reappearance. On the day of *El Cristo Negro,* people come by the thousands from all the surrounding villages and communities to pay homage to *El Cristo Negro.* They come by land or they cross the flowing Papaloapan on barges, primitive ferries, canoes, and boats— and they fill the empty square of Otatitlan.

It was the religious festival where the Spaniard and Indian really converged. The festivals always celebrated some patron saint or miracle of the Catholic Church. They were replete with images, costumes, music, dancing, and plays based on biblical and moral events. Many of these plays and dances dealt with the magi and the birth of the Christ Jesus. But there were dances that were Indian in origin as well. One Pre-Columbian dance, which was performed throughout Mexico, has survived till today. It is performed on the Day of Corpus Christi by the Totonac, Otomí, and

Huaxteca Indians. Atop a 100 foot high pole is a small moveable platform on which stands the captain with his drum and flute. Four ropes are wound around the pole to which are attached the four flyers. This is the Danza de Los Voladores, or the dance of the flyers. As the captain in the center begins to beat his small drum, and play his flute, the flyers fall backward and fly around the pole, moving their arms and bodies to resemble flying birds. The four flyers make thirteen turns around the pole. Since four times thirteen is fifty-two, it is apparent that the number of revolutions correspond to the fifty-two year cosmic life cycle of the Pre-Columbian civilizations.

An area in which the Indian found collective security and spiritual identity was with the *cofradia*. These Indian brotherhoods were a rather late development in the colonial period. The cofradia was one organization introduced by the Catholic clergy to which the Indian truly responded positively. This religious brotherhood was a parishioners association which offered financial and spiritual security in addition to emotional solidarity. The Indians could readily identify with families within a given parish—and they could gain security and recognition as additional benefits.

The cofradias acted as a subordinate religious and economic structure both within and outside of the Catholic Church. The members of the brotherhoods, like any fraternal organization, at once gained a distinct identity. As a group they sponsored religious festivals, paid for masses said for deceased members; and they also could guarantee the burial of its members. As a group they bought and sold land; and they invested in other profit making ventures as a means to support their organization. They acquired the funds for investment just as any other organization would; through the collection of dues, donations, and bequests. Of course good investments also swelled the coffers of the cofradias. But in times of hardship they would rely on their wealth and their investments to aid the members of the cofradias. There is no doubt that the cofradias were the singularly most important organizations that bound the Indians to Catholicism. And finally, the cofradias acted as a vehicle for the preservation of certain Indian traditions within the Catholic Church. In a sense, they were catalysts for aspects of present day Catholic heterodoxy.

One of the most vital and successful branches of the Catholic clergy was The Society of Jesus, commonly called the Jesuits. This order, which was founded in 1534 by Ignacius Loyola, was originally charged with the responsibility of the counter reformation. Noted as an educated elite, members of the religious order arrived in New Spain in the 1570's. Unlike their other clerical counterparts, the Jesuits invested mainly in rural estates which they themselves managed. The reason for this was that most of the select urban properties were owned by Spaniards or other religious orders.

In all of their investments, the Jesuits were very successful. And it was through the profits gained from their rural estates that the Jesuits in New Spain financed their colleges and missionary efforts. In fact, it was education and missionization which were the two-pronged goals of the Jesuit order. By the eighteenth century, the Jesuits had gained control of the vast majority of secondary schools, and their influence in universities was almost as great.

The irony of this immense success was that the Jesuits became *too* successful. Their economic and educational success made them the envy and enemy of the people of New Spain. And they were also a challenge, for they often appealed over the king to the Pope—and even to God!

But it was their overwhelming desire for profit and insistence on concentrating their investments in rural estates, with consequently efficient management, that led to the final downfall of the Society of Jesus in America. Their organizational structure, their close control over the operation of their estates, and the efficient marketing of their products permitted them to successfully finance their missionary activities and their highly successful educational institutions. This obsession with profits inevitably brought them into direct—and that is the key word, direct—competition and resultant antagonism with the creole landowners and Indian villagers.

A case in point was the huge Jesuit estate called the Colegio Maximo de San Pedro y San Pablo, a corporate structure located near Mexico City. This huge estate came into such competition with the creole and Indian landowners that it led to a series of legal battles. The frequency of these court battles led to a great deal of ridicule of the Jesuit profit making system, and society in general began to question the motives and goals of the Jesuit Order. Probably one of the most dramatic and significant legal controversies took place around 1720 over a grain mill attached to the estate. The case began when an increase in population within the Indian village motivated the Indians to go to court to claim land owned and operated by the Colegio Maximo. The Indians claimed that the land was theirs and that the purchase had been made illegally. The Jesuits countered that the purchase was made during a decline in the village population in the early 17th century. They added that the purchase was legal not only to the land but to the water rights as well. And to prove their point they arrived in court with all legal documents signed and sealed by the Indian representatives. The Indians then went directly to the Jesuit Order, to the managers of the Colegio Maximo, and pleaded their case directly. In effect, the Indians said:

> "The land you took from us may have been purchased legally according to your laws, but to the higher law of morality, it was not. Because force was used in the conquest of this land, all that follows must be considered null and

void. We, who need the land for our people, ask you in the name of right and morality to return it to us, together with all of the water rights as well."

But the Indians' pleas struck no responsive cord. To one Jesuit ". . . the Indian arguments simply presented a rehash of the conquest, relating its injustices and asserting that all Spanish titles were illegal since the conquistadores had forceably usurped Indian property rights."[33]

The courts, and the Jesuits, rejected all Indian arguments! Frustration? Yes, a great deal of frustration. When the Indians found no recourse in the courts or with the moral pleadings to the Jesuits themselves, they turned to what they saw as their only recourse, violence. What followed this decision was one of the most violent and serious riots against the Jesuits' holdings. And who led the riotings? Well, in many cases it was the village priest who, through his religious upbringing, saw the injustices meted out to the Indian. The grain mill? Well, in 1721, it was burned to the ground. But the violence and animosity refused to abate, and the Jesuit resistance to giving up "their" land was fought with equal ferocity—it was a long war of attrition.

The case of the *Colegio Maximo* was only one of many, but it gives some insight as to why such antagonism developed against the Jesuit Order. Finally, by 1767, the order came—directly from Charles III, king of Spain—the Jesuits were to be dissolved. Their land holdings were to be confiscated by the government for the purpose of redistribution, and the members of the Jesuit order were to be removed from New Spain.

Why such a harsh decision for an order of the Catholic Church that performed such good and positive services to the people and the state? First of all, the government was greedy. Bureaucrats saw an opportunity for confiscation which would enrich their own personal states. Secondly, there was a general antagonism felt by the hierarchy of the Spanish state, many of whom were creole landholders who had come into conflict with the Jesuit holdings. All of this was augmented by the alienation felt by the Indians.

But the Church had many successes. It was not a monolithic structure with absolute control from the top. And finally, the Church became the focal point of the family, and in many ways served the needs of the community. Church fathers exerted regional control which provided a flexibility that has helped make the Catholic Church one of Spain's most lasting contributions to the New World.

[33] James Riley, "Jesuit Hacendados: Estate Management by the Colegio Maximo de San Pedro y San Pablo of Mexico City", 1973 MSS—Unpublished Article.

CHAPTER 16

New Spain's Northern Frontier

The Grand Canyon is one of the most awe-inspiring of nature's works. While it is usually thought of as a purely North American landmark, in the fall of 1540, Captain García López de Cárdenas, a member of the famous Coronado expedition, stood on the rim of the canyon and viewed an amazing scene. His chronicler wrote that the river below looked like little more than a rivulet. The obstacle of the precipitous walls was so great that several attempts to descend for desperately needed water failed. So Captain García López de Cárdenas returned to the main encampment to tell his incredible story.

During the colonial period of New Spain, from 1521 to 1821, the frontier was not overlooked. The unexplored regions to the north were the object of curiosity and speculation. Legends of mythical lands and lush islands inhabited by giants, or blond blue-eyed men, or black amazon women, had been repeated so often that it must have been difficult not to believe their accuracy. And the stories told of places where fountains flowed with the water of everlasting youth, while one legend described cities whose buildings were covered entirely with gold and silver. Amazonia, El Dorado, Gran Quivira, The Seven Cities of Cibola or Gold, and the amazing island of California were all part of these legends. Even that great conquistador Hernán Cortés was tempted to explore the north in search of those legendary lands. And he did make several expeditions.

But the most amazing tale of all was told by the survivors of an expedition led by Pánfilo de Narváez which had landed in the area of Florida in 1528. Out of several hundred that began this expedition, only four survived. The two central figures were the expedition's treasurer Alvaro Nuñez Cabeza de Vaca, and a Moorish slave by the name of Estevancio. In April of 1536 a bearded and desheveled group arrived at San Miguel de Culiacan. Their appearance caused a great deal of excitement, but far greater was the excitement caused by their stories. They had wandered for eight years—on foot—across the southern part of the present day United States. They had been threatened, chased, captured, turned into slaves, and revered as wise men. Finally they escaped. They said they had seen "shaggy cows" (buffaloes) and heard of magnificent cities of gold. The listeners were enraptured and they motivated the survivors to embellish their stories with even greater magnificence.

Even the viceroy of New Spain, Antonio Mendoza, became actively involved and several expeditions were planned and executed. One set out under the leadership of an Italian-Franciscan priest, Fray Marcos de Niza. Estevancio, the slave, went along. Their goal was to confirm the existence of the fabled Seven Cities of Cíbola. Although Estevancio was killed by the Indians on the journey, Fray Marcos de Niza did return—and he confirmed the sighting of one of these fabled cities. He reported that some of the buildings actually glittered as if they were made of gold or silver.

Fray Marcos de Niza described what he saw:

". . . I proceeded on my journey until coming within sight of Cíbola, which is situated in a plain at the base of a round hill.
    The pueblo has a fine appearance, the best I have seen in these regions. The houses are as they had been described to me by the Indians, all of stone, with terraces and flat roofs, as it seemed to me from a hill where I stood to view it. The city is larger than the city of Mexico. . . .
    When I told the chieftains who were with me how well impressed I was with Cíbola, they told me that it was the smallest of seven cities, and that Totoneac is much larger and better than all the seven, that it has so many houses and people that there is no end to it."[34]

When the news reached central Mexico, the pressure to conquer the fabulous golden cities heightened. The rivalry between viceroy Mendoza and Hernán Cortés, and various legal difficulties, limited the great conqueror's rights of further exploration and conquest. But Cortés did send a convoy northward under the command of Francisco de Ulluoa and much of this expedition is shrouded in mystery. Some have even accused Cortés of using this expedition to send gold and treasure to be hidden in these unexplored lands so that he could establish his own empire. So great were

[34]Quoted in Herbert Eugene Bolton, *The Spanish Borderlands* (New Haven: Yale University Press, 1921), p. 16.

these tales of buried treasure that it led to the discovery of a treasure map. As recently as 1956, there were major explorations in Southern California attempting to locate the treasure on a map purportedly made by Francisco de Ulluoa. But Ulluoa did make one important discovery on his last fateful journey. The expedition returned without Ulluoa, but with the information that California was part of the mainland; it was not—as popularly thought—an island. Ulluoa's expedition was the first to apply the name California to the area which had been previously called the island of Santa Cruz. But in spite of this, Ulluoa's maps continued to depict California as an island for almost two centuries more.

And what about the fabulous seven cities of gold? In 1540, Viceroy Antonio de Mendoza sent northward one of the most massive land expeditions that had ever been assembled. His choice for leader of this expedition was the youthful governor of Nueva Galicia, Don Francisco Vásquez de Coronado. He led a magnificent party that travelled in several waves, with the main body consisting of more than 230 mounted men with an infantry detachment of 62. Several of the men brought along their wives; and there were the Indian support teams which numbered about eight hundred. Black slaves too were part of this expedition. Everything was provided for occupation and settlement, for Spaniards rarely relied on living off the land, and this formal *entrada de conquista* or expedition of conquest was no exception. Hundreds of animals of all sorts were herded along in order to supply food and even more were added as the expedition moved northward. And to insure that the army would not be lacking, Hernando de Alarcón was sent from Acapulco with several ships of supplies. Alarcón made it all the way up the Gulf of California and into the Colorado River, but he never made contact with Coronado. As viceroy Mendoza waved goodbye, and dispensed his personal blessing, Coronado and his party set out from Compostela late in February of 1540. From there to the Sinaloa outpost of Culiacán—a distance of 350 miles—took them more than a month. Coronado decided to establish a main encampment at Corazones on the Sonora River and take a third of the group at a more rapid pace to the Seven Cities of Cíbola. On April 22, the smaller group pushed forward along this coastal trail. They crossed the river Sinaloa, then the Fuerte, the Mayo, the lower Yaqui, and through the Valley of Sonora into the territory known as Despoblado—or unpopulated. On July 7, with expectations high, they arrived at Hawikuh, the first of the so-called Seven Cities of Cíbola. But the buildings were not of gold nor were they of silver—in fact there weren't many buildings at all. The few structures they saw were of adobe; and the people were the Zuñi—who were less than hospitable. Coronado must have wondered if it was worth the fight he encountered to enter this impoverished village. He already must have suspected that what Fray Marcos de Niza viewed from a distant hilltop was not the Seven Cities of Cíbola with their metallic buildings shimmering in the sunlight, but merely adobes whose whitewashed walls gave the illusion of being made of gold and silver.

In spite of this disappointment, the main body was summoned in the hope of still finding the golden cities. Fables die slow deaths, and as they fought their way through the Hopi towns of northeastern Arizona, rumors abounded of a fabulous land to the west and also to the east. A contingent moved westward and discovered the Grand Canyon, which was more of an obstacle than a spectacle of majestic beauty. Another group moved east across the present site of Albuquerque, New Mexico, and into the edge of the Texas panhandle—but still no fabled cities. This expedition met an Indian who they called *El Turko*, or The Turk. He spoke of a rich land to the north which they called Gran Quivira, and the search was on again. With renewed hope the party moved in an easterly direction and then turned north searching for Gran Quivira. The winter of 1540 was harsh, and was made even more difficult by the raids of the Pueblo Indians encountered along the way. As they moved to the northeast, they came across fierce plains Indians whose fighting skills were far better than the Pueblos. By mid April of 1541, the main group was sent back to the Rio Grande, while Coronado and a smaller contingent pressed on to Gran Quivira. The story of the Indian Turk was now suspect, so he was placed in chains as they moved toward the Arkansas River. By the time they reached the present state of Kansas, the awful truth was learned. *El Turko* confessed that he had fabricated the entire story in the hopes of luring the Spaniards onto the plains; once there, in a weakened condition, they would be easy prey for the Indian inhabitants, and their intrusion would come to an end. Needless to say, the Turk was garroted on the spot. But his execution did not diminish the disappointment these ever hopeful explorers felt. Although some talked of continuing the search, an injury to Coronado sealed the decision to return. The records of the journey were scientifically invaluable for they provided the Spaniards with a wealth of information on the inhabitants, the geography, and the flora and fauna of the land. But the findings were also disheartening. The summers were as hot and dry as the land through which they passed, while the winters were cold and severe. And the inhabitants and their lack of technology offered no relief. In fact they were hostile, and not in great enough concentrations to provide a ready source for labor. And finally, there were no cities of gold—in fact no gold at all.

In the minds of the Spaniards, the Coronado expedition was an unprecedented failure. There were other expeditions to the far northern frontier; Hernando de Soto explored the region of the Mississippi River with more than 600 men; Juan Rodríguez Cabrillo sailed from Acapulco up the coast of California to the region of San Francisco Bay. But none was so grandiose in design and expectations—nor so despondent in its failure to achieve those expectations—as the expedition under the command of Don Francisco Vásquez de Coronado. The publicity received by this expedition was so bad that it effectively halted the Spanish advance into the northern frontier for years to come.

So, New Spain turned its attention to a closer frontier, one that was certain to bring fame and riches to those who would exploit these silver mining regions. The mining centers of Zacatecas, Guanajuato, Aguas Calientes, Queretaro and San Luis Potosi produced so much silver that their mines became essential to the economy of New Spain. Yet the nomadic character of the Indians, and the fact that these regions were generally outside of the mainstream of political and social activity, gave these areas the characteristics of a frontier society. In addition, most of the people who moved to here were from humble origins, for the social elite tended to remain in the central areas of population and development. It is true that some of the political and social structures found in the central areas were found on the frontier, but in a loose and rudimentary fashion. For example, the lack of a large sedentary Indian population precluded the establishment of an encomienda system. Instead, labor was obtained from transients who were always moving northward—constantly searching for more and more economic opportunities; a dream that the discovery of new and richer mines could fulfill. And were there no estates? Quite the contrary. Estate living was as much a part of the frontier as it was the central agricultural regions of New Spain. But there were two basic differences; one was the character of the estates. Because agriculturally marginal lands were given over to grazing, they became ranchos—and large ones at that. The marginal quality of the land often meant that it could support only one or two ranchos per province, sometimes an area covering several hundred square miles. It was not unusual for an estate owner to own or control an entire province. Thus the estate owner became a lord—an absolute ruler. The second basic difference was in the nature of the workers. Because the cost of maintaining permanent workers on these estates was costly, they became part of the transient labor force. The same applied to the mining operations, which ofttimes was owned and operated by the estate owners themselves.

All of this had an effect on the social and political nature of both the colonial and national periods of Mexico. In spite of these regional distances from Mexico City, most social activity and, particularly, most of the economic activity, ultimately affected the capital. These rather loose frontier societies that began to develop as secondary political units would in time become provinces or states; or in the case of Texas, an independent nation. Much of the frontier region of New Spain also developed the prototype of the cowboy—a social concept which antedated the popular North American type by more than two centuries. The horse, chaparreras or chaps, stetsons, and other so-called western paraphernalia are still a part of northern Mexico today, as is the independent nature of the people. For it was these loose frontier regions which were the first to rise up against the government in the Wars of Independence.

So these areas peripheral to Mexico City, mainly silver mining regions, became New Spain's frontier—and it remained the only frontier for many years. The stories of a far northern paradise persisted, but there was always the bitter memory of Coronado.

But in 1579, the appearance of an English privateer caused a renewed surge of interest in finding—not the golden cities—but a northwest passage—the straits of Anian. Sir Francis Drake, sailing on the famous *Golden Hind,* was in search of Spanish treasure. He had sailed around the tip of South America into what was considered a Spanish lake, the Pacific Ocean. Some believed he had discovered a northwest passage to successfully intrude on the domain of Spanish shipping. So New Spain turned its attention once again to the Far Northern Frontier. (Of course, no expedition would be so grand or expensive as Coronado's—the viceroyalty had learned its lesson.) A limited number of ships sailed northward in search of those non-existent straits of Anian, and a port of call for the Manila Galleons.

In 1587 a Manila galleon commander, Pedro de Unamuno, while searching the Pacific for islands of great wealth, which could be made way stations for the Manila Galleon, put in at a bay on the Coast of California. Unamuno, possibly at Morro Bay, ventured inland only to have several of his men killed and wounded. Unamuno returned to Mexico, having established no port of call.

Almost eight years passed before another serious attempt was made to explore California's coast. In the summer of 1596, Sebastián Rodríguez Cermeño, another Galleon commander, sailed from Manila to the Coast of California in the 200-ton *San Agustín.* Cermeño sailed from Cape Mendocino south to Drake's Bay where he remained for about a month, recording the topography of the land and exchanging gifts and embraces with the Indians. But on November 30, shortly before Cermeño was to set sail, a storm drove the *San Augustín* on shore, wrecking it, and spilling its entire valuable cargo onto the beach. Cermeño and his men completed the construction of an open launch—carried on board the *San Augustín*—and set sail for New Spain. During his voyage south, he carefully explored and recorded what he saw along the coast of California; the topography, bays, the flora and fauna, and the Indian inhabitants. While all of his efforts were valuable to Spain, Cermeño's loss of the *San Augustín* was unforgivable. Cermeño, in spite of all of his work, was considered a failure; and it would be the last time that Spain would send a Manila galleon with valuable cargo on an exploration mission.

In 1603, Sebastián Vizcaíno, a merchant contractor, reached Mon-

terey Bay in California—and fell in love with its virtues. Beautifully
protected he said, and large enough to accommodate all of Spain's navy
and merchant fleet. It would also make an excellent stopping-off place for
the ships which sailed from Manila in the Philippines to Acapulco on the
Pacific Coast of New Spain. These Manila Galleons were prey not only to
sea dogs such as Sir Francis Drake, but also to an even greater danger that
lurked on board of every ship which departed Manila with its precious
cargo of silks, ivory and spices; that danger was scurvy. Establishing a
port of call on the coast of California could effectively combat scurvy.
But bickering, indecision, and a game of political musical chairs put the
decision off for another one hundred and eighty years.

There were some moves to settle the northern frontier. After
months of political infighting, Juan de Oñate was given the commission to
settle the area presently known as New Mexico. On January 26, 1598,
Oñate set out with 129 soldiers, some with families, eighty-three wagons
and around seven thousand head of cattle, pigs, sheep, horses, and other
stock animals. Oñate's colony was not a great success during his tenure as
governor, and by 1608 it appeared as if once again the far northern
frontier would be abandoned. But the following year, virtually simul-
taneous with the founding of Jamestown in Virginia and Quebec in
Canada, the settlement at Santa Fé was begun. Oñate, who had spent a
personal fortune on the fledgling colony, did not even share in the glory
of founding this most important northern outpost of New Spain. In
Spain's early colonial period, New Mexico served as a bastion of defense
against Indian and European raiders. In time it was to become a major
trading center for Mexico's northern provinces.

By then, Spain had developed a workable solution to the settlement
of these rather uninviting frontier regions. This was the three part structure of *presidio, pueblo,* and *mission.* The presidio was the military post
which would defend both the mission and pueblo. The mission served as
the civilizing and Christianizing agent for the heathen Indians; and the
pueblo would be the city in which Spain's citizens would live; and Spanish
institutions would develop.

Of course, New Spain was most noted for her missionary activities.
The first Jesuit missions in northwest Mexico began in the 1590's, but
probably the most famous period of Jesuit activity took place almost a
century later under the dedicated missionary, Father Eusebio Francisco
Kino. Father Kino spent twenty-five years exploring and founding missions in Pimería Alta—or upper Pima land—named for the Indians who
lived on the northern frontier of New Spain. Father Kino never founded
any missions in either Baja or Alta California, but he did motivate other
Church fathers to do so.

One of these was the Jesuit priest Father Juan María de Salvatierra, who came to Baja California in 1697 and founded the mother mission of Loreto, here on the gulf coast of the peninsula. With money gathered by the newly established Pious Fund for the founding of the missions, the Jesuits built seven missions in the parched peninsula before Salvatierra's death in 1717. Because the Jesuits were given special political control of Baja California, and because they were permitted to approve or deny all visitations to the peninsula, a great deal of jealousy and suspicion developed around them. While they had relaxed their restrictions by the mid-eighteenth century, rumors persisted that the Jesuits were secretly hoarding massive treasures of gold, silver, and pearls. These rumors, coupled with a change in royal policy in Spain, led to the arrest and deportation of these hard-working fathers.

In Spain, Charles III, a Spanish Bourbon king of French antecedents, was philosophically imbued with French reform policies. Among them was the belief that the Catholic Church must be curbed in its political and economic power. In 1767, in keeping with this anti-clerical fervor that was sweeping Europe, Charles III issued an order which expelled the Jesuits from all Spanish Colonies in the New World. The order was carried to New Spain by the newly appointed *Visitador General,* José de Gálvez. And the expulsion was carried out by Gaspar de Portolá, a military captain who would play an important role in the settlement of Spain's farthest northern outpost, California.

In 1769, Gálvez was granted authority by King Charles III to establish a military outpost in California as a buffer against possible Russian encroachment. The ambitious *Visitador General,* bent on fame and fortune, expanded upon this authority to send a military and missionary expedition into California with the purpose of settling the northern frontier. Two ships were commissioned, the San Carlos and San Antonio; and two land parties were organized. The first land party was led by Captain Fernando de Rivera y Moncada with twenty-five soldiers and the Franciscan priest, Father Juan Crespi. The overall commander, and the leader of the second land party, was Captain Gaspar de Portolá. With him were twelve soldiers, forty-four Christian Indians, and the leader of the Franciscan missionaries, Father Junípero Serra.

On July 1, 1769, Father Serra founded the first Franciscan mission in Alta California, *San Diego de Alcalá.* These first explorations proceeded under great difficulty, and they were beset with illness and shortage of supplies and food. At one point, Father Serra, in ill health, returned to Mexico City to plead with Viceroy Antonio María Bucareli y Ursúa for aid for the struggling mission settlements. Bucareli, himself an appointee of Charles III, provided the necessary assistance by which the first settlements in Alta California managed to endure.

From 1774 to 1776, Capt. Juan Bautista de Anza was sent by Viceroy

Bucareli on several land expeditions to California in order to insure the success of the colony. And in 1776, as the North American War for Independence was beginning, Felipe de Neve, who had been governor of Baja California, was transferred to Alta California where he established the seat of government in Monterey. Neve brought a number of settlers who founded the pueblos of San José in 1777, and Los Angeles in 1781. The success of California was then insured.

The history of California during this period is really the history of the missions. The governors and foreign visitors, the development of pueblos and presidios, all add to the establishment of the province, but the most outstanding institution was the mission system, and its greatest hero was Father Serra.

In the little town of Petra on the island of Mallorca, the largest of the Baleric islands off the coast of Spain, Father Junípero Serra, founder of the California mission system, was born.

The Franciscan influence in Petra was a strong and constant one. Friars from this Order lived in the town for over 225 years, and during that time no less than 79 boys joined the Franciscans, quite a record for a small farm town. As a boy, Junípero attended the school run by the Franciscans where he learned Latin, mathematics, reading, writing, and vocal music, especially the Gregorian chant. Junípero had a good voice and on occasion joined the Franciscans' community choir to sing with them on feast days. The relationship held by the friars and Junípero as the boy grew up was more personal than formal. He and his father would visit the friars for friendly conversations. He came to know of the greater world from visitors who came to see the friars. Junípero, surrounded by the religious influence of the Franciscans, early in his life became interested in becoming a friar. Religion was for him part of his everyday life. On coming home he would announce his arrival by saying, *"Ave, María Purísima"* (Hail Mary, Most Pure). His parents or sister would answer, *"Concebuda* [sic] *sens pecat"** (Conceived without sin). In later life Serra was frequently heard to say *"Benedito"* or *"Alabado sea Dios"* (Blessed or Praised be God). These were expressions learned from greeting farmers on the road or in the fields. His upbringing was for a simple life, based on faith, work, and frugality.[35]

The things he did and learned in Petra would serve him well when he joined the other voyagers on his mission to civilize and Christianize the New World.

---

*[sic] probably a misprint in Geiger's work. Correct word is probably Concebida.

[35]Father Maynard J. Geiger, O.F.M., Ph.D., *The Life and Times of Fray Junípero Serra, O.F.M. or The Man Who Never Turned Back,* (Wash. D.C. Academy of Amer. Fran. Hist., 1959) pp. 10-14.

The main purpose of the mission was to Christianize and Hispanize the Indian neophyte. Of the approximately 135,000 Indians in the Alta California province, the mission fathers were able to recruit approximately half as neophytes. Initially they were recruited with gifts and the promise of a regular food supply. The initial response of the Indian was voluntary, but once he chose to join the mission, he was not free to leave. He was not free to enjoy his traditional freedom if there was work to be done. Many Indians learned trades from the missionaries, such as masonry, carpentry, and agriculture. But they never accepted completely the concept of European civilization. Generally, more Indians died in the missions than were born and had it not been for new converts, the system might have failed very early. Deaths were not a result of cruelty or overwork, but essentially from European diseases, and illness which resulted from the unsanitary conditions within the missions. At the same time, there is little doubt of the unceasing dedication of the padres, of whom Junípero Serra, Francisco Paloú, and Fernín Francisco de Lasuén stand out for their unselfish contributions.

By the time of Mexican independence in 1821, there were twenty missions, four presidios, and three official pueblos or civil settlements. Since the founding of the first mission in 1769, perhaps fifteen or twenty ranchos had been established. Monterey boasted a population of about 700, Los Angeles claimed 650, and San Jose had 240. Villa de Branciforte, which later became Santa Cruz, struggled along with only about thirty residents. California remained a pastoral society and even during the struggle between Mexico and Spain for Mexico's independence, the province of Alta California remained almost completely uninvolved. Only a few raids by a pirate-privateer, who claimed to be on the side of independence, notified California that a revolution was under way. When Spain relinquished California as a possession, the province quietly accepted Mexican rule to become a province of the new nation.

CHAPTER 17

From Enlightenment
to Independence

The *"caballito"* in Mexico City is a statue of Charles IV of Spain cast in 1803 as a single piece of bronze weighing approximately thirty tons. It stands in the glorieta which divides Avenida Benito Juárez from the Paseo de la Reforma. Ironic is it not, that this massive bronze represents the crown's inability to cope with the Spanish colonies. Charles IV, a weak and ineffectual monarch, ascended to power while the entire world was in a state of turmoil; the American War for Independence had effectively separated the thirteen colonies from mother England; and the French Revolution would soon separate the head from Louis XVI's body. The Spanish colonies would also feel the effect of this international instability. Charles IV was incapable of dealing with the crises. And he knew it.

In 1808 he stepped down in favor of his son, Ferdinand VII. In March of that same year France invaded Spain and both Charles IV and Ferdinand VII were forced to renounce the throne. The way was clear for Mexico's movement toward independence.

The English philosopher John Locke, in his *Second Treatise on Civil Government,* penned the following about man's inherent rights and his relationship to government:

"Men being . . . by nature all free, equal, and independent, no one can be put out of this estate, and subjected to the political power of another, without his own consent. The only way whereby any one divests himself of

150

his natural liberty and puts on the bonds of civil society, is by agreeing with other men to join and unite into a community, for their comfortable, safe and peaceable living one amongst another, in a secure enjoyment of their properties and a greater security against any that are not of it. . . . When any number of men have so consented to make one community or government, they are thereby presently incorporated, and make one body politic, wherein the majority have a right to act and conclude the rest."

This early eighteenth century philosopher was both a reflection and a motivator of his time, and his time was called the Enlightenment. But the Enlightenment was not limited to the words and ideas of English philosophers; many see the French philosophers as the major forces of this age. It was an age when people began in earnest to question their import, place, and very worth in governments whose legitimacy flowed from the fountain of divine right. Did in fact kings rule by divine right? Did they receive their power and authority from God? John Locke said no. And the French philosopher Jean-Jacques Rousseau also said no! Emphatically no! In his *Social Contract* which he wrote in 1762, Rousseau said:

"Man is born free; and everywhere he is in chains. One thinks himself the master of others and still remains a greater slave than they. How did this change come about? I do not know. What can make it legitimate? That question I think I can answer. . . ."[36]

Rousseau's answer to what gives legitimacy to any association of people is their voluntary will. For he believed as did John Locke, that people in a state of nature are free with the right to seek out the political convention of their choice.

"This common liberty results from the nature of man. His first law is to provide for his own preservation, his first cares are those which he owes to himself; and as soon as he reaches years of discretion, his is the sole judge of the proper means of preserving himself, and consequently becomes his own master. . . ."[37]

And how did Rousseau view political authority in light of the power structure of the state?

"The strongest is never strong enough to be always the master, unless he transforms strength into right, and obedience into duty. . . . Let us then admit that force does not create right, and that we are obliged to obey only legitimate powers."[38]

[36] Jean Jacques Rousseau, *The Social Contract and Discourses*, trans. & ed. by G.D.H. Cole (New York: E.P. Dutton & Co., 1950), pp. 3-4.

[37] Rousseau, p. 4.

[38] Rousseau, p. 6.

How does all of this affect the movement for independence in the Latin American colonies, and particularly in Mexico? First of all, the so-called "Enlightenment" was a world movement. In spite of the fact that books which challenged divine right were banned by the Catholic Church, they did enter Mexico. Some came in from North America by way of the leaders of the American Revolution—and many were introduced into Mexico by the growing and influential Masonic orders; both the York and the Scotch rites existed in Mexico—and the York rite was fiercely anti monarchy—not anti Catholic, but anti monarchy. So it was this Masonic rite that acted as one vehicle for the introduction of the works of the "Enlightenment."

Prominent members of the court of Charles III and his father Philip V, were disciples of the Enlightenment in general, and of Rousseau in particular. Rousseau was widely read in New Spain before his *Social Contract* was placed on the *Index Expurgatorious,* or list of books which the Catholic Church considered unacceptable to read. And he was even more widely read afterward! Besides attacking the divine right of kings, he also attacked Christianity!

> "Christianity preaches nothing but servitude and dependence. Its spirit is too favorable to tyranny not to profit always from it. True Christians are made to be slaves; they know it and are not moved by it; this short life has too little value in their eyes."[39]

And what Rousseau created, Voltaire and others popularized.

The French reform movement even found expression in Spain's new King of the French Bourbon lineage who ascended to the throne in 1759. Charles III initiated a series of reforms both in Spain and in the New World. Those reforms were equalled by his excellent choice of advisors, particularly José de Gálvez, who arrived in Mexico in 1765 as the *Visitador General,* or Inspector General. Gálvez' most important reform was the introduction of the French intendant system into the political structure of New Spain. Twelve regional intendants took authority over the established *alcaldes, alcaldes mayores, corregidores,* and other local officials who acted as mayors or justices of the peace. All of this was done with an eye toward an economic and political reformation in the colonial empire of Spain; and it worked! So did the liberalized trade policy of José de Gálvez. It caused a massive increase in the exports of New Spain. But the creole bureaucracy deplored the intendants, as well as the expansion of trade which they saw as an attempt by the crown to deprive them of their power—of their wealth. And the beneficiary of all this, the Spanish peninsular, of course!

Under the guidance of Gálvez, New Spain also extended its frontiers

[39]Rousseau, pp. 137-38.

into Texas, New Mexico, Louisiana; and, under the pretext of stemming the tide of Russian expansion, into California as well.

It was logical that the expansion into California would be undertaken by the Jesuit order, which had already established a growing missionary system in Baja California. But in 1767, José de Gálvez received the order to expel the Jesuits from New Spain. The settlement of California went to the Franciscan order and the venerable Father Junípero Serra was dispatched under the political and military command of Gaspar de Portolá. By 1769, California was established as a territory of New Spain; and by 1776, San Francisco was founded as New Spain's northernmost outpost of empire.

But the reform minded and benevolent despot Charles III, could not live forever. When he died in 1788, the world was in the midst of this philosophical revolution known as the Enlightenment. What Spain needed was another Charles III, what she got was his incompetant son, the dullard Charles IV. Charles was already 60 years old as he ascended the throne and, although well meaning, he lacked the ability necessary to pull Spain and her colonies through the historical events which followed. The example for revolution against "divine right" had already been set.

The thirteen British colonies had already successfully overthrown the yoke of the mother country—and much of this had been accomplished in the name of the "Enlightenment." In France, Louis XVI was about to literally lose his head, and the era of Napoleon would begin. The cry of liberty, equality, and fraternity was accompanied by the advent of Napoleon. First, the French Revolution and later Napoleon threatened monarchy everywhere—including Spain. And there was Charles IV, weak, indecisive, and ineffectual. The renowned artist Goya captured something different in the man Charles IV than did Juan de Tolusa in the power expressed in his huge bronze casting of the *"caballito"* in Mexico City. One author described the essence of Charles IV, as captured in Goya's famous painting, as ". . . visibly fonder of eating than of thinking. . . ."

It was Charles' wife, Queen Maria Luisa, who in Goya's works appeared to exercise royal authority, and much of that authority she delegated to her chief minister and intimate friend, Manuel de Godoy. The Spanish people were horrified by the relationship between Queen Maria Luisa and Minister Godoy. But Godoy dreamed of conquering Portugal and possibly acquiring a kingdom for iimself.

Godoy's dreams became momentary reality when on October 27, 1807, Napoleon signed at Fontainebleau an agreement which would lead to the conquest and division of Portugal. Although France and Spain were to receive their share, Godoy saw this as an opportunity to realize his desire for a kingdom of his own. Within less than a year, plots and conspiracies and counter-plots, and counter-conspiracies ensued. Charles IV abdicated in favor of his twenty-three year old son, Ferdinand VII. Then he rescinded his abdication. Ferdinand VII acceded to the throne, and then abdicated to his father Charles IV, who in turn abdicated to Napoleon Bonaparte. Napoleon offered the throne of Spain to two of his brothers who refused. So he ordered his third brother, Joseph Bonaparte, to accept the sceptor of authority. And what happened to Charles the Fourth and his young son Ferdinand the Seventh? Well, Charles, Maria, and Godoy were sent to Marseilles where they lived a royal life under French guard. Ferdinand also was given a "lovely little" guarded chateau in which he could play lord and master.

The imprisonment of the legitimate monarch and his replacement with a Corsican motivated Mexico and Spanish America to take the irrevocable step toward independence.*

Mexico was suddenly freed from the moral and historical tradition of loyalty to the king of Spain. In Mexico, there had already been a growing resentment with all administration from Spain. Joseph Bonaparte increased that resentment.

Historians have generally agreed that much of Mexico's discontent resulted from a class struggle between the peninsular and the criollo. Criollos were disatisfied because they were deprived of equal social status and equal rights with the peninsular, and only because the peninsular was born in Spain did he merit a higher social standing. It is accurately claimed that creoles were being excluded from high political office.

As the late colonial period developed, legal and social class distinctions began to disappear. There was a greater amount of movement up and down the social/economic structure, based more on wealth and ability—and connections—rather than ethnic or racial antecedents. The greatest beneficiaries of this new social freedom were the criollos who dominated the social, economic, and to a great extent the political life of New Spain.

But as the wealth of New Spain grew, the Spanish crown realized the importance of this colony.

The Bourbon kings, particularly Charles III, as part of his reform movement attempted to bring New Spain under tighter control by the crown; this, of course, included sending a host of "trusted" peninsulares to New Spain to replace criollos who held high political office.

Let us examine one case in point: The Audiencia, or high court of Mexico, which also acted in an advisory capacity to the Viceroy, in 1770 was overwhelmingly criollo. Of its eleven members, eight were criollos,

*Joseph Bonaparte spoke hardly any Spanish at all; and many said he was more addicted to alcoholism than to administration. His reluctant subjects laughingly referred to him as "Pepe Botellas," or loosely translated—"Joe Bottles."

while only three were peninsular. And the peninsular Spaniards had been in Mexico for so many years they could almost be considered native. Several of the criollo members were sons of former criollo members. It was obvious to the crown that this kind of self perpetuation could only mean a loss of loyalty to the mother country, Spain. To regain the authority of the crown, and to reaffirm control of a mercantilist colony, the Bourbon kings, particularly Charles III, appointed only peninsulares to fill vacancies on the audiencia. By 1780, only ten years later, of the fourteen members of the audiencia of New Spain, ten were peninsulares, and only four were criollos!

Unquestionably, among the Spaniards that lived in New Spain, the criollos were in the majority. Also without question, they were left bitterly resentful of this turn of events. And the Bourbons tampered with other established patterns of government which also led to resentment—such as the formation of the Intendencies, which resulted in greater efficiency but also resulted in greater criollo disenchantment. Because New Spain's bureaucracy was not a corporate body of professionals, and because bureaucrats benefited financially from the economic arrangements they accrued from their political connections, tampering with the political system meant tampering with the economic system as well. For the local official it meant that his vital economic ties with the Spanish and Indian communities could be disastrously disrupted.

But the Bourbon kings were moving toward total royal control and to insure their power and authority they raised a standing army.

There had been a militia, and the militia continued; but there had never been a standing army. This army of regulars was primarily staffed by peninsular officers and stationed along the coast, and it was supported mainly by the Spanish government. The militia, on the other hand, was staffed with officers who were residents of New Spain—mostly criollos—and was supported by the local cabildos or town councils. Both the regular officers and those of the militia received a special privilege from the crown known as the *fuero militar*. Generally, it meant that an officer would be exempt from taxation and exempt from arrest and trial in civilian courts. Because military courts were lenient toward their own, military justice was often escape from justice. As the ranks of the officers increased, so did the resentment from the less privileged classes of mestizos, Hispanized Indians and other racial mixtures. And, indeed, jealousy and distrust developed between the officers of the militia and the newly formed regular army.

The Bourbon kings also attempted to extend their power and authority by curbing the power of the Catholic Church. By placing a heavy tax on the Church, the crown could both raise revenues and limit the economic power of the Church. However, it is clear that the Bourbon kings understood very little about the structure and operation of Catholicism in New Spain. Indeed, they saw the Church as a monolithic institution, much the same as it was in Spain. Nothing could be farther from the truth; and nothing could be more dangerous than a precipitous act on the part of the crown that would diminish the economic standing of the Church in Mexico. New Spain's Catholic Church was an integral part of the colonial economy. Since there were no private banks, the religious orders of the Catholic Church had become the sole bankers of New Spain. While the religious orders were wealthy, the vast majority of their money was invested in loans to members of the community, with urban property as the collateral.

If a proposed heavy ecclesiastical tax were imposed, the orders would have to call in their loans and cease being lending institutions. The result to the economic community would be disastrous. It would have meant a restriction of business capital. Thus, it was not unusual that prominent members of the community joined with the clergy in protesting a tax imposed on the Church.

And while the crown's policy of expanding commerce and trade seemed beneficial on the surface, it too met with vigorous protest. Certainly, the opening of ports and freeing New Spain from the fleet system meant more products would be sold in Spain, and more European products would be arriving in New Spain. So why the antipathy? Well, through most of the eighteenth century, commerce in New Spain was handled by great merchants called *almaceneros.* (The word *almacenero* is literally a warehouseman. *Almacen* is a warehouse or storehouse.)

The almaceneros maintained huge stockpiles of goods which they purchased from Spain. Sometimes, they would purchase a ship's whole cargo with the vast sums of silver which they also stockpiled. Some of these goods the merchant sold immediately to provincial merchants. Another part he distributed to the northern mining areas. And still other parts he sold slowly in Mexico City where he maintained his home base. Almost all almaceneros were peninsular-born Spaniards. How could this be? What about the sons and daughters, the heirs, who were born in New Spain? As the colonial period developed, the wealth and prominence of the merchants increased dramatically. With their surplus capital they purchased a hacienda or haciendas, partly to enhance their credit; partly to have something to leave to their heirs; and partly for prestige. Because Spanish inheritance patterns called for division, that is, something for everyone, a series of haciendas would be most beneficial.

And it was here that the perpetuation of peninsulares as great merchants took place. Because the lion's share of the estate went to the oldest son, it was traditional for him to exclude himself from commerce and lead a rather lordly life. And the second son usually went into the priesthood. Therefore, it was often left to the daughter to inherit a good portion of the business. So the key figure became the nephew. The nephew, usually still in Spain, was often a poor yet ambitious person whom the merchant would send for. He would initiate him into the business, eventually turning the management over to him. Then in order to bind the agreement, the nephew would marry the merchant's daughter which would perpetuate peninsulares as merchants.

How did this affect the movement toward independence—toward revolution? Simply, the new liberal and expanded trade policy of the Bourbons created such an influx of European goods into New Spain that prices dropped drastically. Many of the merchants were forced to divest themselves of their commercial enterprises and leave Mexico City. This created animosity against the crown of Spain by the Spanish merchants and by their criollo sons as well, since they were deprived of their inheritances and of their lordly lives.

But it was in the mining areas that unrest and discontent turned into action. Mining in New Spain was still very primitive and there had been few technological advancements. The mines which produced the greatest wealth were those which had been dug with the longest shafts. Deep hard-rock mining was expensive. It took a great number of men and animals to run the operation. Consequently, it took a great deal of capital. A productive mine might take up to a thousand horses and mules to power the machinery necessary to run the mine. The Valenciana mine in Guanajuato employed more than three thousand men. With an operation of this magnitude, there was an increased need for credit—credit on a long term basis. But the financier-suppliers based in Mexico City preferred short-term credit. The crown attempted to encourage credit by placing heavy price controls on mercury. Cheaper mercury, which came from the Almaden mine in Spain and which is essential to the efficient separation of silver from ore, would motivate the financier-suppliers to increase their credit. With cheaper mercury, more marginal mines could be put into operation and thereby increase the flow of silver to Spain. And it worked.

But government intervention also meant government controls; something that the fiercely independent mine worker resisted. Paid three times as much as the hacienda workers, they resented any attempts to restrict their social and physical movements. These people, frontiersmen in essence, were unsettled and resentful. They were all too easily motivated toward revolution; and many of them would take part in the actual fighting that was to come.

So a highly complex set of tensions and animosities developed regionally between the old established areas and the developing frontier mining regions. Animosities developed not between the old criollo and the old peninsular, but between the criollo in general and the new peninsulares sent to insure the crown's control over her colony. As events in Europe moved toward the explosion of the French Revolution, the fire of discontent smoldered in New Spain. It is no accident that the movement toward Independence began in Mexico's major mining region, Guanajuato. For there on the frontier—as with any frontier—there is a loose and riotous nature to society itself. Constraints of government lie not only in authority but in power as well. And with the downfall of Ferdinand VII, Spain and New Spain could not effectively muster the power to prevent the spark, and the eventual explosion which began on September 16, 1810, in Guanajuato, Mexico.

CHAPTER 18

Death to the Gachupines!

In the early morning hours of September 16, 1810, Father Miguel Hidalgo y Costilla looked over the courtyard of his church of Dolores in what is now called Dolores-Hidalgo and asked his poor parishioners to right the wrongs that had been perpetrated against them and their ancestors for more than three hundred years. The exhorted crowd responded with "death to the gachupines!" That same morning, the fighting began. Some have called it merely an uprising; others, a rebellion; still others refer to it as a full scale revolution. But for those who fought, it was at least the beginning of the struggle for independence that was to last for more than ten years. On every September 16th the president of the republic, and the governors of all states, stand on the balcony of their state residences and repeat the "grito," Hidalgo's call to arms in the year 1810.

This church of Dolores-Hidalgo is located in one of the most prosperous mining areas of Mexico, the present states of Queretaro and Guanajuato. And it is no wonder that rebellion would begin in a successful mining region. The people who worked in the mines, although poor, still had a better standard of living than most agricultural workers. Furthermore, their very location outside of the central area of control imbued them with a frontier attitude that was fiercely independent and a character that was intrepid. The Bourbon kings with their reformed governmental structure had created more affluence and efficiency than had been known for decades, in both the colony and in Spain. That is, until 1804 when the crown attempted to place controls on Church investment. And because the church acted as the major banking institution in New Spain, the new taxes had a disastrous effect on the economy until they were repealed in 1809. Furthermore, efficiency meant controls on people; their status; their freedom to move about; their accountability. For the people of Queretaro and Guanajuato this was both frustrating and infuriating.

The events in Europe and in Spain had also created frustration. In 1808 Napoleon's invasion of Spain had deposed the legal king, Ferdinand VII, and he had placed his brother Joseph Bonaparte on the throne.

Many intellectual criollos were saying that the deposing of Ferdinand VII meant that New Spain ought to be ruled by "Mexicans;" that is, by the people of Mexico. What the criollos wanted was a Mexico ruled by them, and not the peninsulares or gachupines who had been sent there in the latter years of Bourbon rule.

Criollos and peninsulares began to struggle for power. The viceroyalty, traditionally peninsular, was held by the weak and corrupt José de Iturrigaray. The peninsulares were fearful he would somehow reach an accommodation with the leading criollos. So while the criollos plotted, the peninsulares took decisive action. On September 16, 1808, the peninsulares in a bloodless coup removed Iturrigaray from office and chose their own successor. Their choice was an eighty year old peninsular, who had spent the last forty years of his life in Mexico. They felt that Pedro de Gariby's antiquity would insure their control over him. But the peninsulares found some of his statements to be sympathetic with the criollos. In frustration, they turned to the *junta* in Spain, a military group which claimed to rule in exile for the exiled king; and they asked the *junta* to replace Gariby. It did. But their choice, an archbishop, was worse than the ancient Gariby. Within a year the archbishop was removed and the government was turned over to the audiencia, which at the time was dominated by peninsulares.

But the audiencia was no better, and concerned peninsulares, particularly of the merchant class, petitioned the Regency in Cádiz—which also claimed to rule in the place of King Ferdinand—to send an able viceroy who would carry out Bourbon policies. Viceroy Francisco Xavier de Venegas arrived in Mexico City on September 14, 1810, less than two days before Mexico struck for independence.

Mexicans at all levels of society were feeling frustration and discontent. All that was needed was a spark to set the fire of revolution burning. That spark was struck by the parish priest Father Miguel Hidalgo y Costilla. Hidalgo was born on May 8, 1753, in Pénjamo, Guanajuato, an important mining region. He studied at the College of San Nicholas

Obispo at Valladolid. Through examination and thesis, he was awarded a Bachelor's degree from the University of Mexico and later taught at these two institutions.

His learning and teaching exposed him to, and directed him toward, French liberalism. In his early career, he taught at both the University of Mexico and at the college of San Nicolas Obispo; and in 1791, he became rector of San Nicolas. But this was the period of Bourbon reform, and Hidalgo's office was almost certainly turned over to peninsula-born Spaniards. Thus, in the following year, he received a small church in Colima, and then at San Felipe in Michoacán, where Hidalgo remained for the next eleven years. He apparently was not unknown, even at this early period, as a result of his French liberalism, for in 1800 a secret file was opened on Hidalgo by the Holy Office of Inquisition. It read that: ". . . he spoke disdainfully of the popes; that he showed little respect for the apostles and for St. Teresa; that he doubted the virginity of the Mother of Christ; that he declared fornication to be no sin; and that he lived an immoral life, forgetting the obligation of priesthood and indulging in music, dances, and game." In addition, several people had referred to Hidalgo's home as "Little France!" There was a measure of truth to the allegations, for Father Hidalgo acknowledged, lived with, and supported, two illegitimate daughters.

After eleven years of serving parishes in Colima and Michoacán, in 1803 he succeeded his brother in the congregation of the Church of Dolores. There, he taught the Indians many crafts and agricultural techniques; and because he planted mulberry bushes and vineyards, he came into active conflict with the government. The cultivation of these were considered government monopolies; and on one occasion, the authorities even destroyed his mulberry bushes so that he might not encroach on the monopoly of sericulture. But Hidalgo was well liked, even loved, by his Indian and mestizo parisioners, with whom he had even developed an orchestra which played for fiestas. Hidalgo's reactions to government restraint were both emotional and intellectual.

In 1810, a number of organizations and *ad hoc* committees had formed, each bent on some kind of action against the disastrous government in Mexico City. Through these organizations, intellectual criollos formed what might be termed committees of correspondence—comittees that would keep each other informed as to the growth of their ideas and progress toward some kind of government reform. The "Queretaro Society for the Study of the Fine Arts" was one of these organizations. Ostensibly it was an innocuous group of intellectuals which gathered together to discuss pertinent social literature. In reality, it was, like so many other groups, made up of disenchanted criollos who plotted revolutionary action. The conspirators included two captains of the viceroy's garrisons, Ignacio Allende and Juan Aldama. Both of these men had been actively indoctrinating their subordinates against the "corrupt" peninsular government that ruled Mexico. The disenchantment with the central government was widespread, for the wife of the Corregidor of Queretaro, Doña Josefa Ortiz de Dominguez, was also involved, as was an alcalde, Juan Ochoa.

It is probable that Hidalgo was not a major leader in the cause for independence, but events pushed him into that role. The conspirators had planned for a strike on regional peninsular leadership on the first of October, but their plans were disrupted when the government learned of the plot and made arrests. The major conspirators might have been rounded-up had it not been for Doña Josefa Ortiz de Dominguez, the wife of the corregidor, who from an upstairs room, by a pre-arranged signal, stamped three times on the floor with her heel, and warned a messenger that the plot had been betrayed. She then spoke to the messenger through the window and exhorted him to warn the others. The messenger rode forty miles to San Miguel to warn Captain Ignacio Allende. But Allende was with Hidalgo at Dolores some twenty miles away, a distance covered by Juan Aldama, who is considered the Paul Revere of Mexico. When Aldama arrived at Dolores in the early morning hours of September 16, he was surprised to find that Allende had already learned of the government's actions. Hidalgo was supposed to have turned to his friends and said: *"Caballeros, somos perdidos. No hay otro recurso que ir a cojer gachupines."* My friends, we are lost. We have no other recourse but to go and catch the peninsulares.

Early that Sunday morning, Hidalgo rang the church bells and addressed the congregation that gathered in the atrium: "My children, this day comes to us a new dispensation. Are you ready to receive it? Will you be free? Will you make the effort to recover from the hated Spaniards the lands stolen from your forefathers 300 years ago?" Then Hidalgo shouted the famous Mexican grito: "Long live independence! Long live America! Down with bad government!" The Hispanized Indians and mestizos shouted back *"Muero a los gachupines!"* Death to the gachupines!

While the subsequent actions of the Hidalgo forces constituted "mobocracy" pure and simple, they were not Indians in the classic sense. Rather, they were Hispanized Indians who were reacting not to pure emotion, but to government attempts to force them to pay tribute and wear traditional Indian clothing. Many of these Indians had migrated away from the central areas of New Spain into the "northern" frontiers in order to escape Indian identification. Thus it was perfectly logical that they would join the Hidalgo movement.

It was probably accidental that Hidalgo was placed in command of what turned out to be a bloody rebellion; with fighting and violence which he clearly did not anticipate. The immediate objective of the "army" of Hidalgo was to take San Miguel in order to capture military supplies, which they accomplished. Their next objective was Guanajuato where they arrived one week later. By now, his army had become a mob number-ing around 50,000. Even with experienced military leadership it was impossible to maintain control. Armed with guns, lances, picks, shovels, machetes, and even slings and stones, the unruly mob descended upon the government grain storehouse, the Alhóndiga de Granaditas. The intendent had gathered the frightened gachupines and wealthy criollos inside the compound for protection, and armed with artillery, the gauchupines inflected heavy losses on their attackers, but they in turn were massacred. The story says that a soldier named Pípila placed a stone on his back for protection and with a torch in hand he set fire to the wooden doors of the granary. When the angry mob had finished, four to six hundred men, women, and children inside the walls of the Alhondiga lay dead. And for the attackers losses were immense, as more than two thousand gave up their lives on the attack of this now famous shrine. What followed was an orgy of violence. For two days the mobs of Hidalgo looted the city carrying off anything of value and destroying buildings. The revolutionary army now split into two groups. One numbering 20,000 inflicted a similar fate on Zacatecas as the Spaniards fled before the fury of the revolutionaries. San Luis Potosí also suffered the same fate as did Valladolid which was abandoned at the sight of Hidalgo's 60,000 man army.

But the victories were hollow. They were examples of what destruc-tion a mob could inflict. They failed to achieve what they needed most for a successful revolution—cooperation from the people of the cities they captured; for without cooperation, occupation was ineffective. And al-though the criollo population outnumbered the peninsular by fifteen to one, the actions of the undisciplined mob created a revulsion on the part of those from whom they should have received their greatest support. Even the sedentary Indians refused to participate in a revolt in which they saw no benefit to themselves. Thus it was that Hidalgo's army marched from city to city accomplishing little in the way of permanent change. And here lay Hidalgo's greatest pitfall; the failure to establish a power base beyond the uncontrollable army which they "commanded." Fear by the general population resulted in the lack of true national support that caused the demise of this early revolution.

Militarily, Hidalgo's failure to act decisively and capture Mexico City was also a fateful decision. His successes took him to the neighboring town of Toluca, where the great market is still held; and the road to Mexico City was clear. Why he turned west instead is speculative, but he probably would have been successful. In the high mountain road which separates the basin of Toluca from that of Mexico City, his army engaged a smaller army of peninsulares, which they defeated. In this six hour battle, the Spaniards inflicted heavy losses of somewhere between two and four thousand before retreating. Whether fearful of even greater losses or weary of the fighting and bloodshed, Hidalgo did turn west and moved to the more familiar territory of Guadalajara. Ignacio Allende became so angry over Hidalgo's decision that he departed, temporarily leaving Hidalgo without artillery. Nevertheless, the residents of Guadalajara fled before the surging mob. Many escaped the city, but some of the peninsulares were captured and taken out in the middle of the night in groups of thirty or forty to be executed. For more than a month this revenge was exacted and somewhere between 350 and 1,000 peninsulares were given summary executions.

By November of 1811, the tide had turned when the royalist general, Félix Calleja, recaptured the city of Guanajuato. The afternoon before he entered the city, a mob had killed and multilated two hundred peninsular prisoners who had been held captive in the Alhóndiga. In a fit of rage, Calleja ordered the city to be destroyed along with all of its inhabitants. Before the order was rescinded as an act of humanity, many lay dead in the streets. But the carnage continued with public executions of the so-called guilty parties. For many their guilt was established by a mere drawing of lots; for some, it was the gallows; for others the firing squad. Calleja had many shot at the Alhóndiga as a symbol of reprisal. Because there was so much blood on the pavement, the executions had to be temporarily halted so the carnage could be cleared away. But the cruelty of Calleja was even exceeded by other royalist generals who literally put whole towns to the sword if they gave any kind of assistance to the revolutionaries. As the revolutionary forces learned of these reprisals, they too increased the severity of their own assaults against the peninsulares. Writing in 1850, Lucas Alamán, the intellectual conservative, described the events of 1811:

> "As the revolution became more extensive and general, the war came to be more cruel and sanguinary on both sides: the insurgents put to death all Spaniards whom they could catch, all the members of the corps raised to guard the towns, and on many occasions the people in the countryside who refused to make common cause with them; the commanders of the royal troops treated in the same manner all the captured chieftains of the insurgent forces, many of the prisoners, many of the town residents who were adherents of the cause or who were understood to have given them aid. All executions were performed without any attempt at judicial procedure . . . the commanders arbitrarily disposing of the lives and fortunes of all."[40]

[40]As quoted in Charles Cumberland, *Mexico, The Struggle for Modernity,* (London: Oxford Univ. Press, 1968), p. 120.

It was apparent that Hidalgo had no idea of what he had wrought when he gave his *"grito"* on that early September morning. He was more of a romantic than a revolutionary; and he somehow believed that a magical transformation would take place that would insure equal rights for all men. Hidalgo never saw the revolution developing into class warfare between the castes and the Spaniards, whether they be criollo or peninsular. To him, if the corrupt Spaniard could be removed from power, there would be a general rapproachement between all classes. He did not understand the anger and hatred felt by the lower classes toward crillo and peninsular alike. His religious upbringing and humanistic teachings he took seriously. He devoted much of his life to the poor and unfortunate because that is where his heart was . . . not because he was committed to a philosophical and intellectual levelling of society. In a sense he was like many priests—paternalistic; and that paternalism led him to do what he did. It also led him to offer himself as a decoy for his escaping congress—and that cost him his life.

The end was in sight on January 17, 1812, when a brush fire destroyed Hidalgo's ammunition stores in a field near Guadalajara. At the bridge of Calderón, on the banks of the Lerma river, Calleja's 6,000 man army completely routed the insurrectionist force of more than 80,000. Hidalgo and Allende fled northward as did the other leaders of the failing rebellion. Hidalgo was betrayed and captured by one of his own ex-insurgents, Colonel Ignacio Elizonda, because of a petty quarrel Elizondo had with Allende. Hidalgo, along with Allende, Aladma, and Jiménez were executed and decapitated. Their heads were staked, encaged, and placed on the four corners of the Alhóndiga, in Guanajuato.

While Hidalgo's rebellion died with him, and while he failed to establish a power base, the movement for independence was far from over. Within a year the revolution was assumed by the leadership of Father José María Morelos y Pavón. Morelos had been a student of Hidalgo at the college of San Nicolas Obispo, and he had assumed a leadership role in Hidalgo's rebellion. Also like Hidalgo, Morelos was also a humanist; a true Christian who took the Bible seriously. But unlike Hidalgo, he was not a romantic; he was not a dreamer. He was a disciplinarian. Philosophically he was committed to the abolition of all classes. He was a genuine revolutionary. He firmly believed in popular sovereignty by Mexicans and that peninsulares should have no hand in the national decision making. He believed that land should be owned by the people who worked that land and not by the hacendados who exploited the labor of others. On this subject, he said that, "All should work in that occupation which will render a person most useful to the nation. By the sweat of our brows we must work so that all of us will have bread to eat. The women should busy themselves in their own honest household labors; the priests must take care of souls; the laborers must be employed in agriculture, and the artisans in industry; the remaining men should devote themselves to the army or the government."[41] To the conservative Lucas Alamán, Morelos was nothing more than a dangerous rabble rouser. He wrote: "Since Morelos had come to regard the war as a struggle between proprietors and proletariat, there was attempted nothing less than the complete destruction of all property and the distribution of it among those who had nothing."[42]

But Morelos' words, as radical as they might appear to Lucas Alamán, had a traditional ring to them. He was at heart a Catholic and did not wish to see the destruction of the Church. Because he wished to distribute some Church land; because he wished to curb the power and wealth of the gachupin hierarchy; and because he suggested that tithing be voluntary "out of love for the Church," all of these beliefs did not make him an atheist nor even a diest. He was a Catholic, and remained so to his death.

In September of 1813, a congress of revolutionaries met in the city of Chilpancingo where a young Yucatanese scholar, Andrés Quintana Roo, along with Anastacio Bustamante, drew up a manifesto which denounced Spain and Spanish rule and called for Mexican independence. This document has been considered Mexico's Declaration of Independence. Morelos attended the early meetings of the Congress of Chilpancingo. On one occasion he addressed the members on the significance of their task: "Spirits of Las Cruces, of Aculco, Guanajuato, Calderón, Zitacuaro and Cuautla! Spirits of Hidalgo and Allende should be witness to our flood of tears! You, who govern this august assembly, accept the most solemn pledge which we make to you today—that we shall die or save the country . . . Spirits of Moctezuma, Cacamatizin, Chauhtemoc, Xicotencatl, and Caltzontzin, take pride in this august assembly, and celebrate this happy moment in which your sons have congregated to avenge your insults. After August 11, 1521, comes September 8, 1813. The first date tightened the chains of our slavery in Mexico-Tenochtitlan; the second one broke them forever in the town of Chilpancingo . . . We are therefore going to restore the Mexican empire, and improve the government; we are going to be the spectacle of the cultured nations which will observe us; finally, we are going to be free and independent."[43]

And the Congress did adopt Quintana Roo and Bustamante's Declaration on November 6, 1813. It concluded that "the dependence on the Spanish throne should be dissolved . . . for better government and domestic happiness. . . ." The Declaration also said the new govern-

[41]Wilbert H. Timmons, *Morelos, Priest, Soldier, Statesman of Mexico.* (El Paso, Texas: Texas Western Press, 1970), pp. 100–101.

[42]Timmons, pp. 100–101.

[43]Timmons, p. 118.

ment did not ". . . profess nor recognize any religion other than the Catholic, nor will it tolerate or permit the use of any other in public or in secret. . . ." and that it would maintain the "purity of the faith and its dogmas. . . ."

The Congress also adopted a decree abolishing slavery and one which restored the Society of Jesus for the purpose of education. It set to work writing a constitution—a task that was never completed at Chilpancingo. Morelos suffered a humiliating defeat in Valladolid at the hands of a rising star in the royalist army, Augustín de Iturbide. The Congress relocated in the remote hamlet of Apatzingan and there promulgated the Constitution of 1814. In 242 articles, it proclaimed Mexico a republic with leadership determined by popular sovereignty. Like the United States Constitution it proclaimed a separation of powers and an indirect system of elections. In fear of one man rule, it established a weak three man executive. And in keeping with the Declaration of Independence, Catholicism was to be the nation's faith with no other religion being tolerated. But tithing was to be voluntary. Slavery and caste differences were to be abolished; and the law was to be applied equally to all. Everyone should have the right to own property, for that right is sacred. And this representative government was to be financed by a 5 percent income tax and a 10 percent import duty. Although the Constitution of 1814 was never fully adopted, the document gave legitimacy to the insurgent forces and was a strong morale booster. Furthermore, "it gave legality and dignity to the insurgent regime, particularly in the eyes of foreign powers," who saw the constitution as an act of faith and sincerity. And to the insurgent leaders it gave a feeling of faith and ultimate triumph.

But that triumph would not be effected by this congress nor the men of Morelos. The royalist forces of Calleja and others were thoroughly shocked by the Constitution of 1814, and they intensified their efforts to crush the rebellion. On November 5, 1815, while permitting his fleeing Congress to escape, Morelos permitted himself to be captured. The leader of his captors was a lieutenant who had served under Morelos in Acapulco and Cuautla. As Morelos surrendered, he eyed his captor and said: "Señor Carranco, it appears that we know one another."

Morelos was duly tried by a joint tribunal which represented both the civil and the ecclesiastical authorities. The ecclesiastical trial, which included an interrogation before the Holy Office of Inquisition, lasted less than four days, after which Morelos was publicly degraded in an *auto de fé*. The civil trial began on November 28, and it lasted for three days, at the close of which the death penalty was sought. On December 20, 1815, after a short trial, Felix Calleja approved the execution. On December 22, Morelos was bound and forced to kneel in the courtyard. His eyes covered, his face tilted upward, he spoke his final words: "Lord, thou knowest if I have done well; if ill, I implore thy infinite mercy." Four shots were fired, and Morelos fell to the earth.

The death of Morelos was an awesome display of vengence by the state and government he sought to abolish. Ironic is it not, that the very leaders he fought would eventually join the struggle for Mexican independence.

CHAPTER 19

Augustín Primero, Emperor of Mexico

In the National Cathedral of Mexico rests the body of Augustín de Iturbide, Mexico's first emperor and leader of Mexico's first independent government. Iturbide had been a royalist officer who had served the Spanish viceroy. He was responsible for the decisive defeat of Morelos at Valladolid, and struggled fiercely against other insurgents. And then, he and those he represented suddenly became the champions of Independence. On his tomb is inscribed: "Here lies Augustín de Iturbide, stranger admire him, compatriot weep for him for here lies the remains of a hero."

By 1815, the two most famous leaders of Mexican Independence had been shot and their armies defeated and scattered. Hidalgo and Morelos had been more than revolutionary leaders, they were symbols; they were men of hope; they were leaders who engendered hope in the minds and hearts of thousands of Mexican insurgents. As the year 1820 approached, only two insurgent leaders of any force and authority remained, Guadalupe Victoria and Vincente Guerrero.

Guadalupe Victoria was a criollo whose real name was Miguel Fernández y Félix. Known as Félix Fernández, he rechristianed himself Guadalupe Victoria in honor of the virgin Guadalupe and his intention to win victory over the gachupines. Victoria's army was scarcely more than a band. He and his people remained in the hills between Puebla and Veracruz, where they inflicted some damage, but spent more time running and hiding, than fighting.

Vicente Guerrero with a ragtag band of 2,000 continued to fight in the mountains of the Sierra Madre del Sur in the region of Acapulco. Guerrero was a disciple of Morelos, and he steadfastly believed in his values of social reform, particularly land reform. There is a touching story of Guerrero's father, an ex-royalist soldier who was sent by the viceroy with an offer of amnesty and reward if Guerrero would end his guerrilla warfare. When his father came to the encampment there was a great deal of excitement among the men. After son and father greeted each other, Guerrero turned to his men and said: "My compadres, this old man is my father. He came in presentation of the Spaniards to offer me rewards and employment. I have always venerated him but I will not accept anything from the enemies of our cause. My Country is first."

In spite of the fact that Victoria and Guerrero continued the struggle, all appeared hopeless. Then in 1820, events in Spain changed the whole complexity of the struggle for independence in Mexico. These events had their antecedents in the government of Joseph Bonaparte in Spain in 1812. In accordance with the ideals of the French Revolution, a constitution had been written that would abolish convents, the inquisition, tithes, and the *fueros*—those special privileges granted the clergy and the military. The constitution also guaranteed freedom of the press—and certain liberal agricultural reforms. Ferdinand VII, the landed aristocracy and the Catholic hierarchy of Spain were bitterly opposed to such moves. However, the Constitution of 1812 never really had an opportunity to be tested, for the government of Joseph Bonaparte abruptly ended with the defeat of Napoleon in 1814. With the movement in Europe toward restoring legitimate monarchs, young Ferdinand VII, now thirty, again became Spain's king. But during his six years of exile, the world—and Spain—had changed dramatically. Ferdinand found that peaceful accession meant he had to recognize the Constitution of 1812, even though he saw it as only temporary. When eventually Ferdinand felt his position was strong enough to revoke the Constitution, he did so, but not without opposition. And it was this opposition in Spain—not in America, but in Spain, that led Mexico to declare for independence.

As 1820 began, a number of liberal rebellions started throughout Spain. The most successful was led by Colonel Rafael del Riego in January. It began in Cádiz and spread throughout much of Spain including Segovia and Barcelona. By March, it became apparent to the vacillating king that this was no small insurrection and he succumbed to the revolutionaries by publishing a document restoring the Constitution of 1812. The result was that the new cortes or representative assembly became dominated by intellectuals and Masons imbued with the ideals of the Enlightenment and the French Revolution. They lifted censorship and released many political prisoners. But the worst was to come. Burdened with a heavy military debt, the new government turned to that institution which traditionally had the funds to support and maintain the system, the Catholic Church. Their first move was to abolish the Holy Office of Inquisition. They then called for an end to monastery building and the confiscation of the property of the regular orders. In addition with an eye to further weakening the power of the orders, they offered a bonus to any monk who would become secular. When the papal nuncio of Spain denounced the actions of the government and returned to Rome, even Ferdinand complained about the embarrassment he had been caused by the liberal constitutional regime.

All of this had a direct effect on Mexico's movement toward independence. The hierarchy of the Church in Mexico and the gachupin dominated government were terrified that these radical actions would spread to the colonies. This terror was heightened when Mexico's viceroy, Juan de Apodaca, took an oath to the new constitution and then duly dissolved the Holy Office of Inquisition. Thousands of Mexican revolutionaries accepted pardons in return for their allegiance to the viceroyalty. Mexico appeared to be heading toward a measure of peace and stability. But the clerics and gachupines saw this peace as a destruction of the foundations of Catholic New Spain.

In a complete about face, they decided that Spain's government had become radical and corrupt, and it would be better for Mexico to take independence from Spain—not for the reasons of the Enlightenment, or of the French and American Revolutions; certainly not for the reason of popular sovereignty. They believed that Ferdinand VII had been deceived, and they felt that if offered it, he would accept the crown as king of an independent Mexico. And thus the plotting began.

While the gachupines plotted, the viceroy was attempting to crush the last vestige of revolution in Mexico. Vicente Guerrero and his band were thorns that had to be removed, and for that job, he chose the able colonel, Augustín de Iturbide. After all, had not this criollo officer been instrumental in the final defeat of Father Morelos? Iturbide, although able and charismatic soon found himself embroiled in a dispute with the viceroy over a matter of six thousand pesos which Iturbide felt was due him. At the suggestion of the conspiring conservatives, and in spite of the dispute, the viceroy selected Iturbide as the man to corral Guerrero, either through peaceful surrender, or by force of arms.

Actually, the clerics and peninsulares who suggested Iturbide to the viceroy had already met at a convent in Mexico City, called La Profesa. At La Profesa, they planned to strike for independence, with Iturbide as their tool. They wanted to offer the crown of Mexico to Ferdinand VII, and if he refused, they would extend the offer to a member of his family or someone else of royal blood. They called their plan, La Profesa.

It was a great opportunity for Iturbide, probably greater than he originally suspected and in the waning months of 1820, he marched against Vícente Guerrero. After a series of engagements, he proclaimed great victories although the evidence is that he might actually have suffered a number of defeats. And to continue the flow of ready cash—for himself—he appropriated a shipment of silver bound for Acapulco and the Manila galleon, a shipment for which he had guaranteed safety.

But Iturbide still had the problem of Guerrero whom he could not defeat in battle. He also failed to convince him to surrender. So on January 10, 1821, from his headquarters at the town of Iguala, Iturbide—on his own authority—wrote the following letter to Vicente Guerrero:

"You are in a position to contribute to . . . the future of Mexico . . . in a special manner by ceasing hostilities and by submitting with your troops to the orders of the government with the understanding that I shall allow you to remain in command of your force and shall even secure for you some provision for its support. This measure is proposed in view of the fact that, animated by the grandest ideas of patriotism and liberty, our representatives have started for the Spanish Cortes. There they will energetically present our needs. Among other matters they will propose that, without exception, all the sons of Mexico should enjoy the same privileges as the citizens of Spain. Now that his Majesty Ferdinand VII cannot become our sovereign, perhaps his august brother Senor Don Carlos or Don Francisco de Paula will proceed to Mexico. If this should prove to be impossible, you may be certain that the deputies will omit nothing which will lead to the complete happiness of our native land. But, if contrary to our expectations, we should not be granted justice, I shall be the first person to aid with my sword, with my fortune, and with my ability in the defense of our rights. I swear this to you and to all the world on my word of honor which you can trust; for never has it been broken, and never will it be broken."[44]

Guerrero's answer came on January 20. In it he repeated his principles of the revolution—those which had been formulated by Morelos. He said he would never accept pardon from the Spanish government and that his motto was independence or death. He furthermore declared that Iturbide should not wait for emissaries to return from Spain but should take decisive action now. In a series of meetings which followed, Iturbide convinced Guerrero to join him in a movement for Mexican independence under his now famous Plan de Iguala in spite of Guerrero's skepticisms and suspicions.

On February 24, 1821, Augustín de Iturbide formally proclaimed for Mexican Independence under his *Plan de Iguala,* or the Plan of the Three Guarantees. The first guarantee was that Mexico was to be inde-

[44]Bustamate, *Cuadro Historico,* v, p 100; as quoted in Robertson, *Iturbide of Mexico.* p. 63.

pendent with Ferdinand VII or another royal monarch as its king. Secondly, the Church would retain all privileges or fueros; and thirdly, there would be equality of all the races—that is, Mexicans would be Mexicans, regardless of their racial mixture. As an addendum, there would be an army of the Three Guarantees, and a new tri-color Mexican flag: green for independence; white for religious purity; and red for the union of blood, Spanish and Mexican. As a tribute to their Indian heritage, the center of the flag would be adorned with the Aztec eagle wearing a royal crown.

So by the summer of 1821, all of Mexico except Mexico City, Veracruz, Perote and Acapulco, proclaimed for *Plan de Iguala*. On June 8, 1821, Don Juan O'Donojú sailed from Cádiz toward Veracruz, appointed by Ferdinand VII, as Captain General of New Spain, "with all the privileges and distinctions which viceroys of that kingdom had enjoyed." He had also been appointed Superior Political Chief of the Viceroyalty. In effect, he was to replace Juan de Apodaca. A valiant Spanish soldier of Irish lineage, O'Donojú's attitude before leaving Spain was conciliatory. Upon arriving in Veracruz he was convinced he would support the Spanish royalist cause. But on his way to Mexico City while lodged in the town of Córdoba, O'Donojú met with Iturbide, became convinced of the fact of Mexican Independence and so accepted it. On August 24, 1821, O'Donojú formally recognized Mexican Independence by the Treaty of Córdoba.

Under the terms of Iguala, O'Donojú notified Spain of his decision stating that it was not his intention to have Spain lose Mexico. He concluded, however, that independence was a fact and therefore a limited monarchy would be better than none at all. But to Spain, the Treaty of Córdoba was totally unsatisfactory, and it is probable that Iturbide suspected that Ferdinand VII would denounce independence as illegal and refuse the offer of the crown of independent Mexico.

In spite of Ferdinand VII, Guerrero's acceptance of *Plan de Iguala* inspired other revolutionaries to support the plan; the most significant was Guadalupe Victoria. Approached by messenger, Victoria recognized the Trigarantine Army and declared for *Plan de Iguala*. And Anastasio Bustamante, the criollo commander who had fought many insurgents, joined his viceregal army with that of Iturbide in a massive parade in Guanajuato. To Viceroy Juan de Apodaca, the events were confusing and incomprehensible; but there was little he could do. Independence was a fact. On September 21, 1821, Iturbide marched into Mexico City. On one side of him was the disciple of Morelos, Vincente Guerrero; on the other, the undefeatable Guadalupe Victoria. The Church, of course, hailed independence, for with the guarantee of a Bourbon king, and the guarantee of all of their property and fueros—what more could they want?

Thus it was that independence was achieved not by Hidalgo,

Morelos, nor any of their followers. All of them lacked the power base nece ⸜y for a successful revolution. Rather, Independence was achieved by those people who defeated the early insurgents.

For the peninsulares, the *Plan de Iguala* had almost everything they wanted, a retention of the social and economic system and assurance of a Bourbon king. For the criollo landowner or mineowner, *status quo* was just fine. True, some criollo intellectuals wanted change, and they were assured that the Constitution of 1812 in Spain would prevail in Mexico. It was scarcely a wave in the ocean of the Enlightenment, but it seemed to satisfy many. And for the poverty stricken Indian—well, there was more poverty.

On the morning of September 28, one day after marching triumphantly into Mexico City, Iturbide summoned his hand picked deputies to meet in the main hall in the National Palace. After attending a solemn ceremony at the National Cathedral, they crossed the Zocalo and returned to the National Palace where they unanimously elected Iturbide president of the Junta. The following day, a regency was formed with Iturbide, as president, and four other members. The Regency conferred a number of honors and powers on the new president including the right to create titles; and back pay for all of his services. Iturbide rose in his seat and in a gesture of magnanimity he dismissed all claim to the money and asked that it be distributed amongst his soldiers instead. Clearly, he was endearing himself to the Regency which now passed a resolution praising the "sublime virtues of its liberator."

As the days of the Regency wore on, Iturbide lavished titles on deserving colleagues. And the regency continued to bestow titles on Iturbide. He became "Generalissimo of the Army and High Admiral of the Navy, with the title of His Serene Highness." The titles gave Iturbide virtual control of all administrative and military affairs with total power of appointment. There appeared to be general satisfaction with his glorification except for a small but significant group of republicans. They were led by a Scottish Rite Freemason who had come from Spain with Juan O'Donojú. Manuel Cordorniu counted among his followers such revolutionaries as Nicholás Bravo and Guadalupe Victoria.

Iturbide's total disregard for republican principles led several within this group to meet with the idea of taking action. Their course of action was innocuous enough; they would send a mild protest. If he ignored them, they would publish a manifesto. On the evening of November 26, 1821, as they sat writing their protest in the home of Manuel Domínguez, the old corregidor of Queretaro, a group of soldiers entered and arrested all of them. None of them remained in jail for more than one month, but the intimidations and threats were severe. However, for Guadalupe Victoria, who had been one of the republicans arrested,

His Serene Highness and the Regency represented all that was repugnant to Victoria's idea of independence. He retreated to the hills once more to continue the struggle for real Mexican Independence.

On the evening of May 18, 1822, a sergeant of the Celaya Battalion in Mexico City, led his men into the streets with shouts of "*¡Viva Augustín Primero!*" "*¡Viva Augustín Primero!*"—"Long live Augustin I!" "Long Live Augustin I!" Almost simultaneously, a Colonel Rivero entered the municipal theatre and exhorted the audience to also proclaim that Augustín de Iturbide be made the emperor of Mexico. At the same time, similar demonstrations were engendered throughout the City. Soon thousands were milling about the streets shouting "*¡Viva Augustín Primero!*" "*¡Viva Augustín Primero!*" *¡Viva el Emperador!*"

Because the demonstrations appeared simultaneously, Iturbide and his supporters have been accused of planning the whole event. It has been reasoned that because of the schism that had developed between Iturbide and the Congress over the size of the army and the make-up of the regency, Iturbide felt the time for action had come. He was aware that Congress was about to pass a measure which would have virtually eliminated his power over the armed forces, and this would be intolerable. But Iturbide and his supporters denied any complicity. He did enjoy immense popularity with the military and the Church and the populace, of that there is no denial. He himself described the events of that evening in May:

"Augustín I was the universal cry that astonished me, for it was the first time in my life that I experienced this kind of sensation.

Immediately, as if everyone shared a similar sentiment, the city was illuminated, the balconies were adorned and filled with people who repeated with joy the acclamations of the multitude in the streets, especially those near the house where I then lived. Not a single citizen expressed disapprobation, proof of the weakness of my opponents and of the unanimity of public opinion in my favor. There was no misdeed, no disorder of any kind. Augustin I filled the minds of all. My first thought was to refuse a crown seemingly burdensome, but from this I was dissuaded by the advice of a friend who was then with me: 'The people are easily made irritable by what they construe as ingratitude. You must make this new sacrifice for the public good; the country is in danger; a moment of indecision may change their acclamations to cries of death.' Seeing that I must resign myself to the circumstances, I employed the rest of the night calming the popular enthusiasm and persuading the public and the troops to give me time to make a decision."[45]

Iturbide then retired from the balcony and requested advice from the generals, the Regency, and some deputies. Accordingly, they all urged him to accept, and to the wild rejoicing of the crowds, he did! However,

[45]Breve Deseño from Caruso, *Iturbide,* pp. 247-48.

when Congress convened the following morning to debate the issue, the Republicans and Bourbonist representatives were noticeably absent. But the display that followed assured Iturbide of the crown of Mexico. As the deputies debated, throngs of people packed the galleries and many more gathered outside of the hall. The debate was met with shouts of approval to those who supported Iturbide and jeers of disapproval to those who did not. Some members of Congress even questioned the legality of electing an emperor and they insisted their authority was limited to passing legislation. At one o'clock in the afternoon, a group of monks burst into the hall shouting: "Emperor or death! Emperor or death!" As others took up the same cry, the deputies quickly voted; sixty-seven for and fifteen against. The public acclaim was wild. And for those who did not support him? Well, either they locked themselves in their homes or clandestinely left the country—one of these men was the Archbishop of Mexico, Pedro Fonte.

Everywhere, there was praise. Antonio López de Santa Anna, who later would be the first to revolt against Iturbide, wrote: "Long live Your Majesty for our glory, and let his expression be so gratifying that the sweet name of Augustín will be transmitted to our descendants, so that they may have record of the memorable deeds of our worthy liberator."[46]

Vincente Guerrero, in speaking for those people whom he represented, wrote: "After dragging their chains for three centuries, they see themselves fully free, thanks to the genius of Your Imperial Majesty and your forces, with which you took off the yoke. . . ."[47]

Valentin Gomez Farias, who later became a leader for the radical liberals also called for great acclamation; as did the Catholic Church. Although Hidalgo's revolution had envisioned the creation of a democratic state, what was achieved was far different. Mexico began its national existence as a monarchy with a vast empire which included, not only much of what is now the United States, but also Central America to the Panamanian border. Four years later, Brazil in its strike for independence from Portugal also chose a monarchical form of government with a vast empire as well. So it was that two nations in the Western Hemisphere began their independence not as New World democracies, but as Old World empires.

Unfortunately for Iturbide, his Old World empire was doomed from the beginning, for this monarchy was formed by the elites to govern Mexico for their own interests. It did not speak to the larger concerns for the nation as had Morelos and Hidalgo; therefore, it could not enlist the support of the vast majority of the population. Furthermore, Iturbide's task from the beginning was impossible. Neither Iturbide nor any other person had the ability to heal the wounds of more than ten years of

[46]Caruso, p. 251.
[47]Caruso, p. 251.

revolution. The scars ran deep. The gachupines would not forget the slaughter of the Alhóndiga, nor would the revolutions forget the sight of the staked heads of their leaders hanging on the walls of that government granary. The carnage perpetrated by Calleja and other gachupines officers could not be erased by a document that stated that "Mexicans would be Mexicans" regardless of racial make-up. Furthermore, class and caste was too deeply ingrained in the minds and hearts of the gachupines and criollos to accept such a doctrine of equality. And their fear of the unruly mobs of Hidalgo was not assuaged by the election of a handsome emperor.

Furthermore, Mexico was in a state of economic devastation. The War for Independence began in the major mining areas of Mexico, and mining was the backbone of the economy. The mines in the vicinity of Guanajuato had been abandoned and their shafts filled with water— ruining the structural timber as well as the machinery used in extracting and processing. Shovels, picks, axes, and other tools had been gathered by the mobs for use as weapons in the early days of the revolution. The Valenciana mine, the wealthiest in Mexico, was virtually shut down. Its only production after the revolution was picking pieces of silver out of what were once rubble heaps. The cities which these mines directly supported were also in a state of ruin. The prosperous and beautiful town of Guanajuato which had an affluent population of 80,000 before the war, now supported 35,000 poverty-stricken people amidst incredible destitution and rubble.

The destruction of mining had an effect on the entire economy—for it deprived Mexico not only of jobs but of capital necessary for foreign trade. Not only did mining suffer, but business and agriculture also felt the effects of the scorched-earth policy practiced by both sides. An English mining official described the ruin on the road from San Luis Potosi to Zacatecas:

> "We . . . saw the houses roofless and in ruins blackened by fire, and had ridden over plains still bearing faint traces of the plow; but the Rancheros who had tilled the ground had been murdered with their whole families during the war. In the space of forty miles we passed no fewer than fifteen crosses set up at the roadside, to mark the spot where an assassination had been committed."[48]

Joel Pointsett, the first United States minister to Mexico, writing after 1825, observed the devastation of the village of San Felipe, thirty-five miles north of Guanajuato:

> "San Felipe presented another melancholy example of the horrors of civil war. Scarcely a house was entire; and, except for one church lately rebuilt,

[48]Cumberland, *Mexico's Struggle for Modernity*, p. 134.

the town appeared to be in ruins. We stopped in the principal square and passed through arches built of porphyry into the courtyard of a building which had once been magnificent; nothing but the porticoes and ground floor remain."[49]

Added to all of this was the graft and corruption which was perpetrated by many military leaders, including Augustín de Iturbide, himself. Forced loans became the favorite of the royalists; looting was the option of the insurgents. It is little wonder that the Emperor, who had entered with such fanfare and glory, was completely and totally unable to cope with the social and economic ills which befell Mexico. And as the military and bureaucratic budget skyrocketed, revenues drastically diminished. The foreign and domestic debt became staggering—literally impossible to fund.

And if the social and economic aspects of the empire were impossible to deal with—so was the political. The Republicans and Bourbonists continued their attacks on his Royal Majesty. And they were joined by anti-Iturbide newspapers, some of which were supported by the powerful Masonic orders. The newspapers, Iturbide surpressed. Deputies who disagreed with him, he jailed, more than fifteen in all. And finally, after Congress failed to pass his suggested legislation, just four months after his coronation on October 21, 1822, Iturbide dissolved that august body. But the first signs of a real challenge to his authority came from the commander of the military garrison at Vera Cruz, Antonio López de Santa Anna. Santa Anna had enthusiastically endorsed the crown of Iturbide shortly after Congress had conferred it. But to Iturbide, Santa Anna's scheming to assume greater personal power in the area of Veracruz was a threat. Iturbide arranged a meeting with Santa Anna in early December of 1822, the ostensible purpose was to cover Santa Anna with glory—to permit him to remove the last of the Spaniards from the island of San Juan de Ulúa off the coast of Veracruz. But the emperor said he needed Santa Anna in Mexico City to plan strategy. Santa Anna was not fooled, and on December 6, 1822, the Napoleon of the West, as Santa Anna saw himself, pronounced against the Empire, and requested that His Royal Majesty resign. Within a short time, Vicente Guerrero, Guadalupe Victoria, and Nicolás Bravo followed suit. Initial successes in crushing the rebellion were followed by devastating defeats, including the loss of support from the Catholic Church. On March 20, 1823, the inevitable happened, Augustín de Iturbide, His Royal Majesty, resigned. On May 11, 1823, the deposed emperor sailed aboard the English merchant ship *Rawlins* into exile in Italy. From there he went to England where he became convinced he should return to Mexico in order to bring a measure of tranquility to

[49]Cumberland, p. 135.

his country. But his country had proclaimed him "a traitor and outlaw.
. . .," and anyone who aided his return would also be treated as traitors
and invading enemy. Iturbide was forbidden to return to Mexico "on pain
of death." On July 15, 1823, Iturbide landed just north of Tampico, not
knowing that a sentence of death had been placed upon him the previous
April. By the afternoon of July 19, Iturbide lay lifeless—a firing squad
having executed him just outside the little town of Padilla. His body was
carried to a roofless church in Padilla and buried.

The death of Iturbide brought no respite to the social, economic,
and political ills which plagued Mexico. It did decisively mark the end of
Mexico's criollo emperor, and little more. He was succeeded by a new
republicanism which also failed to cope with Mexico's problems. For the
next fifty years, chaotic conditions prevailed. Neither federalism, nor
centralism, nor a foreign-imposed empire could solve them.

CHAPTER 20

The Constitution of 1824
and the First Federal Republic

      The Mexican flag was created by an act of the constituent congress of Mexico on April 14, 1823. The national coat of arms adorns the center of the flag with an eagle perched on a cactus. The cactus is growing out of a rock in the middle of lake Texcoco. In his right claw is a serpent; and the eagle is in the act of devouring a serpent. The colors of the Trigarantine army were preserved: green for independence; white for the purity of Catholicism; and red for the union of the Spaniard with the Mexican. The original horizontal bars were changed to a vertical position. The flag measure passed without much opposition. It was about the only thing this constituent congress passed that did not engender a hostile reaction.

      Shortly after the abdication of Augustín de Iturbide, the national constituent congress appointed a triumverate to act temporarily in place of an executive. In addition to appointing a cabinet, they saw as their task the elimination of every vestige of the empire that had been established by Iturbide. The Council of State which he had created to act in lieu of congress was abolished as were the political and military districts of the former regime. Political prisoners were released and the Royal Orders, designed to emulate a European court, were also abolished. It was clearly assumed that the new form of government would be a republic, and it was also assumed that a republican form of government would in some way solve the many and complex problems which the new nation faced. This attitude was strangely similar to that of the *criollo* prior to Independence. "Rid the country of *gachupin* rule, and our problems will be solved." But the end of colonialism brought only new problems with which the government of Iturbide failed to grapple, and those problems continued. They were mainly economic such as how does one finance an independent bureaucracy and a mammoth military establishment which devoured nearly eighty percent of the budget? During the ten months of Iturbide, it appeared that Mexico had a balanced budget. But in reality, the cost of operating the government far exceeded revenues from normal taxation. In fact, the cost of collecting taxes at the local level, exceeded the amount collected, so the government sought both foreign and domestic loans. Agents of Iturbide attempted to borrow from European sources, but they found no one willing to loan money to his Royal Majesty. Next they turned to local lenders, many of whom obliged at interest rates of six to seven percent per month, rates that were ruinous to the new government with an almost empty treasury. On the day the provisional government took office in 1823, there was exactly forty-two pesos in the national treasury.

Where Iturbide's agents were unsuccessful, the provisional government found succor. British bankers having just read Alexander von Humboldt's glowing description of Mexican mineral wealth, saw an opportunity to turn a quick profit. From a banking firm in England, Mexico received a loan for sixteen million pesos, payable at five percent interest; fair enough on the surface. However, most of the money quickly disappeared as the provisional government attempted to fund the revolutionary debt of forty-five million pesos. And so a second loan was authorized for another sixteen million pesos by Barclay and Company of England. Out of this, four million was used to reduce the original debt and an even larger portion was spent on military hardware at inflated prices. The actual cash placed in the treasury from this second loan amounted to only a fraction of the loan itself. If revenues had equalled expenditures, it would have been possible to fund the debt, but expenditures were more than double revenues, which created an ominous picture for the future.

Still, the new congress went about the business of creating a new form of government, selecting a single executive, and drawing up a federal constitution. Two political parties had emerged and both were represented in the newly elected congress, the federalists and the centralists. The federalists held the majority and they undertook the tasks of writing Mexico's first federal constitution. The most influential contributor was a clerical-liberal—a representative from the northern area of Coahuila—Miguel Ramos Arizpe.

Under the influence of Ramos Arizpe, the constitution adopted in 1824 paralleled the federal constitution of the United States, and it was even titled the Constitution of the United States of Mexico. It contained most of the traditional guarantees embodied in the U.S. constitution: Freedom of the press was guaranteed; cruel and barbarous punishments were abolished; copyrights and patents were established; and a system of justice with a supreme court and state courts was established. In addition, there would be nineteen states and four territories. The constitution also provided for secular education, but still endorsed Catholicism as perpetually the only religion of the Mexican nation. This was not unusual in light of the tradition of the Catholic Church in Mexico. The constitution also differed on trial by jury; because Mexico was established upon the tradition of Roman law, the practice of trial by judges prevailed. Representation would be embodied in a two-house legislature: a senate and a chamber of deputies. The deputies were to be elected by the populace at the ratio of one for every eighty thousand. Two senators for each state, however, were to be elected by the state legislatures. The election of the president and vice president and congress was almost identical to that of Mexico's northern neighbor.

Two candidates emerged for the high office of president. Guadalupe Victoria was the favorite of the federalists, while the centralists supported Nicolás Bravo. Guadalupe Victoria, the honored revolutionary, with whom many identified the ideals of Hidalgo and Morelos, was elected by a majority of the votes cast. Bravo then became the vice-presidential candidate along with the warrior from Acapulco, Vicente Guerrero. Neither candidate received a majority, so congress selected Nicholás Bravo. At the governmental level, there was a sense of optimism and expectation; even the people saw the election of these two honest revolutionary leaders as a solution to the many problems which had befallen Mexico. Tradition and heritage focused hope on the person, the individual savior rather than the general policies of the nation. Three hundred years of colonial rule by a divine monarch coupled with the presence of an almost divine viceroy had left a lasting impression on the thinking of the population. Added to this was the paternalism of the Catholic Church, a paternalism that was especially true of the Indian population in the villages associated with the encomienda.

The problems Mexico faced could not be solved by one individual, let alone one whose experience was revolutionary-military and not political. Neither Guadaulpe Victoria nor Nicolás Bravo could drain the water from the flooded mineshafts. Neither could they remove the rust from the massive pieces of processing equipment that had been left in the open field to disintegrate; nor could they replace the thousands upon thousands of men who died fighting for one cause or another—and the fighting continued. It wasn't as widespread as before independence, but there were constant little rebellions with which to contend. The loss of so many men kept population growth exceedingly low.

Through this early period of the republic, the Catholic Church maintained its wealth and power, but respect for the Church had eroded. Its immense landed wealth, whether or not it directly worked that land, caused many to question—why should the Church, traditionally the protector of the people, own all that land? Why should the land not be distributed among the people? A number of liberal generals, both before and after independence found this an enticing idea. But the popularity of the Church with the people, led them to be cautious. Independence also had an effect on the numbers and the quality of the clergy. With a diminishing of the missionizing efforts of the monastic orders, many of the convents were either closed or maintained with small staffs. The regulars generally moved into the cities and lived off either their investments or the contributions of the people. As respect for the monastic orders diminished, so did the quality and number of its members.

Even the restoration of the Jesuits did not mean their educational establishments would suddenly produce the scholarship familiar to the mid-colonial period. And although the Constitution of 1824 gave the Catholic Church absolute dominance of religion in Mexico, many intellectuals, along with the rapidly growing Masonic lodges, challenged that singularity. Even independence itself had a disruptive effect on the Church, as a new national Mexico would receive ministers and consular officials from protestant countries, or countries where religious freedom had been guaranteed. And if Mexico were to sustain any kind of immigration, her religious policy of Catholic singularity would have to change. It finally did with the Constitution of 1857.

For all of the problems faced by the new federal republic, politics and economics were the most difficult—and each had an effect on the other. In the first seven months of 1825, government expenditures exceeded twenty-one million pesos, while revenues amounted to about nine million pesos. Of the twenty-one million pesos, ninety percent was earmarked for the military. The late historian Charles C. Cumberland did a comparative study of Mexico's pre-independence budget with that of first federal republic. The results are astonishing. At no time during the colonial period, even at the height of revolutionary activity, did the viceregal budget exceed ten million pesos; and yet, the expenditures for the first seven months of 1825, were nineteen million pesos. For the full year, they would be over thirty-one million. Why? Did the Spanish occupation of the island of San Juan de Ulúa in the harbor of Veracruz necessitate a fully equipped army of fifty thousand men? Certainly not. Cumberland believed, "They may be better explained as incidents of national politics—jealousies, fears of insurrections, sources of lucrative positions—than as reflections of genuine concern over national security. This is particularly true in view of British investments and the well-publicized English foreign policy which served as a counterpoise to any possible French aid to Spain."[50]

Probably because of the military budget, the government failed to expend anything on internal reconstruction. Roads, bridges, harbors, water supply projects, and public buildings were in a state of decay and destruction which resulted from the prolonged war for independence.

Sadly, little respite could be seen from this state of affairs. There was little hope in increased internal revenue from taxation for most of that collected went to the agencies for collection—and sometimes even more than that collected. The graft and corruption engendered during the colonial period did not suddenly die with the advent of Independence. By greasing the palms of a tax collector, the amount owned to the government could be significantly diminished. Those who gave and those who accepted did not have the capacity to see the magnitude of the problem they were creating. Foreign loans at ruinous rates, loans that would lead to future foreign intervention, had to be met with even greater expenditures in money and life. In many cases, domestic loans were even worse— short term ninety-day notes payable at fifty percent interest. As the national debt increased, inventors were loathe to develop mining and industry. There was some rejuvenation of mining by British investors and some mines were even staffed with British personnel. But these efforts could not possibly solve the gigantic economic problem Mexico was experiencing.

The political situation appeared to be even worse. In the decades to follow, presidents came and went with amazing speed and regularity as the *pronunciamento* or pronouncement became a monthly event.

There were regular *cuartelazos* or barracks revolts. *Golpe del estado* the *coup d' état* against the government was the result of the pronouncement by general after general—and many were not even generals. The major tribute which can be accorded to Guadalupe Victoria was that he served out his four year presidential term—he was the first and last to do so for decades to come.

During these first years of the republic, two distinct political factions emerged: the federalists and the centralists. The federalists wanted a government patterned after the United States, based on Anglo Saxon democracy. They believed that the powers of the federal government ought to be limited by the sovereignty of the states, and they believed in popular sovereignty—that is, representatives ought to be elected by all of

[50]Cumberland, p. 146.

the people. The centralists on the other hand, looked more to the tradition and heritage of Mexico. One could evade the issue as is often done, and say that they "yearned for the good old days of the Spanish monarchy." And there would be a measure of truth to that. But there were many conservatives who reasoned that neither the heritage nor the educational level of Mexico could handle full democracy and popular sovereignty. They asked, how could a large illiterate caste population decide on complex and social and economic issues? They reasoned that *their* votes would be either guesses or reflections of those for whom they worked. From these two political factions emerged the so-called liberals and conservatives. Generally, historians have treated the liberals as the "good guys" and the conservatives as the "bad guys." While there might be a measure of truth to this, some conservatives were sincere and very capable.

The liberals split into two separate groups. The more traditional members were appropriately called the *moderados* or moderates. Other than supporting a republican form of government, the moderados were reluctant to tamper with the status quo. Most of the *criollo moderados* were property owners and they had little knowledge of the majority of the landless, illiterate agrarian population. A major leader of the moderados was General Manuel Gómez Pedraza, Minister of War in the government of Guadalupe Victoria. In time, the conservatives seeing their chances of winning an election as dim, supported Gómez Pedraza.

The more radical element of the liberals was the *puro*, or pure liberals as their name implies. The puros felt that Mexico's problems had to be solved by direct action. At times their programs curdled the blood of the conservatives who saw the puros as a potentially destructive force. For their part, the puros wanted to distribute land to the landless through government expropriation of Church and hacienda estates. The puros also wished to curb the power of the Catholic Church, and the military, both politically and socially. They called for an end to the *fueros* or privileges which the military officers and clergy had enjoyed for some time, privileges that literally exempted the clergy and military from civil action in the courts and privileges that exempted them from taxation. This intellectual doctrinaire group saw the fueros as the very antithesis of enlightened democracy. Education, they felt should be strictly secular. But this was only one part of the whole conception of separation of church and state. The puros had many outstanding leaders, but three in particular stand out. Valentín Gómez Farías was a physician from the mining area of Zacatecas. As a politician, he was respected by liberals and conservatives alike for his honesty and intellectual capacity. Major reforms that were instituted during the period of Reform, in the 1850's, were mainly programs initiated by Gómez Farías. He was in effect, the real leader of the liberals for more than thirty years. He was associated with one of the great theoreticians of the puros, José María Luis Mora, an outstanding economist. But even the economic knowledge of Mora, could not raise Mexico from her economic morass. Finally, there was Lorenzo de Zavala. He was a mestizo from the Yucatan who had excellent political insight. In spite of his theoretical talents, he was a man of action. He believed the puro program could be implemented—and that it would work.

Unfortunately, the centralist role of honor is almost non-existent. There were generals and politicians who fought sincerely for what they believed. But all too often, centralist leaders were self-adulating and all too ready to gain whatever profits their position would permit. Nevertheless, one centralist leader stands far above all others, Lucas Alamán, a mining engineer, who had been Minister of Foreign Relations, was indeed a brilliant politician. His observations were dispassionate and clear. He was firmly convinced that Mexico could only survive with a foreign monarchy or an indigenous dictatorship. He is the author of a classic multi-volume history of Mexico, in which he is critical of the liberals and conservatives alike. His history of Mexico is still regarded as the most honest of that period.

Liberals and conservatives notwithstanding, neither could solve Mexico's problems. During the four years that Guadalupe Victoria served as president, the government consistently sank deeper into debt and as the economy floundered, the conservatives conspired to overthrow his government. In 1827, Nicolás Bravo, a grand master of the Scotch Rite Masons, was motivated to remove the York Rite Masons from positions of authority in government. This included Joel Pointsett, the American Minister to Mexico, who was an active *yorkino* and a fiery supporter of democratic federalism. Even as a foreign diplomat, he worked for the York Rite cause. Bravo, believing his cause was to gain a strict fulfillment of the constitution led a rebellion in which he demanded the dismissal of the president's cabinet and the dismissal of Joel Pointsett as America's Minister to Mexico. The Minister of War, Vicente Guerrero, acted quickly and decisively, and the rebellion was crushed. It was a tragic event in the otherwise patriotic and honorable career of Nicolás Bravo who was promptly impeached and exiled.

If this political circus was ominous for the future of Mexico, there were even more ominous signs pointing to foreign intervention. Spain, which had never recognized the independence of Mexico, made one last futile attempt to recapture her lost colony. The invasion was planned by Spanish merchants both in and out of Mexico. In June of 1829, when the Spanish General Isidro Barradas arrived in Cuba with an invasion army, reports reached Mexico of an imminent invasion by the Spanish troops now based in Cuba. When the reports proved correct, the Mexican press called for unity in the face of this foreign threat. While the condition of the Mexican army was wretched, nature and fortune did not smile upon the invaders. Shortly after landing, a storm separated five hundred soldiers from the main body. Lost, and unable to get food, they were quickly defeated by Mexican guerrillas. The main forces were equally unfortunate; as they endured the tropical climate of Tampico, their ranks were decimated by malaria and yellow fever. It became impossible to obtain food from the hostile population. On September 11, 1829, before their weapons and fighting ability could even be tested, the Spanish general surrendered his army to the Mexican forces, led by Antonio López de Sauta Anna. The Mexican journalists found a hero in Santa Anna, as a result of this almost comical invasion. Santa Anna became known as "the hero of Tampico." His influence as a political figure was growing.

At the same time, the government of Vincente Guerrero, Mexico's second President, disintegrated rapidly. Conservatives, who wanted a restoration of a monarchy, contemptuously alluded to Guerrero's alleged lower-class origins and lack of education. In November, a pro centralist rebellion began in Campeche. By December 4, the Vice President Anastasio Bustamante openly declared against Vicente Guerrero on the grounds that Guerrero had abused his power and misused public funds. His fate sealed, Guerrero fled to the mountains above Acapulco. The moderate Bustamante had recognized that opportunity outweighed morality and on January 1, 1830, Bustamante became President of Mexico.

Guerrero continued his fight; but within a year he was captured, placed on an Italian merchant ship in Acapulco, and literally sold to the government for fifty thousand pesos. Guerrero was marched to Oaxaca where a kangaroo court leveled seven charges against him, mostly for rebellion and treason. On the fourteenth of January, 1831, in the little town of Cuilapa, near Oaxaca, the deposed Constitutional President Vicente Guerrero was placed on his knees, read the sentence of the court, and was shot.

Guerrero's tragic end signaled Mexico's descent into the politics of coup and counter-coup. While the majority of Mexico's population suffered social and economic indignities, an elite group of politicians and military leaders attempted to create a self-serving bureaucracy. The Church, wishing to maintain the elitist role, joined with the conservatives in their effort to solidify their power. The assassination of a president was only an event in what would become a protracted struggle for the definition of Mexico's government, goals, and philosophy.

CHAPTER 21

Antonio López de Santa Anna, Hero of Tampico

In the area of Jalapa in the state of Veracruz are the remnants of what once was the great hacienda of Antonio López de Santa Anna. The massive rambling rancho called Manga de Clavo, literally translated into shaft of the nail, was his home, his retreat, and in time, his very identity. If Santa Anna wasn't pronouncing—that is declaring a revolution against some political leader, if he wasn't fighting a glorious war, if he wasn't running for the presidency or playing the role of a dictator, he was at his hacienda, Manga de Clavo. Antonio López de Santa Anna's influence on the course of Mexican history has been so great that historians generally refer to the time of his control over Mexico, as the "age of Santa Anna." He began his career as a royalist soldier for the viceroyalty and joined in the suppression of Mexican independence. Later, he joined in the struggle for separation from Spain and participated in establishing the first Mexican Empire under Augustín de Iturbide.

Interest in Santa Anna lies not only in the man but in the era with which he is generally associated. These are his own thoughts about his early years and his exotic rise to power:

"I have, since my earliest years, been drawn to the glorious career of arms, feeling it to be my true vocation and calling. On the ninth of June, in the year 1810, with my parents' blessing, I enlisted as a first-class cadet in the permanent infantry regiment of Vera Cruz. Thus, from the age of fourteen, I belonged to the Royal Army of New Spain. I had already proved my gentlemanly qualifications—an indispensable asset in those times."[51]

It was the period of the Enlightenment; of the American, French, and Latin American Revolutions. In the midst of this turbulence, on February 21, 1794, Antonio López de Santa Anna Pérez de Lebrón was ushered into this world in the province of Veracruz in New Spain. With little or no formal education, Santa Anna, as he called himself, found an early fascination with the military. In 1810, he became a cadet in the *Regimiento Fijo de Veracruz* or the Fixed Regiment of Veracruz. As early as 1811, he led the royal government forces against revolutionary insurgents, wounded, he was promoted to second lieutenant in the following year. He continued to suppress guerrilla bands and small insurrections including one in Texas in 1813. Up to the moment of independence, Santa Anna had been decorated several times and even invited to the Capital to be aide-de-campe to the viceroy.

"I knew that I had been favored by the vice-regal government and I was very grateful. But, even so, when the Plan de Iguala was made public, by proclamation of Colonel Augustín Iturbide on February 24, 1821, I hurried to sponsor it, wishing to contribute my own little grain of sand to our great political rebirth."[52]

And so, Santa Anna changed sides. Until 1821, he had maintained absolute loyalty to the Spanish crown and viceroyalty. Suddenly he switched. He declared for Plan de Iguala, engaged in open warfare against the viceregal government which he had served, and supported Iturbide in the Regency and later as Emperor of Mexico. When Iturbide appointed Santa Anna as permanent Commanding General of the Province of Veracruz, it appeared as if Iturbide had his absolute loyalty, but it only appeared that way. Within seven months of his appointment, the two were at odds as Iturbide became aware that Santa Anna was seeking power for himself instead of merely supporting the Empire. For Iturbide, the last straw came when Santa Anna concocted a fantastic scheme to defeat and eject the Spaniards from the fortress in the harbor of Veracruz, the island of San Juan de Ulúa. Spain had never recognized the independence of her colony and she continued to maintain a well-armed garrison at San Juan de Ulúa.

Its strategic location permitted the Spaniards to periodically bombard the city of Veracruz. Santa Anna's plan was to conspire with the commander of the Spanish garrison and feign the surrender of Veracruz

[51]Ann Fears Crawford, ed., *The Eagle: The Autobiography of Santa Anna.* (Austin, The Pemberton Press, 1967), p. 7.

[52]*The Eagle,* p. 9.

in hopes of luring the Spanish soldiers into the streets of the city. He dressed his own troops in Spanish uniforms and then waited to initiate his surprise attack, but the plan failed. So ill conceived was Santa Anna's plan, that a general Iturbide sent to Veracruz to investigate the matter was almost captured by the Spanish forces. Iturbide was infuriated, and although his wife was expecting a child at any moment, he rushed to Jalapa for a meeting with his Commanding General of Veracruz, seeking an explanation. Santa Anna's reception at Jalapa was far greater than the emperor's and it led Iturbide to remark that "this scoundrel here is the real emperor." At the meeting, Iturbide feigned a need for Santa Anna at the capital. The emperor's real intention was to reprimand Santa Anna and relieve him of his command at Veracruz. But Santa Anna suspected that Iturbide wished to lure him to the capital in order to strip him of command. He pleaded with the Emperor for a short amount of time during which he could settle his affairs and Iturbide, apparently satisfied that Santa Anna would comply, returned to the capital. But this master of duplicity had other ideas:

> "Knowing my disapproval of his coronation as Emperor, 'His Majesty' stripped me of my command and ordered my transfer to Mexico City, without extending to me the mere vestiges of courtesy. Such a crushing blow offended my dignity as a soldier and further awakened me to the true nature of absolutism. I immediately resolved to fight against it at every turn and to restore to my nation its freedom.
>
> I knew that my resolve would mean great effort and personal sacrifice, but I was determined to gain freedom at any price. I hastily made a public appearance in Vera Cruz in order to address the people. Before my troops, I proclaimed the Republic of Mexico on the second of December, 1822. I published the *Plan de Vera Cruz* and a manifesto in which I expressed my intentions, carefully stating that these were only to be temporary, in order for the nation, itself, to be the true arbiter of its destiny."[53]

And so Santa Anna switched again. First against independence; then for it. First for Iturbide's empire; then against it. But the social, political, and economic conditions in Mexico had deteriorated so badly that Santa Anna found more allies than adversaries. Guadalupe Victoria and Vincente Guerrero both denounced the government of Iturbide, and within a few months the Emperor ruled only in Mexico City. Shortly thereafter he abdicated. Santa Anna had been successful in overthrowing the empire; he had demonstrated his ability to lead, to attract and command loyalty. He was a force to be reckoned with:

> "My victory could not possibly have been more splendid! Judge and jury that I was in these momentous times of the destiny of my country, I remained faithful to every promise in the program that I had proclaimed

[53]*The Eagle,* pp. 16-17.

for the Republic. With a zeal that was almost religious in nature, I followed it to the letter!"[54]

After the abdication of Iturbide, and as the Constituent Congress began its work on the Constitution of 1824, the interim government appointed Santa Anna to be Comandante General and Governor of Yucatan. It appears that the appointment was made in order to exile him from the capital and the center of political power.

Santa Anna spent a turbulent year in the Yucatan during which he was involved in an abortive military campaign against Cuba. After tendering his resignation in 1825, Santa Anna moved to the area of Jalapa where he managed his newly acquired estate of Manga de Clavo. He remained there in semi-retirement with his fourteen-year-old newly wed wife, Doña Ines García, who bore him four children and managed the estate of Manga de Clavo until her death nineteen years later. In his early thirties, Santa Anna was described as ". . . tall and thin, with black darting eyes, a perfect nose and yellow-colored skin." Lorenzo de Zavala, a leader of the liberal movement in Mexico, wrote one of the most incisive descriptions of the man and his personality:

"The soul of General Santana does not fit in his body. It lives in perpetual motion. It permits him to be dragged along by the insatiable desire to acquire glory. It estimates the value of his outstanding qualities. He gets angry with the boldness that denies him immortal fame. . . . From his childhood he has distinguished himself by a courage that never has deserted him. One could say that his courage touches the summits of recklessness. On the battlefield he is a resemblance of Homer. He studies the enemy in his smallest movements. He casts gazes of indignation on the field that he occupies. He encourages his soldiers with the sensitive request of a friend. He is infuriated in moments of defeat, and then faintheartedly, he capitulates. . . . He ignores strategy. Presented with the occasion, he unrolls in front of the enemy the immense resources of his genius. Santana has not perfected the study of his military talents. If he becomes convinced that the war is undertaken for principles, and of the fact that skill is necessary to kill thousands, or hundreds of thousands, then he will come to achieve a place among the generals of superior fame."[55]

Santa Anna not only achieved superior fame, but also he became infamous! That infamy was best described by Fanny Calderon de la Barca, wife of the first Spanish minister to Mexico. Her description of Santa Anna is in contrast to that of Lorenzo de Zavala!

[54]*The Eagle*, pp. 17-18.
[55]Oakah Jones, Jr. *Santa Anna* (New York: Twayne Publishers, Inc. 1968), p. 45.

"In a little while entered the General Santa Anna himself, a gentlemanly, good-looking, quietly dressed, rather melancholy looking person, with one leg, apparently a good deal of an invalid, and to us decidedly the best looking and most interesting figure in the group. He has a sallow complexion, fine dark eyes, soft and penetrating, and an interesting expression of face. Knowing nothing of his past history, one would have said a philosopher, living in dignified retirement—one who had tried the world and found that all was vanity, one who had suffered ingratitude and who, if he were ever persuaded to emerge from his retreat, would only do so, Cincinnatus-like, to benefit his country. It is strange, and a fact worthy of notice in natural history, how frequently this expression of philosophic resignation, of placid sadness, is to be remarked on the countenances of the most cunning, the deepest, most ambitious, most designing and most dangerous statesmen I have seen."[56]

The next thirty years would reveal the cunning of this man. When Vice President Nicolás Bravo and Vincente Guerrero rebelled against Guadalupe Victoria in the latter part of 1827, Santa Anna came out of retirement to offer his services in support of the Republic. Although the rebellion was quickly crushed and Bravo was captured, Santa Anna's offer placed him back in the political limelight. When the following year his old enemy, Manual Gómez Pedraza, was elected president over Vicente Guerrero, the puro liberal, Santa Anna demanded strong republicanism, and declared the election to be fraudulent. Guerrero should be Mexico's president!

"At the time of the election, I was in charge of the government of Vera Cruz. Nothing that I could do to preserve order in this grave situation was sufficient. I knew that revolution was inevitable!

"In order to spare the lives of the people and to quell the whirlwind of revolution, I adhered to the pleadings of the people that Vicente Guerrero be declared constitutional President of the republic."[57]

And declare he did. But somehow he failed to convince the population of Mexico to rise in revolt over this so-called injustice. His initial attacks were met with reverses, and Santa Anna finally retreated to Oaxaca where he was besieged. The situation appeared desperate, even critical. This one would be lost. But with the arrival of a Spanish invasionary force near Tampico, Santa Anna convinced the commanding officer besieging Oaxaca, to lift that siege so together they might save Mexico. So it was off to Tampico to save the nation! But the Spanish invaders were disorganized, unsupported by the local population, and utterly decimated by malaria and yellow fever. The kindest thing the

[56]Fanny Calderón de la Barca, *Life in Mexico*, edited and annotated by Howard T. Fisher and Marion Hall Fisher (Garden City, N.Y.: Anchor Books, Doubleday and Co., Inc., 1966), p. 65.
[57]*The Eagle*, p. 20.

commander, General Isidro Barradas, could do would be to surrender immediately. With scarcely any serious confrontation, he did just that. For Santa Anna's part, he became known as the "Hero of Tampico"; and, if you believe his words, he deserved the accolade!

> "Leading fifteen hundred soldiers, I commanded the general to surrender. His haughty reply infuriated me, and I attacked his forces furiously, disregarding his entrenchments and barricades. A bloody battle, lasting eleven full hours, from six in the evening to five in the morning, ensued. When their boastful leader was wounded, he surrendered unconditionally."[58]

Unquestionably, Santa Anna was a hero in the eyes of most Mexicans and he could have easily entered the political arena, but he chose not to. The turbulent political conditions of the Guerrero presidency might have had an influence on the decision of the "Hero of Tampico," to retire to his rambling estate, Manga de Clavo. He remained there during the revolution that Vice-President Anastasio Bustamante initiated against Vicente Guerrero. Guerrero fled in January of 1830, after just two years in office. Once again Mexico had a non-elected president. In his memoirs, he condemned these events—but he remained aloof, for he was aware of the support that Bustamante enjoyed, and was reluctant to chance any open defiance.

Within another two years, disatisfaction with Bustamante led to renewed rebellions throughout Mexico. Taking stock of the conditions favorable to overthrow, Santa Anna came out of retirement and formed his own revolutionary army. It was an ill-kempt, rag-tag mob, with either antiquated weapons—or no weapons at all. Bustamante's army soundly defeated Santa Anna's "troops," and forced him to retreat to Veracruz. But the attacking general made the error of laying siege to Veracruz in the middle of May, as the humid summer approached. His soldiers suffering from yellow fever, he was forced to lift the siege and allow Santa Anna to escape the trap. The interlude was long enough. Within a short time rebellions broke out all over Mexico, and the end was in sight for president Bustamante. By December, 1832, Santa Anna decisively defeated the government forces and extracted both a surrender and resignation from Anastasio Bustamante. And who would be the interim president, who would enter the Capital arm-in-arm with Santa Anna in a grand gesture of victory and glory? The deposed Manuel Gómez Pedraza, the man he had overthrown nearly four years previously. Gómez Pedraza, his old arch military enemy returned from his exile in Bedford Springs, Pennsylvania, just long enough to oblige the ambitions of the "Hero of Tampico." But Santa Anna wanted to gain absolute power for himself, and that became clear when in March of 1833, sixteen of the eighteen

[58]*The Eagle*, p. 23.

state legislatures voted not for Gómez Pedraza but for Antonio López de Santa Anna Pérez de Lebrón as president, with Valentín Gómez Farías, the liberal puro physician from Zacatecas, as the vice president.

> "By the free and unanimous election of the legislature, I was chosen con-
> stitutional President of the Republic. According to the provisions of the
> Constitution, I assumed my office in April of 1833, despite the fact that I
> had not reached the age required by law."[59]

Well, at least he recognized that the law was broken by his election to the presidency. As for his assuming the office, it didn't happen. Instead of attending the inauguration, he claimed that he was obliged to suppress a rebellion that had broken out in the area of Veracruz. He subsequently retired to his rancho at Manga de Clavo.

Valentín Gómez Farías, in the absence of Santa Anna, now assumed the presidency. And at his behest, Congress passed a series of reform laws the enactment of which the Church denounced as heretical and which increased disatisfaction within the Republic. Had Santa Anna been committed to a truly liberal program based on the ideals of the Enlightenment, he might have supported these laws, and Mexico's political course might have been more secure. But Santa Anna had no deep political commitments, and he only waited to see the reaction to his vice-president's legislation. The program of Gómez-Farías, essentially became the backbone of nineteenth century liberalism, and much of it was later incorporated in the Constitutions of 1857 and 1917. While many saw this legislation as an attack on the very foundation of the Catholic Church, its supporters argued that they merely sought to remove the Church from the political and economic sphere of Mexican life. In addition to limiting the powers of the Church, the power and privileges of the military would also be curbed. It was a formidable challenge to tackle the two most powerful institutions in Mexico, and it was doomed to initial failure. Capsulized, the program included the complete elimination of *compulsory* tithes, while monks and nuns would be free to retract their vows *only* as far as the state was concerned. That is, it would not be a criminal offense to give up one's benefice in the Catholic Church. As part of the liberal program to secularize education, a department of public education would be established. And the old Royal Pontifical University of Mexico would be removed from the authority of the Church and made public. The frontier missions, particularly those in California, would be secularized or taken away from the regular clergy which had political and religious authority, and handed over to the secular clergy—which had only religious authority.

It was really an attempt to reduce the power of the orders which had held great social and economic sway. And finally, the *fueros ecclesasticos*, or

[59]*The Eagle*, p. 46.

religious privileges, which had also become military fueros, would be terminated. But certain aspects of the Royal Patronage would be retained by the state, particularly those which referred to the nomination of benefices of the higher clergy. The reasoning was that these rights legitimately were given to the crown of Spain and his subordinates by the Holy See. Therefore, a change in governments did not automatically terminate the rights of patronage. The Mother Church in Rome countered that rights of patronage granted by the Pope may be revoked at any time by the Pope:

The reaction of the clergy and military was loud and clear. Their slogan became ¡*fueros y religión! ¡religión y fueros!* Some officers openly pronounced against the government, while others made ready to join in a rebellion. Members of the clergy proclaimed these laws to be anti-Christian and anti-God. Some even seized upon a widespread cholera attack as a punishment from God. As thousands died from the spread of Asiatic Cholera (On one day alone, August 17, 1833, the burials in Mexico City alone, exceeded 1,220), the superstitious listened to the warnings of the conservative clergy. And their demands were communicated to Santa Anna. They pleaded with him to take over the presidency and to assume extraordinary powers, maintaining that the reform program of his vice-president, Gómez-Farías, was ruinous to the Church and the nation. The exhortations and pleadings of the clergy finally had their effect. In December of 1834, Santa Anna was ready to listen. Before the year was out, he had displaced Gómez Farías and had revoked the liberal legislation of the congress.

> "When I returned to the capital, I encountered stormy sessions of the Congress. One faction was endeavoring to confiscate the property of the church and to deny to the clergy its rights and ancient privileges. The public was dismayed by these actions and opposed violently any usurpation of the clergy's rights. Obeying the dictates of my conscience and hoping to quell a revolution, I declined to approve the necessary decree to put these edicts into law. . . .
>
> These careless reforms of the Congress caused turmoil among the people. In Cuernavaca a *Plan* was issued and swiftly accepted by all the states. Under this *Plan*, the President was granted extraordinary powers. Meanwhile, Congress was able to convene, and once more the government gained the people's confidence and was able to preserve the peace."[60]

What Santa Anna had opted for was a Centralist Republic. Now at home with his military centralist policies, liberal federalism had come to a temporary end. But again his political career was interrupted by war, for by 1835 events in Texas, demanded his attention in that northern department.

[60]*The Eagle*, pp. 48-49.

CHAPTER 22

The Catastrophe
of Centralism

Late in 1833, Santa Anna had returned to Mexico City from his hacienda at Manga de Clavo with the Constitution in hand, and he pledged to "sacrifice himself" for the good of the nation. Inaugurated as President of Mexico, he followed his established pattern and remained in office just long enough for the new Mexican congress to be installed on January 4, 1834. Santa Anna again pleaded ill health and turned the reigns of government over to General Miguel Barragán who would act as interim president. Then he went back to Manga de Clavo to wait, as he had done before and as he would do again.

When Santa Anna came out of retirement he quickly revoked all of the laws passed by the national congress and restored to the Church and military their *fueros* or privileges. The frontier missions were returned to the regular orders and the educational system—made public during the two years of Gómez Farías—was restored to the Church. The newly elected congress which was dominated by conservative-centralists, worked in concert with the military clerical establishment, to create a strong centralist republic. The state legislatures were dissolved as were town councils. Governors who refused to support the centralist regime were deposed, and the office of vice-president was declared vacant. These actions returned Mexican society to its colonial patterns. They represented a fear of change prevalent among large sectors of society. Although Santa Anna gave his blessing to all of these "reforms," he did so from his hacienda at Manga de Clavo. Once again feigning illness, he had supported the appointment of General Miguel Barragán as the interim president to act in his stead. Barragán had officially proclaimed centralism and the total suppression of federalism. As a measure of implementation, state governors would serve only at the sufference of the central government; and state legislatures would cease to exist entirely. They would be replaced by an appointed council of five from each district.

   To solidify their control, the centralists adopted a new constitution in 1836, which made centralism absolute. Its core was manifested in seven laws which the centralists called *"Las siete leyes,"* and which the federalists dubbed *"Las siete plagas,"* or the seven plagues. The new bicameral legislature required property ownership as a qualification for its own members; and the president was selected by the legislature and the Supreme court for a term of eight years. States would become departments and would be entirely subordinated to the "Supreme Government."

   The state governments did not relinquish their authority without a struggle although most resistance was merely verbal. But occasionally, resistance turned into open violence such as the events which took place in the "departments" of Zacatecas and Texas. Zacatecas was part of the mining frontier and its inhabitants were early fighters for independence, and committed to the ideals of the Constitution of 1824. Even before the *"siete leyes"* were passed, Governor Francisco García refused to be cajoled by the new centralists. Antonio López de Santa Anna had been called upon to "teach the governor a lesson." At the head of an army, he had marched to Zacatecas and soundly defeated the forces of Governor García. Santa Anna's troops, then sacked the town, after which they made a symbolic triumphal march through Guadalajara, Queretaro and Morelia. For the centralists he was the Messiah. For the federalists, he was the devil.

   The Texas rebellion was far more complex and far more difficult to handle. In an attempt to populate the frontier regions of New Spain, the Spanish government had offered empresario or free land grants to groups of settlers who would colonize the frontier. As early as the 1820's Moses Austin the Connecticut born frontiersman, appealed for and received an empresario grant, and attempted to bring colonists in from the United States. The conditions of the grant were designed to insure a certain amount of loyalty from the newly arriving colonists. They had to be of good moral character; they had to take allegiance to the Catholic Church, to the crown of Spain, and to the laws and authorities in the province of Texas. Moses Austin, a Connecticut frontiersman had gathered three hundred families to enter Texas in 1820, but before the move was made he died and many of the colonists scattered. But his son Stephen renewed the grant under the newly independent Mexican government, which had passed a colonization Act of 1824. By that act, the Mexican Congress delegated the authority of making *empresario* grants to the individual states. Since Texas was part of the frontier state of Coahuila and without the restraints of the central government, very liberal empresario grants were made. The empresario or colonizer—in this case Stephen Austin—would receive a very large tract of land for his efforts. Each colonists would also receive 177 acres for agriculture and 4,251 acres for grazing. The cost of the land to the colonist was minimal and payments were spread over six years. The colonists would be exempt from paying tariffs on agricultural implements, and from total taxation for a period of six years. For the next six years, their taxes would be cut in half. It is no wonder with these liberal provisions that colonists from the United States were moved to settle in the area of Texas. Stephen Austin was given permission to colonize three hundred families in Texas. Within a few years, eight thousand colonists had settled in Texas from different parts of the world; but they were predominantly Anglo-American.

In time it became obvious to the Mexican government that such large numbers of Americans in Mexican territory contiguous to American territory could pose a problem. Without naming Texas, a law passed on April 6, 1830, which prohibited colonization by foreigners in Mexican territory that was adjacent to their own national territory. It was clear that the act was addressed to Texas. Furthermore, the law fostered the establishment of convict colonies in these frontier regions. Military posts and customs houses were to be established immediately. And the Mexican government now insisted that its anti-slave laws be upheld in the northern frontier regions; an act which caused great resentment since many Texas immigrants were from America's Southern States. The resentment felt by the Texans led to talk of a greater degree of federalism—a greater degree of autonomy. By the end of 1831, an extra-legal, provisional government had been established in Texas.

These acts, coupled with the downfall of the federalist government in Mexico, ultimately led to confrontation and finally separation. The cultural chasm between Anglo-Americans and Mexicans widened. Although Stephen Fuller Austin spoke of the colonists' desire to remain loyal to the Mexican government; he also spoke of Mexico's disdain for their rights as Mexican citizens. He spoke of the militia formed by the Texans to protect their exposed frontier from hostile Indian attack—and how this militia had been ordered to dissolve. He spoke of the political turmoil in Mexico's central government and the attendant waves of anarchy that had wracked the stability of the nation. And finally he spoke of the absence of trial by jury which was a basic cultural difference between the two peoples. His closing remarks held little hope for settlement between the Texans and the central government in Mexico:

"A total interregnum in the administration of justice in criminal cases may be said to exist. A total disregard of the laws has become so prevalent, both amongst the officers of justice, and the people at large, that reverence for laws or for those who administer them has almost entirely disappeared and contempt is fast assuming its place, so that the protection of our property, our persons and lives is circumscribed almost exclusively to the moral honesty or virtue of our neighbor."[61]

To Austin and the Convention, the answer was separation from the state of Coahuila. It meant the creation of a separate and independent state of Texas. While this may have had some possibility during the Federalist regime, it had no possibility under the Centralist government of Antonio López de Santa Anna. Nevertheless, in April of 1833, Stephen Fuller Austin traveled to Mexico City in order to present the demands of the Second Convention, which included reforms in the judicial system and a separate state of Texas. Austin commented on his mission:

"I left Texas in April, 1833, as the public agent of the people, for the purpose of applying for the admission of this country into the Mexican confederation as a state separate from Coahuila. This application was based upon the constitutional and vested rights of Texas, and was sustained by me in the City of Mexico to the utmost of my abilities. No honorable means were spared to effect the objects of my mission, and to oppose the forming of Texas into a territory, which was attempted. I rigidly adhered to the instructions and wishes of my constituents, so far as they were communicated to me in the labyrinth of Mexican politics. . . ."[62]

Austin and the Texans mistakenly saw the accession to power of Santa Anna as a victory for liberalism. They truly believed he would grant their demands. And when Santa Anna removed the immigration restrictions, they were certain he would also permit them to have statehood. But Santa Anna's pretenses as a liberal were exposed when he overthrew the Federalist government in 1834, and supported a Centralist regime that would effect even further restrictions on Texas.

Austin's arrival in Mexico City on July 18, 1833, coincided with Santa Anna's overthrow of Gómez-Farías—and Austin found himself playing an exasperating waiting game. He became so impatient with the congress and the president, he wrote a letter to the Central Committee in

[61]Eugene C. Barker, ed. "The Austin Papers," in the American Historical Association's *Annual Report for the Year 1922* (Washington, 1928), Vol. 2, pp. 935-938.
[62]Dudley G. Wooten, *A Comprehesive History of Texas, 1685-1897*, (Dallas, 1898) Vol I, pp. 501-504.

Texas urging that they complete their plans for state government. Finally on November 5, 1833, Austin attended a meeting of ministers convoked by Santa Anna, for the purpose of considering Texas' request for separation from Coahuila. He was apparently satisfied that his petition would receive favorable consideration.

He started his journey homeward but was apprehended and arrested in Saltillo—apparently for promoting revolutionary acts. His letter to the Second Convention in Texas had been intercepted by the Mexican authorities who now jailed Stephen Austin. Austin remained in jail for almost two years before he was allowed to return to Texas. By then, his desire for compromise had come to an end. He and other Texans believed that the only answer to their problems, was total separation from Mexico. After returning to Texas, Austin wrote the following report:

> "My Friends, I can truly say that no one has been, or is now, more anxious than myself to keep trouble away from this country. No one has been, or is now more faithful to his duty as a Mexican citizen, and no one has personally sacrificed or suffered more in the discharge of this duty. I have uniformly been opposed to having anything to do with the family political quarrel of the Mexicans.
>
> Texas needs peace and a local government; its inhabitants are farmers, and they need a calm and quiet life. But how can I, or any one, remain indifferent when our rights, our all, appear to be in jeopardy, and when it is our duty, as well as our obligation as good Mexican citizens, to express our opinions on the present state of things and to represent our situation to the government? It is impossible. . . ."[63]

In late 1834, Santa Anna repudiated any reforms he might have promised the Texans; and in a move to stem the tide of resentment, he ordered military units to move into Texas immediately. Several clashes took place. In some the Texans prevailed; in others the Mexicans. Still hoping for a rapprochement, on November 3, 1835, the representatives of the Texans met and passed a "Declaration of Causes" for taking up arms. Santa Anna's response to these events was to gather a rag-tag army and force march them to Texas, where he would "avenge the honor of Mexico:"

> ". . . With the fires of patriotism in my heart and dominated by a noble ambition to save my country, I took pride in being the first to strike in defense of the independence, honor, and rights of my nation. Stimulated by these courageous feelings, I took command of the campaign myself, preferring the uncertainties of war to the easy and much-coveted life of the palace."[64]

[63]Wooten, pp. 501-504.
[64]*The Eagle* p. 50.

And to war he went. The Texans, frustrated by their inability to convince the Mexican government that they deserved an independent state, and suffused with an anti-Mexican attitude, declared their Independence. Santa Anna force-marched his poor Indian conscripts to an old Franciscan mission at San Antonio where The Alamo, as it was called, became the blood-bath for all who decided to remain.

And again at Goliad, Santa Anna slaughtered another three hundred Texans in a "no-quarter" attack. But the Texans were to achieve their revenge and their independence as well.

While Santa Anna was in the midst of overthrowing his vice president Gómez-Farías in 1832, Samuel Houston appeared in Texas. Houston, who had served with Andrew Jackson in the War of 1812, had an early successful military and political career. His future appeared to be bright. He had been a major general, a member of Congress and was elected governor of Tennessee at age thirty-four. But, within two years of his election, he married and within three months of that event he resigned, deserted his wife, and departed for Indian country where he took an Indian spouse. Rumor was that he had been involved in a love affair which had been discovered by his wife. Houston finally ended up in Texas territory. He was an imposing man of over six feet tall, well built, handsome, and with a deep voice. He also had the qualities of a natural leader; and he became the leader of the military forces for Texas independence. It was Sam Houston, with an army of six or seven hundred that surprised Santa Anna's forces on April 21, 1836. At the battle of San Jacinto, Houston's sword swinging Texans slaughtered six hundred Mexicans and captured Santa Anna himself.

In the agreement of Velacco, which followed the victory of San Jacinto, Texas received its independence. Although Santa Anna signed the agreement, a cloud remained over the treaty because the Mexican congress refused to ratify it. Nonetheless, for all intents and purposes, Texas was independent. After signing the agreement, Santa Anna was taken to Washington, D.C., where he met with President Andrew Jackson. The records of the Jackson meeting are non-existent and little is known of their discussions. Santa Anna then returned to Mexico and promptly retired to his rancho at Manga de Clavo.

But his retirement was short lived for within one year he called upon himself to again come out of retirement to "save" his country. The incident which touched Santa Anna's patriotism took place in the middle of Bustamante's Centralist Republic.

The incident began when Mexico failed to meet the claims of French citizens who lost property during the military insurrections in 1828. It focused in particular on a French pastry shop in the suburbs of Tacubaya on the outskirts of Mexico City. Under the pastryman's proddings, the

French government demanded special treatment to French retailers, and tendered a bill to Mexico for six hundred thousand pesos—payable immediately for the loss of the pastry shop and the pastries. If not honored, France would be obliged to satisfy its honor. It was not honored and France did satisfy its honor. In 1838, a French squadron that had been maneuvering off the coast of Veracruz, bombarded that city and captured the island fortress of San Juan de Ulúa. Santa Anna who was peacefully ensconced in his nearby hacienda at Manga de Clavo responded to the challenge of the French—These are his words:

> "Honor declared that I accept the challenge. Justice was on the side of Mexico! We must meet force with force! Now that the conflict had begun, it was the duty of every loyal Mexican to protect his flag. I knew that I was wearing the sword of Mexico and the insignia of a general, and I was not engaged in the national struggle. As if by magic, I seemed to forget all the wrongs my country had done me. It could not be otherwise, as love for my country had been uppermost in my heart from an early age. Carried away with the same enthusiasm which had first driven me into battle, I hurried to the combat field. I presented myself to Commandant Manuel Rincon, and my services were quickly accepted."[65]

In the events that followed, Veracruz surrendered to the French and then retracted that surrender. Santa Anna arrived and then retreated. The French fought and then fled. And it was in their flight that they fired a cannonade which scored a direct hit on the left leg of Santa Anna which had to be amputated. And now the "Hero of Tampico," who was the villain of Texas Independence, became the "Hero of Veracruz!" Santa Anna graphically described the "glorious" event:

> ". . . The bones in the calf of my left leg were mangled, one finger of my right hand was broken, and my entire body was covered with bruises.
>
> I, too, thought I was dead! Ah, how we deceive ourselves! I rejoiced in the enthusiasm that we had a decided advantage over our enemy, who had thought our forces could not measure up to his. I prayed to God to let me die in a blaze of glory.
>
> How many times since have I bewailed that fact that God failed to accept my humble pleas!
>
> But the ways of the Almighty are wondrous! My unworthy life was spared, while the nine men wounded with me died shortly afterward. Also, the five surgeons who had operated on me and held no hope for my recovery went to their deaths."[66]

The leg which was amputated was preserved for a macabre event which would take place in the Capital a few years later. The amputation restored some of the luster to the tarnished career of Santa Anna. Within

[65]*The Eagle,* p. 59.
[66]*The Eagle,* p. 64.

two months of the event, Santa Anna was called to Mexico City by Guadalupe Victoria to defend the Centralist government of Anastasio Bustamante. Bustamante survived this rebellion but fell to the second in 1841; which was now led by the generals who defended him in 1838; including the perennial "master of the pronunciamiento," Antonio López de Santa Anna. The revolution began in Guadalajara but soon spread to Mexico City where the revolutionaries occupied the building called the Ciudadela, government armory. From the plaza in front of the Ciudadela, where now stands the statue of Morelos, the bombardment of the National Palace took place. Unfortunately, the innocent, who had no part in the political musical chairs being played, were caught between the combatants. Many fell dead—and many of the beautiful buildings of the city were damaged as well. Finally, on October 6, 1841, Bustamante's government fell. And the provisional president? Santa Anna of course.

Fanny Calderón de la Barca, wife of the first Spanish minister to Mexico, described the events of the revolution from her lodging in the center of the city:

". . . every turret [of every building] and [every] belfry is covered with soldiers, and the streets are blocked up with troops and trenches. From behind these turrets and trenches they fire at each other, scarcely a soldier falling but numbers of peaceful citizens—shells and bombs falling through the roofs of the houses, and all this for *'the public good.'*

. . . Now there is neither principle, nor pretext, nor plan, nor the shadow of reason or legality. Disloyalty, hypocrisy, and the most sordid calculation are all the motives that can be discovered; and those who then affected an ardent desire for the welfare of their country have now thrown aside their masks, and appear in their true colours; and the great mass of the people, who thus passive and oppressed, allow their quiet homes to be invaded, are kept in awe neither by the force of arms, nor by the depth of the views of the conspirators, but by a handful of soldiers who are themselves scarcely aware of their own wishes or intentions, but that they desire power and distinction at any price."[67]

On the morning after Bustamante's surrender, the minister's wife observed:

". . . . Santa Anna is triumphant. He made his solemn entry into Mexico last evening. . . . Not a solitary *viva* was heard as they passed along the streets; nor afterwards, during his speech in congress. *Te Deum* was sung this morning in the cathedral, the Archbishop in person receiving the new president."[68]

[67]Fanny Calderón de la Barca, *Life in Mexico,* pp. 499-500.
[68]Fanny Calderón de la Barca, *Life in Mexico,* pp. 516-17.

The following year, a *moderado* congress was elected so Santa Anna again retired to his hacienda at Manga de Clavo. And he waited. He waited until 1843, when a new constitution was written which gave the president of Mexico virtual dictatorial powers. He then came out of retirement to be elected president of the republic, an office which made him dictator.

Santa Anna's dictatorship was marked by the most corrupt government Mexico had yet experienced. The military was expanded and the officer class was enlarged. Salaries were raised and new uniforms were purchased. There were parties and military parades; grand fiestas and national ceremonies. Even the amputated leg of the dictator, which had been preserved in Veracruz, was brought to the Capital and it was interred in the National Cathedral with full military honors. In 1844, when Santa Anna's wife died there was another massive parade, again with full military honors. And all of this was paid for by taxation and more taxation. Loans and more loans. There were taxes on dogs and cats, windows and doors—so the citizens boarded up their entry ways in order to avoid payment. Loans from outside and loans from within—particularly those from the Catholic Church—did little to endear the dictator with the powerful elements of Mexico. As the treasury was drained government employees were threatened with a loss of salaries. For the generals in particular, this was unforgiveable. In 1844, they raised the flag of revolution that was to be Santa Anna's undoing. Cornered in the mountains of Veracruz, he was captured and exiled to Havana, Cuba, for a ten year period. The *leprosos* or lepers in Mexico, disinterred his grisley leg, tied it to a rope, and dragged it around the city in a display of open contempt. His statue was also destroyed and it appeared to be the end for Santa Anna's military and political career. But on August 16, 1846, a little over one year after he was exiled, Santa Anna again returned to Veracruz.

And so it began as it had ended. The military hero had arrived, not to fight the Texans, not to fight the French, nor even the Spaniards. But his glory this time would be directed against the giant to the north, the United States of America—or would it be glory?

CHAPTER 23

El Rincón Del Mundo

By the time Mexico had achieved independence from Spain in 1821, her far northern frontier had only small, sparse settlements. Saint Augustine, Florida, founded in 1565, had never developed into a major Spanish outpost; and by the time of independence, its sovereignty and existence was challenged by the expanding power and population of the United States of America. Texas, the site of five Franciscan missions—including one called the Alamo—had just been opened to colonization; and by 1821 a man named Stephen Austin had recruited several hundred families for settlement there. New Mexico could boast two main settlements, Santa Fé and Taos. Until independence, both of these settlements had welcomed only few traders from the American east. But after 1821, Santa Fé suddenly became a major trading post for caravans from Independence and Saint Louis, Missouri, and El Rincón del Mundo, or the end of the world as California was called.

All of these frontier settlements shared one common denominator—they were remote from the mainstream of political, social, and economic activity in the more populous central regions of Mexico. How could a newly emerging nation, beset with internal turmoil, and the constant threat of foreign intervention, maintain these remote frontier regions? Even before independence, Spain had recognized the futility of keeping Florida in the face of United States expansion. In 1819, Spain concluded the Adams-Onis Treaty with the United States in which Spain received five million dollars in return for Florida, and a definite boundary which recognized the northern and eastern limits of the Spanish frontier. Just two years later, because of Mexico's Independence, this Spanish border line became the limit of Mexico's far northern frontier. Thus, with the loss of Florida, Mexico's frontier consisted of California, New Mexico, and Texas. Because of its location on the Pacific Ocean, California was by far the most valuable geographically.

California under Spanish rule is characterized as the mission period. The period of time that the province formed a part of Mexico is known as the era of the great ranchos. More than eight hundred rancho grants were issued by the Mexican government—or by the governor of California. They varied from just a few acres to the incredible size of almost fifty thousand acres. While some of these grants were never established as working ranchos, many became highly successful, particularly in the hide and tallow trade. Because they were isolated from Mexico, California settlers depended upon merchant ships from New England to supply them with manufactured goods. In return, the "Boston Men" as the ship captains were known, obtained hides and tallow. The hides were to be used in shoe manufacture and the tallow for candle-making.

A Harvard student, by the name of Richard Henry Dana, decided to leave his studies and gain experience as "a Boston Man" traveling the seven seas. In a colorful and exciting book, *Two Years Before The Mast*, Dana described his visit to California in the early part of 1835. Although he wrote of the importance of hides, he was also impressed with the large amount of silver he saw in the province.

> ". . . Another thing that surprised me was the quantity of silver that was in circulation. I certainly never saw so much silver at one time in my life, as during the week that we were in Monterey. The truth is, they have no credit system, no banks, and no way of investing money but in cattle. They have no circulating medium but silver and hides—which the sailors call 'California bank notes.' Everything that they buy they must pay for in one or the other of these things. The hides they bring down dried and doubled, in clumsy oxcarts, or upon mules' backs, and the money they carry tied up in handkerchief,—fifty, eighty, or an hundred and half dollars."[69]

A number of wealthy California immigrants got their start in the hide and tallow trade because California did not exclude foreigners. William E. P. Hartnell, a native of England is a good example. Hartnell, who arrived shortly after the Mexican period began, married María Teresa de la Guerra, much to the chagrin of his family, who disowned

[69]Richard Henry Dana, Jr. *Two Years Before The Mast,* ed. by John Haskell Kemble. (Los Angeles, The Ward Ritchie Press, 1964), Vol. I, p. 85.

him. Nonetheless, Hartnell, who was a representative for the worldwide trading company of John Beggs, decided to remain in California; and he opted for Mexican citizenship in 1830. And he and his wife did much to increase the population of the province since she bore him twenty sons and five daughters.

John Forster, another Englishman, arrived in California in 1833 at the age of only fifteen. On his own initiative he embarked upon a career as trader, rancher, and landowner. He married Isadora Pico a member of a prominent California family. Over a period of time, Forster acquired more than 100,000 acres of land, including Mission San Juan Capistrano and for many years he and his family resided at this beautiful ex-mission. John Forster was successively a citizen of England, Mexico, and after 1848, the United States. He was liked and respected by everyone, and his genial hospitality was typical of the rancho period. His life in California spanned the period from pastoral days to the new technological developments of the 1880's.

Americans too entered California and became permanent residents, as did Frenchmen, Russians, and Swiss. All helped to make California the romantic outpost of the Mexican nation, and that romance was founded upon the rancho.

The rancho period was the time of the vaquero, the rodeo, and a fascinating life style which included romance, fandango dances, and dazzling displays of horsemanship. Rodeos were once-a-year round-ups by cattle owners. The main purpose was to brand the cattle and to castrate the young calves. It developed that while the work was being done—and it took several days—the young vaqueros or horsemen, had an opportunity to display their horsemanship. And so it became traditional that rodeos were not only for practical purposes, but for competitive display of horse and rider as well. And some of the finest horsemanship was exhibited by the California vaquero. An American soldier who entered California in 1848, was an eyewitness to the skill of the California vaquero. He aptly described the catching and breaking of a wild horse:

"It is a saying in Chihuahua that 'a Californian can throw the lazo as well with his foot as a Mexican can with his hand,' and the scene before us gave us an idea of its truth. There was a wild stallion of great beauty which defied the fleetest horse and the most expert rider. At length a boy of fourteen, a Californian, whose graceful riding was the constant subject of admiration, piqued by repeated failures, mounted a fresh horse, and followed by an Indian, launched fiercely at the stallion.

His lareat darted from his hand with the force and precision of a rifle ball, and rested on the neck of the fugitive; the Indian, at the same moment, made a successful throw, but the stallion was too stout for both, and dashed off at full speed, with both ropes flying in the air like wings. The perfect representation of Pegasus, he took a sweep, and followed by his pursuers,

came thundering down the dry bed of the river. The lazos were now trailing
on the ground, and the gallant young Spaniard, taking advantage of the
circumstance, stooped from his flying horse and caught one in his hand. It
was the work of a moment to make it fast to the pommel of his saddle, and by
a short turn of his own horse, he threw the stallion a complete somersault,
and the game was secure."[70]

California was growing politically more isolated. Since 1781, hostile
Indians prevented movement from Mexico to California by a land route;
so the main avenue of commerce was by sea. And because the currents
and winds from Mexico to California were contrary, passage was slow and
dangerous. It could take months to make a journey that should be completed in days.

This isolation resulted in the development of a feeling of independence on the part of the *Californios* who tended to view outsiders with
suspicion. That suspicion extended to Mexican politicians dispatched to
California to govern the province. This distrust was partly responsible for
the turbulent state of California politics in Mexico's post-independence
period. The political rivalries in Mexico were also responsible for the
unsettling condition of California's politics. As a result, there emerged
during this period a feeling by many residents that California ought to be
independent from Mexico. Needless to say, this view was held by many
key politicians in the United States as well.

Not only were Californians suspicious of the Mexican governors
sent to administer the territory, but to some they seemed unequivocally
hostile. And why not? Except for one or two, the calibre of politicians sent
to California was somewhat less than acceptable. To prominent Mexican
families, California was "Rincón del Mundo."—the end of the earth. The
territory's isolation and lack of economic development, made it fairly
unpopular with prospective governors—and with colonists as well. It is
not hard to see why Mexico had such a difficult time recruiting qualified
settlers, in spite of the pleasant climate. And when new governors did
arrive, they found that their political tenure was at the sufferance of the
residents; residents who would have preferred that Mexican governors
remain in Mexico City. Several governors found themselves escorted to
the nearest waiting ship and deported from California.

Governor Manuel Micheltorena, who arrived in California in 1842,
was no exception. General Micheltorena was a man of rank, heritage, and
stature. He brought with him an army of 300 soldiers recruited from the
poorer areas of Sonora and Sinaloa. They were to protect California from

[70]From William H. Emory, "Notes of a Military Reconnaissance," 30th
Cong. 1 sess., Senate Exec. Doc. No. 7 (Washington, 1848), pg. 97 as quoted in
John W. Caughey & La Ree Caughey, *California Heritage* (Itasca, Ill., F.E. Peacock
Publishers, 1962) p. 149.

foreigners—particularly Anglo-Americans. But the unruliness of these soldiers offended the native Californios. Events inevitably led to a confrontation between the native Californios and Governor Manuel Micheltorena and his army. On February 20th and 21st of 1845, the opposing forces met in Los Angeles' Cahuenga Pass just overlooking the Hollywood Freeway. The cannonading continued through the evenings—but the adversaries remained far enough apart to prevent any real casualties. But there was at least one casualty, Governor Micheltorena's horse (or mule). With the loss of the animal, the forces of Micheltorena surrendered. Micheltorena and his men were escorted to the nearest ship and exiled forever from California. Micheltorena was the last governor to be sent from Mexico, for the following year the war between the United States of America and Mexico placed California into the hands of the expanding giant to the north.

During the Spanish period, the Territory or Department of New Mexico acted mostly as a buffer between the far northern frontier and America's Louisiana territory. Except for the last few years of Spanish rule, New Mexico was sparsely settled and relatively unimportant. However, the fact that a usable land route existed between Mexico and this territory tended to create a climate of greater political control. Interest in this area grew dramatically, with the inception of the so-called Santa Fé Trade which began at the time of Mexican Independence.

So important was this trade that wagons were introduced along the trail in 1824, the same year that the United States made overtures to New Mexico for a regular trade system. And the following year, the United States even began the survey of a road that was eventually to carry caravans of wagons from Independence, Missouri to Santa Fé, New Mexico. Unofficial, but regular trade had been established.

The trading caravans began their eight hundred mile journey along the Santa Fé Trail, in Independence, Missouri. From here they traveled west-south-west along the Kansas River toward the Arkansas River. About midway, they crossed the Arkansas and then moved directly to the town of either Taos or to the main trading post of Santa Fé. These caravans mainly carried cotton and a variety of dry goods and hardware. The residents of New Mexico paid for this cargo in gold and silver coin. But the tradesmen from Independence also accepted wool, furs, and blankets in return for their cotton. In the nineteen year period from 1824 to 1843, the number of wagons increased annually from twenty-six to more than two hundred and thirty while the value of merchandise increased from 35,000 dollars to about 450,000 dollars. It is no wonder that both sides wished to avoid a conflict that would endanger this important trading system.

But, as with California, North Americans made overtures toward settling areas of New Mexico; overtures that were officially declined.

Nonetheless, settlement by foreigners did take place; and some American traders made permanent residence in New Mexico's three largest settlements, Santa Fé, Taos, and Canada.

Like California, New Mexico suffered from political turbulence, including a full scale revolt in 1837. But unlike California where the revolutions were generally limited to bombast and threats—this one in New Mexico became bloody. Governor Albino Pérez, found himself abandoned when he attempted to quell the insurrection. While trying to flee the rebels, he and his associates were killed. His head was severed and taken to rebel headquarters as a trophy. Within the year, a Pueblo Indian from the town of Taos was installed as the revolutionary governor. However, the tenure of Governor José González did not last long either. A counter-revolution cost José González the governorship, and on January of the following year it cost him his life. And talk of revolution continued, although the traders who supported Santa Fé objected strongly. Many felt that full scale revolution could disrupt the lucrative trade they enjoyed.

In spite of this, stories of revolution reached independent Texas. In 1841, the president of the Republic of Texas, Mirabeau B. Lamar, actually sent an army of three hundred men to New Mexico with the ostensible purpose of liberating the territory from Mexico. The entire venture was an embarrassing failure—and almost all three hundred were eventually captured and sent as prisoners of war to Mexico. Governor Manuel Armijo, who had defeated the earlier revolutionaries, won even more accolades in Mexico by defeating this Texas invasionary force. But to the Texans, it was a matter of vengeance. A force of more than eight hundred was organized to make reprisals against Governor Armijo and the New Mexicans. But this army dwindled to less than two hundred—and had to content itself with pirate-like raiding of the Santa Fé trade caravans. Many of the actions of these raiding parties were detested in both Mexico and the United States of America, which looked upon New Mexico with covetous eyes.

Yet the Santa Fé trade continued, although President Antonio López de Santa Anna issued a decree in 1844, closing the Santa Fé Trail—and trade. So important was the trade—even to California since goods brought to Santa Fé were passed on to California—that the decree was revoked in principle almost as soon as it was issued. And thus it was that in 1846, New Mexico, like Texas and California, became the object of United States expansion. It is estimated that the white population of the territory at that time exceeded seventy thousand. New Mexico was indeed an important outpost of Mexico's far northern frontier.

The territory whose events sparked a war between the United States of America and Mexico, was Texas. Like California, and New Mexico, Texas was isolated from Mexico by distance and by the independent attitudes of its settlers. These were attitudes which began almost as soon as the territory was settled. When Spain attempted to populate Texas shortly before Mexico achieved independence, mostly Americans took advantage of the opportunity. In retrospect, it appears rather odd that Spain planned to maintain a buffer against North American aggression by inviting North Americans to settle in Mexico's northern regions.

But with the advent of Moses and Stephen Austin, the colonization of Texas began. Within ten years the population of Texas had climbed from three thousand to more than thirty thousand. And most of these people were North Americans who had taken the pledge to Mexico and the Catholic religion.

By 1833, twelve years after Mexican Independence, it became apparent to many that these colonists were not securing the territory for Mexico; rather, they posed a real threat to the government to which they had given their pledge. Instrumental in alerting the authorities to this threat was the British Ambassador to Mexico, H.G. Ward. This highly respected diplomat—wishing to enhance Britain's economic position in Mexico—warned the Mexicans that they might lose Texas if immigration were not controlled. Ambassador Ward's warning persuaded the Mexican government to impose restrictions on the inhabitants of Texas. Customs duties which had not been charged along the Louisiana frontier, were now made mandatory. Finally, administratively and judicially, Texas was made a part of Coahuila. This meant that civil and criminal disputes had to be settled in Coahuila—a great distance from Texas.

The Texans protested; formed a convention; and sent Stephen Austin to Mexico City to request repeal of the Law of 1830. All efforts of the Texans and their representative, Stephen Austin, failed as Mexico's president Antonio López de Santa Anna attempted to enforce Mexican law in the area of Texas. Two Mexican generals were empowered to do just that. The first general, Mier y Teran met with such failure that he committed suicide. The second, Martin P. Cos was driven south of the Rio Grande. Santa Anna, in order to avenge the honor of Mexico, decided to lead an expedition to Texas himself.

". . . the colonists of Texas, citizens of the United States, declared themselves in open revolution and proclaimed independence from Mexico. These colonists were in possession of the vast and rich lands which an earlier Mexican Congress—with an unbelievable lack of discretion—had given them. In declaring themselves independent, they claimed that other favors, which they demanded, had not been granted them. . . .

I, as chief executive of the government, zealous in the fulfillment of my duties to my country, declared that I would maintain the territorial integrity whatever the cost. This would make it necessary to initiate a tedious campaign under a capable leader immediately. With the fires of patriotism in my heart and dominated by a noble ambition to save my country, I took pride in being the first to strike in defense of the independence, honor, and rights of my nation. Stimulated by these courageous feelings, I took command of the campaign myself, preferring the uncertainties of war to the easy and much-coveted life of the palace."[71]

Santa Anna forced thousands of poor Indian conscripts who were inadequately clad, armed, and fed, to march through the northern deserts of Mexico. In February of 1836, Santa Anna attacked an old Franciscan mission called the Alamo. This resulted in a needless bloodbath on both sides. For Texas and for Mexico, there was no turning back. That same month, Texas officially declared independence. An American, David Barnett was chosen president and a Mexican, Lorenzo Zavala, vice-president. Sam Houston was proclaimed the military commander.

Within two months Santa Anna signed the agreement of Velasco, which granted Texas independence. It was just the first incident in a series of events that would divest Mexico of all her far northern frontier.

[71]*The Eagle,* pp. 49-50.

CHAPTER 24

The Mexican-American War

The Castle of Chapultepec is located on a hill overlooking the city of Mexico. Generals Worth and Pillow began bombarding the Castle at dawn on the morning of September 12, 1847. The fusillade was fierce on both sides, and in the exchange, General Pillow was wounded. This drove his men into a state of vengeful frenzy. The defenders were commanded by that old independence hero, Nicholás Bravo. But they were mostly young military cadets who, nevertheless, fought and died bravely. The bronze statues in the courtyard are representations of national heroes, the young cadets, who fought to the bitter end—their lives and hopes dashed on the rocks below. They are the *Niños héroes*—or heroic young men. But their sacrifice was all for naught. Bravo saw the futility of continuing the battle, and on the 14th of September, he surrendered. The end of the war was in sight.

For some time Americans had coveted California and other Mexican frontier territory. Some felt that geographically what Americans call the Southwest should belong to the United States. They believed that the United States would be geometrically more perfect if Mexican territory belonged to the United States rather than to Mexico. And then there were all those early "public relations" men: Yankee sea traders, American frontiersmen, mountain men, the fur trappers, and even some adventurous emigrants. They reported about the fine climate, the spectacular harbors; the grandeur of the redwoods and mountains; and the sparsity of the Mexican population. Some wrote home, urging their families to migrate—to settle. Others felt we ought to attempt a purchase from Mexico. And still others felt we ought to take it outright—by force, if necessary.

Early in 1835, the young Harvard student who took time out from his studies for adventure and "improvement" of his eyesight, sailed from his hometown of Boston to California. Several years later, Richard Henry Dana wrote of his experiences in a series of well-known newspaper articles, which were later published in the book, *Two Years Before the Mast.* His praise of the land was widely read in the eastern United States:

> "The bay of Monterey is very wide at the entrance, being about twenty-four miles between the two points. . . . The shores are extremely well wooded, (the pine abounding upon them,) and as it was now the rainy season, everything was as green as nature could make it,—the grass, the leaves, and all; the birds were singing in the woods, and great numbers of wild foul were flying over our heads . . . There are in this place, and in every other town which I saw in California, no streets, or fences . . . so that the houses are placed at random upon the green, which . . . gives them a pretty effect when seen from a little distance."[72]

Dana praised the climate and the ability of the land to produce, but he held little more than contempt for its inhabitants:

> "The Californians are an idle, thriftless people, and can make nothing for themselves. The country abounds in grapes, yet they buy bad wine made in Boston and brought around by us, at an immense price . . . Their hides too, which they value at two dollars in money, they give for something which costs seventy-five cents in Boston; and buy shoes (as like as not, made of their own hides, which have been carried twice round Cape Horn) at three and four dollars, and "Chichen-skin" boots at fifteen dollars apiece.. . ."[73]

Dana's comparison of a remote frontier region with that of the bustling port city of Boston—bathed in European culture—was clearly unfair. Nevertheless, his *Two Years Before the Mast* was a success. It was widely read, and had great influence on America's thinking about Mexico's possessions and their settlers.

A noted fur trapper, Antoine Robidoux loudly sang the praises of California's virtues, especially the miraculously healthful quality of the climate. Addressing a meeting in Platte County, Missouri, in the fall of 1840, Robidoux extolled the climate of California as an "earthly

[72]Dana, Vol. I, pp. 76-77.
[73]Dana, Vol. I, p. 81.

paradise." He went on to say that there was no one in California with the shakes, except one man—who brought the disease from Missouri. So unusual was he, maintained Robidoux, that people came eighteen miles from Monterey to see him shake.

How could anyone resist living in a land like that! Then, in the 1840's there was a revival of the American conception of "Manifest Destiny." Many people, especially many intellectuals believed that it was not only America's destiny—but it was her manifest or absolute destiny—that the United States acquire Mexico's frontier territory. Americans, it was argued, had no choice! They must expand—they must "civilize!" A leading proponent of this theory was President James K. Polk. He saw the southwest as a safety valve for the continued growth and expansion of the United States. California, its harbors and the territory's strategic location, he believed, made it essential that it become part of the United States of America.

America's annexation of Texas on December 22, 1845, set the stage for war between the United States and Mexico. An infuriated Mexico recalled her minister to Washington immediately. Talk of war became louder in both capitals. All that was needed was an incident.

The region here between the Rio Grande and the Nueces rivers was long an area of contention between both nations, and it provided the setting for that incident. Independent Texas claimed her southern and eastern boundary lay on the Rio Grande. But Mexico had always maintained that the provincial limits of Texas lay to the north and east on the Nueces River—never on the Rio Grande. When General Zachary Taylor entered this disputed territory under the direct orders of President Polk, Mexico's president, Mariano Paredes, ordered his troops into action. In a brief skirmish on April 25, 1846, General Mariano Arista's forces killed and wounded sixteen Americans. Mexican losses were light. This was the excuse Polk needed to ask the United States Congress to recognize that war existed between the two countries. Actually, he felt that war would be justified even without overt hostilities. On the morning of May 9, 1846, President Polk made the following entry in his diary:

> "The Cabinet held a regular meeting today; . . . I stated to the Cabinet that up to this time, as we knew, we had heard of no open act of aggression by the Mexican army, but that the danger was imminent that such acts would be committed. I said that in my opinion we had ample cause of war, and that it was impossible that we could stand *in statu quo,* or that I could remain silent much longer; that I thought it was my duty to send a message to Congress very soon and recommend definite measures. I told them that I thought I ought to make such a message by Tuesday next, that the country was excited and impatient on the subject and if I failed to do so I would not be doing my duty. I then propounded the distinct question to the Cabinet, and took their

opinions individually, whether I should make a message to Congress on Tuesday, and whether in that message I should recommend a declaration of war against Mexico."[74]

Polk was never forced to resolve this dilemma, for on that same evening news of the clash between Taylor and Arista reached the American President. Two days later, President Polk's war message was read to a congress already resigned to action.

> ". . . The cup of forbearance had been exhausted even before the recent information from the frontier of the Del Norte. But now, after reiterated menaces, Mexico has passed the boundary of the United States, has invaded our territory and shed American blood upon the American soil. She has proclaimed that hostilities have commenced, and that the two nations are now at war.
> As war exists, and notwithstanding all our efforts to avoid it, exists by the act of Mexico herself, we are called upon by every consideration of duty and patriotism to vindicate with decision the honor, the rights, and the interests of our country. . . ."[75]

And events and attitudes in Mexico? Political, social, and economic conditions were so chaotic that assessment is difficult. Mexico was slowly recovering from the excesses of Santa Anna's dictatorship and the struggle between federalists and centralists. Mexico's president, General Mariano Paredes, had achieved his office by "revolutionary" methods and consequently, he was insecure in his own leadership role. Paredes had even been suspected of forcing a war with the United States, in order to solidify his position. But the people of Mexico did not want a war. The majority was apathetic, and the years of internal struggle which they had survived made the war an unpopular issue. Apathy toward war however, did not mean Mexico harbored no ill will toward the United States, for indeed, the opposite was true.

The loss of Texas, aided and abetted by Americans, precluded any warm feelings between Mexico and her neighbor to the north. An example may be found in the newspaper *El Tiempo*, written on February 4, 1846: "We are not a people of traders and adventurers, the scum and dregs of all countries, whose only mission is to rob the Indians of their land and then sieze the fertile regions opened to civilization by the Spanish race." But rallying a nation to war in a time of internal chaos, is a difficult proposition. Plans for war consisted mostly of talk. When General Arista met with defeat in northern Mexico, there were explanations and reasons, but most felt there was no cause for alarm. After all, had not

[74]James K. Polk, *Diary*, pp. 81-82.
[75]James D. Richardson, ed. *A Compilation of Messages and Papers of the Presidents.* (N.Y. Bureau of National Literature, 1897), Vol. V, p. 2292.

the British press reported that it would be folly for the North Americans to invade Mexico? Had not the English minister indicated that England would tender aid to Mexico? Was not the government in the hands of the military? Everything would be all right.

With such attitudes pervasive it was almost impossible for General Paredes to rally the people behind the government's efforts to wage an effective war. When Mexico's army suffered defeats in the north, there was a national reaction of dismay and disgust. By May of 1846, the centralists had all but abandoned Paredes, who now proclaimed for a conservative federalist republic. On July 6, amidst serious rebellion against his government, Paredes finally executed a congressional declaration of war. Exactly one month later, Mexico was under the command of General José Mariano Salas, who was really a supporter of Antonio López de Santa Anna.

And how could a nation so wracked by internal dissention fight an effective war? How could the moral courage of a sturdy and gallant people be directed toward the enemy when the enemy was both within and without? Barely a score of years had elapsed since the trauma of independence—an independence that was constantly challenged by foreign interests and by a number of Mexicans as well. And then, there was Antonio López de Santa Anna. He had been exiled in 1845 for a period of ten years. But scarcely one year had passed since the sentence of exile had been imposed.

James K. Polk had been assuring congress that Santa Anna was in Havana; that he was blockaded by American picket ships so he could pose no threat. The war would soon be over and Mexico would have no Napoleon of the West behind whom to rally. Santa Anna's military leadership had come to an end—or had it?

As the sun shone overhead on the 16th of August, 1846, in the port city of Veracruz, the guns boomed from the fortress of San Juan de Ulúa. The silence of the gathered crowd was in marked contrast to the crashing artillery and muskets. Wearing the uniform of a major general, Antonio López de Santa Anna disembarked. With his young and pretty wife preceding him, the exiled leader made his way through the files of onlookers and immediately traveled to his hacienda. Within a month he arrived at the National Palace where he offered to "sacrifice himself" for the welfare of the nation. After all, had not General Salas invited him to return?

". . . When war was declared, faithful Mexicans recalled me to head the army.
     No veteran of the War for Independence could refuse a call to arms for his beloved country. No matter how humble my services might be, I answered the call. I chartered a ship—paying all expenses from my own

purse—and sailed to Vera Cruz, defying the blockade . . . The applause of
the people let me know they had forgotten that fatal December 6. I journeyed to the capital amidst a continous ovation, and my heart was overjoyed."[76]

Overjoyed indeed! Ovation indeed! And Blockade indeed! Santa
Anna did not defy the blockade. Capt. David Conner, commander of the
United States squadron had direct orders from the White House to
permit Santa Anna to slip through. Why would President Polk promise
congress that Santa Anna was unable to leave Cuba while at the same time
order the blockade to look the other way? In fact, Polk had spoken to a
friend and representative of Santa Anna. It appears that Santa Anna had
convinced Polk that if he were allowed to return to Mexico, he would
negotiate a peace that would be very favorable to the United States. On
the day that war was declared, President Polk had his Secretary of the
Navy send the following message to the commander of the squadron
guarding Cuba:

(PRIVATE AND CONFIDENTIAL)
NAVY DEPARTMENT, MAY 13, 1846
Commodore; if Santa Anna endeavors to enter the
Mexican ports, you will allow him to pass freely.
GEORGE BANCROFT

Santa Anna returned, and he had no intention of negotiating a
favorable peace with the United States. In fact, he began immediately to
raise an army which would repel the "invasion" of General Zachary
Taylor. In the north, Taylor had already met with victory in several
engagements with the Mexican forces. In September, Taylor defeated the
Mexican army in Monterrey, and shortly thereafter Saltillo fell to the
invading forces. All the while, Santa Anna was in San Luis Potosí, the
frontier mining area, raising troops with which to march northward. And
once again, history repeated itself. In December, for the fourth time in
Mexico's history, Santa Anna was elected President of the Republic.
Again, he was a president in absentia; and again the presidency was
turned over to his vice-president, Valentín Gómez Farías.

On January 28, 1847, Santa Anna's undisciplined, ill-equipped and
under-supplied army moved north toward Saltillo. With hundreds of
soldaderas and women camp followers, Santa Anna's eighteen-thousand-
man army marched 240 miles through deserts, desolation, and severe
storms. Almost four hundred died in one storm alone, and there were
desertions—by the hundreds. The army stayed intact only because rein-
forcements replenished his shrinking forces.

[76]*The Eagle* p. 89.

Santa Anna's plan was to trap Taylor at Saltillo and his plan nearly worked. Taylor, having learned of Santa Anna's advance, prepared a strong defense at a place called Buena Vista just south of Saltillo. On February 22 and 23, 1847, Santa Anna's seven divisions engaged the firmly entrenched army of Zachary Taylor. Wearing an old straw hat and a white duster, Santa Anna rode to strategic locations and attempted to inspire his men. He almost carried the battle, but food and munitions coupled with desertions, determined the outcome. On the 24th, under the cover of night, Santa Anna retreated. One thousand eight hundred dead or wounded and two hundred and ninety-four captured were minor losses compared to the four thousand desertions. Santa Anna's forces straggled back toward the capital as he attempted to turn his defeat into a victory. "Taylor had lost over two thousand men," he reported. "The American invaders had been routed." And Santa Anna's explanation for the retreat was to stabilize the political turbulence in the capital.

In the midst of his defeat, there was a conservative uprising in Mexico city—once again against the liberal-puro vice president, Valentín Gómez Farías. Governing in the absence of Santa Anna, Gómez Farías had confiscated church property in an attempt to maintain the deteriorating military and political situation. Santa Anna arrived in the capital just in time to accept a two-million peso offer from the clergy to overthrow Gómez Farías and rescind the anti-clerical laws. Victory into defeat—rebellion into victory!

But the situation became desperate as news arrived that General Winfield Scott had landed at Veracruz with ten thousand marines. Again Santa Anna could escape the rigors of government and gain some glory for Mexico—and, of course, for himself. He immediately issued a manifesto:

> "My duty is to sacrifice myself, and I will know how to fulfill it! Perhaps the American hosts may proudly tread the imperial capital of the Aztecs. I will never witness such opprobium, for I am decided first to die fighting! Mexicans! You have a religion—protect it! You have honor—then free yourselves from infamy! You love your wives, your children—then liberate them from American brutality! But it must be action—not vain entreaty or barren desires—with which the enemy must be opposed. Mexicans! Your fate is the fate of the nation! Not the Americans, but you, will decide her destiny! Vera Cruz calls for vengeance—follow me, and wash out the stain of her dishonor!"[77]

Believe it or not, Santa Anna was able to gather peons, regulars, guerrillas, and volunteers in order to put an army together. Twenty miles

[77]Senate Exec. Doc. No. 1. 30th Cong. 1st Sess. pp. 259-61; also in Calcott, *Santa Anna*, p. 257; also in Jones, Jr., *Santa Anna*, p. 113.

east of his hacienda at a highland plateau called Cerro Gordo, Santa Anna
set up his defenses. Contrary to the best advice from his subordinate
officers, he left his flank exposed when he failed to fortify a position above
him. It proved fatal. Scott attacked at that exact position and routed the
defenders completely. Santa Anna retreated to Puebla and then to the
capital where he was denounced as a coward and incompetent. Congress
forbade him from negotiating directly with the enemy. In spite of this
degradation, he was still given unlimited political control over the nation!

But Santa Anna was not through with his duplicity. As Scott
marched inexorably toward Mexico City, Santa Anna decided upon a
ruse. It had worked with President Polk, why not with General Winfield
Scott? If Scott would pay Santa Anna a substantial amount of money, he
would permit the American Army to take a few outposts symbolically.
Then he would offer very attractive peace terms from the capital.
Through Nicolas P. Trist, a recently arrived chief clerk in the U.S. State
Department, Scott coughed up several thousand dollars to Santa Anna.
Neither the exact amount demanded nor the total amount paid is known.
Estimates are that Scott paid Santa Anna from two to three hundred
thousand dollars of a proposed million in an effort to end the fighting and
gain a negotiated peace.

While all of this was going on, Santa Anna continued his political
struggle within the capital. The moody, petulant general resigned and
then withdrew his resignation—he threatened and cajoled. All the while
Mexico was attempting to repel a foreign invader. Yet Santa Anna did
prepare for the defense of Mexico City. He brought in supplies from as
far north as New Orleans and as far south as Honduras. He emptied the
prisons and conscripted all men between the ages of sixteen and fifty. Still
when the struggle began, Santa Anna was again outflanked as he attempted to maintain one defensive position. Because of an argument with
General Gabriel Valencia, Santa Anna refused to come to Valencia's aid.
The result was that both men suffered massive defeats at Contreras and
Churubusco. But Santa Anna's bag of tricks was not empty yet. Holding
the carrot of peace in front of Scott and Trist again—he obtained a formal
truce on August 23, 1847, the purpose of which was to effect the surrender of Mexico and a negotiated peace! Once again, Scott and Trist
accepted! Exactly what Santa Anna planned is impossible to assess. But as
negotiations began, each side accused the other of bad faith and duplicity
and Santa Anna prepared for the final defense of Mexico City. The
political and military situation was chaotic and a number of rebellions
broke out against Santa Anna himself. On September 7, Scott ended the
truce and struck toward the heart of Mexico City. At Molino del Rey the
fighting was hard and the casualties were heavy on both sides. Finally, the
assault was made at the Castle of Chapultepec on September 12th and
13th. It ended with the heroic defense of the Castle by "Los Niños héroes"

or the heroic young cadets. While some recent revisionist Mexican historians have attempted to debunk the niños héroes—for Mexico, this symbol of heroism remains.

On the 14th of September, Scott entered Mexico City. Before escaping, Santa Anna ordered the populace to engage in house to house fighting. He also began guerrilla warfare in the mountainous eastern region of Mexico. While fighting continued for some time after the capitulation of Mexico, it was only a matter of months before Santa Anna requested and received safe conduct to go into exile. On April 5, 1848, Santa Anna left for Jamaica, supposedly for good.

During the Mexico City campaign, other United States invasionary forces had moved into Mexico's frontier regions. Colonel Stephen W. Kearney led an Army of the West with 2,700 men from Fort Leavenworth to Santa Fe, New Mexico. There, 3,000 troops led by Governor Manual Armijo prepared for battle. But the far frontier of Mexico had been separated from the center of political power for so long, that it had developed a political independence of its own. There was little heart for fighting and bloodshed; and when a wealthy Santa Fé merchant, James Magoffin interceded, the struggle—which never began—ended. So confident was Col. Kearney, that he sent a contingent of his army south to Chihuahua under Colonel Alexander Doniphan in order to occupy that city.

With 300 of his dragoons, Kearney marched from Santa Fé to Mexico's extreme northern province of California. On his way, Kearney met an American military scout, Kit Carson, who was bringing news to Washington, D.C., that California had surrendered to Commodore John D. Sloat after a short struggle. Again Kearney's confidence was bolstered and he sent two hundred of his men back to Santa Fé.

Yet neither California nor New Mexico were happy with their American occupiers, and neither really gave up without a struggle. The antipathy felt by the residents of both California and New Mexico was less of a patriotism toward Mexico than it was a dislike for the attitudes and actions of the American invaders.

Insulting and haughty, the Americans generally felt disdain and disgust for the inhabitants of their conquered lands. Therefore, both areas revolted. In California, the American occupation almost ended in total disaster. On December 6 and 7, at the battle of San Pasqual, Kearney's forces were almost cut to pieces by Mexican insurgents armed with a few guns and a number of homemade willow lances. Kit Carson and Lieutenant Edward Fitzgerald Beale were able to escape and obtain help from American forces in San Diego averting total disaster. Several other less serious engagements ensued before the Mexican-Californians finally surrendered in Studio City, California at the place called "Campo del Cahuenga."

Meanwhile, in Santa Fe, New Mexico, Colonel Diego Archuleta's failure to gain political control of New Mexico, coupled with his belief that the New Mexican's honor had been tarnished by their hasty surrender, spawned an insurrection. On the eve of the uprising, Governor Charles Bent caught wind of the plot and arrested the conspirators. Believing the conspiracy to be thwarted, Governor Bent relaxed his guard. But on January 19, 1847, Pablo Montoya, who called himself "Santa Anna of the North," led the Taos Pueblo Indians into an uprising during which a number of Americans were killed. Governor Bent himself was killed and scalped. Ultimately, the American forces prevailed at Taos, but not without significant losses on both sides. Recriminations continued for some time afterward. But the Mexican defeat at Taos and the *Californio* surrender at "Campo del Cahuenga" marked the end of the so-called Mexican American War in the northern provinces.

With the fall of Mexico City, the War had come to an end. Manuel de la Peña y Peña, the interim president, realized the folly of continuing the struggle—in spite of Santa Anna's exortations to the contrary.

The Congress, which gathered at Queretaro, acceded to Peña y Peña, and named him president of the Supreme Court and interim President of Mexico. While insurrections and general anarchy continued throughout Mexico, the negotiations between the United States and Mexico continued. The Mexican commissioners Bernardo Couto, Miguel Atristain, and Luis G. Cuevas finally concluded a favorable treaty with the American commissioner, Nicolas P. Trist, even though his commission had been revoked. On February 2, 1848, at the Shrine of Guadalupe, in a suburb of Mexico City, the Treaty of Guadalupe Hidalgo was finally signed.

Under the terms of the Treaty, all Mexican territory generally north of the Rio Grande and Gila rivers, was ceded to the United States. That included the present areas of California, Arizona, Nevada, New Mexico, and parts of Wyoming and Colorado. Uninterrupted passage by American citizens was guaranteed in the Gulf of California and the Colorado River. The United States would pay Mexico fifteen million dollars for the newly acquired territories; and the United States would assume all claims against Mexico by American citizens.

There were those who were dissatisfied on both sides of the Rio Grande. Some in Mexico wanted to continue the struggle, although it was obvious that would be a disaster. And there were those in the United States who felt the Treaty of Guadalupe Hidalgo did not go far enough. Some talked of conquering all of Mexico, others wondered why not at least take Baja California. But the die was cast. "The Mexican-American War" or "The American Invasion" had come to an end.

CHAPTER 25

The Continuing Controversy

On the wall of a building, in the plaza of San Angel located in a suburb of Mexico City there is a bronze plaque. Upon close inspection one sees that the names are all American, and yet they are heroes to the Mexican government and its people. They are the *San Patricios* or Saint Patrick's Batallion. These men were deserters from the American forces who wound up fighting on the Mexican side. Fifty-nine were captured by Scott's army and fifty were hanged. The rest received fifty lashes. To the Americans they were traitors—to the Mexicans they were heroes. This incident is one of many that is testimony of the great controversy the Mexican-American war engendered, then—and—now.

In Mexico they call this war the American Invasion—because that is exactly how they view the entire episode. Americans were generally satisfied that the fault of the war lay with Mexico. In Mexico just the opposite view was held. The signing of the Treaty of Guadalupe Hidalgo in 1848 officially ended the Mexican-American War. It set the boundaries between the United States of America and the United States of Mexico; and it set forth the rules of adjudication of citizenship and land ownership in the territory ceded by Mexico to the United States. But the controversy engendered by the war did not end, and the assessment of guilt remains as a pervasive issue. Indeed, the controversy has spread to the very force and interpretation of the Treaty of Guadalupe Hidalgo itself.

In recent years, Mexican scholars are digging deeper into the causes, meaning, and effect of this struggle that took place more than a century ago. And questioning is not limited to Mexico. In the United States, the past few decades have seen a greater awareness and influence by Americans of Mexican descent. Scholars are actively re-establishing the richness and value of their Mexican heritage and customs. This has led to a re-consideration and re-evaluation of the issues involved in the Mexican-American War.

But it has not been just a case of American historians versus Mexican historians. Historians and political scientists on both sides of the Rio Grande have supported varying theories. A good example of a distinguished American historian who placed the guilt of the war squarely on the United States, was Hubert Howe Bancroft. Bancroft, in his thirty-nine volumes on the history of the American West is extremely laudatory of the American ethos and the American spirit. But his assessment of the United States' actions in the Mexican-American War held little praise for the government and its representatives. In 1880, Bancroft wrote:

> "It was a premeditated and predetermined affair, the war of the United States on Mexico; it was the result of a deliberately calculated scheme of robbery on the part of the superior power. There were at Washington enough unprincipled men high in office, senators, congressmen, to say nothing about the president and his cabinet, and the vast array of demagogues and politicians, who were only too glad to be able in any way to pander to the tastes of their supporters—there were enough of this class, slave-holders, smugglers, Indian-killers, and foul-mouthed, tobacco-spurting swearers upon sacred Fourth-of-July principles to carry spread-eagle supremacy from the Atlantic to the Pacific, who were willing to lay aside all notions of right and wrong in the matter, and unblushingly to take whatever could be secured solely upon the principle of might. Mexico, poor, weak, struggling to secure for herself a place among the nations, is now to be humiliated, kicked, cuffed, and beaten by the bully on her northern border, whose greatest pride is Christian liberty with puritan antecedents, whose greatest principle at this time finds exercise in hunting about for plausible pretexts to steal from a weaker neighbor a fine slice of lands suitable for slave labor. . . ."[78]

Bancroft believed the so-called slave conspiracy thesis: that the War resulted from a Southern conspiracy to extend the institution of slavery. The acquisition of Mexican territory would be a fulfillment of the conspirators' plans. The main exponent of the conspiracy thesis was a Northern historian who wrote at the turn of the century. James Ford Rhodes believed the genesis of the War came from Henry A. Wise of Virginia, a

[78]Hubert Howe Bancroft, *History of Mexico,* Vol. V, pp. 307-308; or Vol. XIII of *Works,* pp. 307-308 (San Francisco: A. L. Bancroft & Co. 1885).

confidential friend of President John Tyler. Wise had advised Tyler to appoint the pro-slave Democrat, South Carolinian John C. Calhoun to the office of Secretary of State. Here the conspiracy began. Historian Rhodes wrote:

> ". . . Calhoun became the master spirit of the cabinet. The man of one idea, and that idea the extension of slavery, had a large share of executive direction. The annexation project no longer lagged; it galloped towards consummation. Calhoun was appointed and confirmed March 6th (1844). On April 11th, although Mexico was at peace with us, he complied with a request, made some months previously, and promised to lend our army and navy to the President of Texas to be used in her war against Mexico. On the following day, the treaty of annexation of Texas to the United States was signed. What Texas had vainly sought, and what the extreme Southern party had ardently desired for eight years, was accomplished, so far as it lay in the power of the executive department of the government."[79]

Rhodes carefully laid out the progression of the conspiracy, he included the election of James K. Polk and the support of Southern slave holders for war in hopes of gaining the southwest and, thus more slaveholding territory. This was a popular view in both the United States and Mexico for many years. But at the turn of the century, historians began to question the conspiracy thesis as too simple. The complexities of the war could not be summed up in the word "slavocracy." Today, most historians on both sides of the Rio Grande have generally discredited the "conspiracy" theory as inconsistent with the facts before and after the war.

Probably one of the most pervasive theories was that of Manifest Destiny. It was a belief that United States expansion into Mexico's territory was inevitable; it was ordained by some inexplicable force, possibly the force of Heaven itself. Harvard's noted historian Frederick Merk has spent a lifetime in the study of Manifest Destiny, particularly as it applied to the Mexican-American War and its results. Professor Merk, in explaining Manifest Destiny, wrote the following paraphrase of an article on the subject:

> "It meant expansion, prearranged by Heaven, over an area not clearly defined. In some minds it means expansion over the region to the Pacific; in others, over the North American continent; in others, over the hemisphere. . . . It attracted enough persons by the mid 1840's to constitute a movement. Its theory was more idealistic. . . . It was less acquisitive, more an opportunity for neighboring peoples to reach self-realization. It meant opportunity to gain admission to the American Union. . . . If properly

[79]James Ford Rhodes, *History of the United States from the Compromise of 1850.* Vol. I of 7 Vols. (New York: Harper & Row, Publishers, Inc., 1892-1922).

qualified, they would be admitted. Some—the Mexican, for example—might have to undergo schooling for a time in the meaning and methods of freedom before they were let in."[80]

And the key to entry was desire—desire and a willingness to accept federalism and republicanism over centralism and monarchy. This, of course, would also mean freedom, especially freedom of religion. And certainly it meant democracy, representative government with frequent elections the key to a democratic state. It was because of Manifest Destiny that the United States elected James K. Polk, an ardent expansionist, to the presidency in 1844.

Many historians have accused Polk of plotting—or rather "manufacturing" a war with Mexico. The evidence is weighty, and the indictment awesome. Yet the guilt that could be assumed by President Polk must be mitigated somewhat by his absolute and sincere belief that "The American mission . . . was literally a divine mission." Polk truly believed that God had chosen the United States of America to carry out His divine will through the American system of government. In his Third Annual Message to Congress, Polk said:

> "No country has been so much favored, or should acknowledge with deeper reverence the manifestations of the divine protection. An all-wise Creator directed and guarded us in our infant struggle for freedom and has constantly watched over our surprising progress until we have become one of the great nations of the earth."[81]

The speech was not political—in the traditional sense. Polk was not fishing for votes. He was saying what he truly believed to be correct—even absolute. Thus Polk was not just an advocate of Manifest Destiny, he was a prime mover of it.

And it is here that Polk stands accused as the agressor by scholars both in the United States and in Mexico. Some of the most damning testimony against him was given by the last president of the Republic of Texas, Anson Jones, M.D. Jones believed that Polk's actions constituted a conspiracy to start a war in which the United States could come to the protection of Texas. President Jones believed that the war between the United States and Mexico was pure robbery—and that it was not justified. He believed that contrary to popular opinion, Polk wanted war not peace. He wanted war in order to expand the territory of the United States at the expense of Mexico.

[80]Frederick Merk, *Manifest Destiny and Mission in American History.* (N.Y. Vintage Books, 1966), p. 24.
[81]James D. Richardson, *A Compilation of the Messages and Papers of the Presidents,* Vol. V, (N.Y.: Bureau of National Literature, Inc., 1897), p. 2383.

From March through May of 1845, James K. Polk sent a number of "agents" to Texas to confer with the military authorities and leaders in the Texan government. In March, 1845, Archibald Yell of Arkansas arrived in Texas. In April, ex-Postmaster General Charles A. Wickliffe, and in May, Polk's friend and confidant, Commodore Robert F. Stockton arrived. Stockton's appearance was ostensibly to extend the protection of his fleet to the Republic of Texas. These men met with President Anson Jones, and with the Texas commander-in-chief, Major General Sidney Sherman. Major General Sherman was in favor of annexation and appeared to be interested in creating hostilities with Mexico. The following is Anson Jones' own words on what transpired:

"In May, 1845, Commodore Stockton, with a fleet of four or five vessels, arrived at Galveston, and with him Hon. C. A. Wickliffe . . . The gentlemen had various interviews with Major General Sherman, . . . the result of which was active preparations at Galveston for organizing volunteer forces, the ostensible object of which was an invasion of Mexico . . . but these gentlemen, it appears, were unwilling to take so great a responsibility: It was therefore resolved that the plan should be submitted to me and my sanction obtained . . . On the 28th of May, General Sherman for himself and associates in the militia, and Dr. Wright, surgeon of the steamer Princeton, and secretary of the Commodore took three days in unfolding to me the object of their visit. Dr. Wright stated that he was sent by Com. Stockton to propose that I should authorize Major General Sherman to raise a force of two or three thousand men, or as many as might be necessary, and to make a descent upon the Mexican town of Matamoros, and capture and hold it; that Com. Stockton would give assistance with the fleet under his command, under the pretext of giving the protection promised by the U.S. . . . that he would undertake to supply the necessary provisions, arms and munitions of war for the expedition, would land them at convenient points on our coast, and would agree to pay the men and officers to be engaged; that he had consulted General Sherman, who approved the plan, and was present to say so; and, besides, that the people generally from Galveston to Washington City had been spoken to about it, and that it met their unanimous approval; and that all that was now wanting was the sanction of the Government to the scheme . . . I asked Dr. Wright if he had written instructions from the Commodore, or any communication from him to me; that the matter was a grave one, and I did not well see how, without them, if disposed even, I would undertake such weighty responsibilities . . . He then stated to me that the scheme was rather a confidential and secret one, that it was undertaken under the sanction of the U.S. Government, but that the President did not wish to become known in the matter. . . ."[82]

President Anson Jones, in his diary, says he then made an explicit charge to Dr. Wright and company—and a charge which they admitted.

[82]Stenberg, *Pacific Historical Review* IV, 1935.

"I then said, smiling, 'So gentlemen, the Commodore, on the part of the United States wishes me to *manufacture a war* for them,' to which they replied affirmatively . . . I suppressed my feelings, and gave no expression of opinion, but suggested every objection and difficulty which presented themselves to my mind . . . I . . . found it necessary to temporize. There was much excitement in the public to annexation . . . also a hatred of Mexico, and a burning disposition for revenge."[83]

In retrospect, Jones pointed out his antipathy to the scheme for war. Jones felt that as President of the Republic of Texas, he should give the people an alternative to war. He felt that Mexico really did not want war—and that war was not necessary.

"The advocate for peace for ten years, I naturally turned with disgust and abhorrence from a proposition of Mr. Polk's through Com. Stockton, 'that I should manufacture a war for the U.S.' The anxiety of Mr. Polk for a pretext for a war with Mexico had been known to me for some time, through the agency of employees of the Texan Government at Washington City. That he was predetermined to have a war with that country so soon as a pretext was found I also well knew, and that such was the feeling of a large party in the U.S. . . . I thought, if she felt such cause existed, she should make the war herself, upon the right grounds."[84]

It appears that Anson Jones, through the good offices of Britain was trying to gain recognition of Texas independence by Mexico—and to the Rio Grande. If such be the case, then there would be no need for war—except of course, if the United States wished to extend her boundaries beyond those claimed by Texas. On June 4, 1845, Captain Charles Elliot, the British consul brought Texas a preliminary treaty of recognition from the central government in Mexico City. Jones immediately issued a proclamation of cessation of hostilities. He points out the disappointment of Polk's agents to this turn of events.

". . . when my proclamation met them at Hamlin's [it] dashed all their expectations, General Sherman returned home from there; but Dr. Wright came on and saw me. *One word* settled Com. Stockton's business, and I assured him I never had the least idea of *Manufacturing a War for the United States.* Soon after which he left our waters and sailed for the Pacific in search of the same *un*pacific object which had brought him to Texas . . . Many had been engaged and promised offices in the campaign to Matamoros, who were disappointed, and laid all the blame on me . . . The public too were disappointed . . . I could have been very popular if I had sanctioned the war scheme . . . and probably there was no personal advantage which the U.S. Government had it in their power to bestow, or no emolument which could not have been stipulated for and received if I had so chosen, by

[83]*PHR*, IV, 1935.
[84]*PHR*, IV, 1935.

acceding to involve the country afresh in war with Mexico . . . It is true, the U.S. made the suggestion *ostensibly* for the *defense* of Texas; but in *reality*, to consummate views of conquest which had been entertained probably for many years, and to wage war which the annexation of Texas afforded a pretext long sought and wished for. Texas never actually needed the protection of the U.S.; and the *protection* so much talked about . . . was all a trick. . . ."[85]

In July of 1845, Texas accepted United States' offer of annexation, and in December, she was formally admitted to the Union. By this very act, Anson Jones was no longer president. As he said, his alternative of peace was not acceptable to the majority of Texans, who had a burning rage for revenge. The ouster of Jones cleared the way for U.S. action. In January of 1846, under direct orders from the White House, General Zachary Taylor occupied the disputed territory between the Nueces River and the Rio Grande. This led directly to a military engagement and ultimately to war. James K. Polk has been accused of engineering the entire event.

Some Polk apologists—those who insist the President was exploring every avenue of peace—point to the emissary Polk sent to Mexico late in 1845. It is true that through John Black, the U.S. Consul in Mexico, President José Joaquín Herrera had said he would accept a commissioner empowered to settle outstanding disputes between the United States and Mexico. Of course this led to the much publicized John Slidell mission. President Herrera of Mexico communicated to James K. Polk:

> "That though the Mexican nation had been deeply injured by the acts of the United States in the department of Texas, his government was disposed with powers to settle the present dispute in a peaceful, reasonable and decorous manner."[86]

But Herrera did not agree to receive an American minister, especially one who came with money and instructions to purchase significant amounts of Mexican territory, including California. John Slidell carried with him a draft for a 3.5-million-dollar down payment on the purchase of California and New Mexico. Herrera was merely an interim president in the midst of a revolution against the dictatorship of Santa Anna. Within months, he was out of office and the man who overthrew Santa Anna was in. General Mariano Paredes, the new president refused to accept the credentials of John Slidell. Polk felt it was an insult to the American people. The rebuff to Slidell was cause enough for war. . . . And yet, as the apologists say, he waited until the acts of agression by Mexico made it impossible for him to wait any longer. This certainly is a precent that has

[85]*PHR*, IV, 1935.
[86]*PHR*, IV, 1935.

been taught to American students, for in a popular high school American history text, the author writes: "Mexico was going to pay dearly for the way she had treated John Slidell!"[87] To Polk's detractors, the Slidell mission was a ruse; and nothing more than an attempt to further confuse the American people and to whip up anti-Mexican sentiment.

In spite of all this, over the years there has been a number of historians who placed the blame for the conflict squarely—or at least equally—on Mexico. There is no question of the instability of the Mexican government before, during, and after the War. This instability, coupled with the great distances from the center of political control to Mexico's distant territories, made those territories in effect, "sitting ducks." Furthermore, many of the inhabitants held little allegiance to the central government because of the distance and because of the neglect that Mexico manifested towards these territories. California is a good example. At the time of Mexican Independence, there were scarcely more than three thousand non-Indian Californios, the majority of them born in that distant province. When the War for Independence from Spain broke out, California played no role at all—save one incident with an Argentine privateer trying to recruit revolutionaries in the province. For California, Independence meant merely a change in flags. The overthrow of Iturbide was another change in flags. In fact, there were some in California who believed the destiny of California lay with the United States not Mexico. Californios also held a certain amount of contempt for the Mexican government. It was not uncommon for the governors sent by Mexico to be overthrown and ceremoniously sent home. This was the case with the last Mexican governor, Manuel Micheltorena, who as late as 1845 was overthrown and deported.

The late professor Justin S. Smith of Dartmouth College spent a number of years researching thousands of documents in both Mexico and the United States. From these he published a detailed two-volume work entitled *The War With Mexico*. Writing in 1919, Professor Smith set to print the following indictment:

> "[Mexico's] treatment of Texans and Americans violated the laws of justice and humanity, and—since there was no tribunal to punish it—laid upon the United States, both as her nearest neighbor and as an injured community, the duty of retribution. In almost every way possible, indeed, she forced us to take a stand. She would neither reason nor hearken to reason, would not understand, would not negotiate. Compensation for the loss of territory, in excess of its value to her, she knew she could have. Peace and harmony with this country she knew might be hers. But prejudice, vanity, passion and wretched politics inclined her toward war; her overrated military advan-

[87]Ralph Harlow & R.E. Miller, *Story of America*, (Henry Holt & Co., Inc. 1957.) p. 188.

tages, her expectations of European aid, the unpreparedness of the United States, and in particular the supposed inferiority of Taylor and his army encouraged her; and she deliberately launched the attack so long threatened.

As was just and natural, Mexico primarily owed her failure in the war to the characteristics that led her into it. From a strictly military point of view her case was not precisely hopeless. . . .

But the military point of view was by no means the only one to be considered. The want of public virtue had filled the army with miserable officers, the legislative halls with dishonest, scheming, clashing politicians, and the whole nation with quarreling factions and wrathful, disheartened people, secretly thankful to find their oppressors, whom they could not punish themselves, punished by the Americans."[88]

Justin Smith continues with an attack on those in the United States who failed to support the war or worse yet, those who spoke against what he saw as a righteous national war. Yet one of the greatest supporters of the war ultimately changed his mind and became a major opponent, Senator Thomas Corwin, a Whig senator from Ohio. Thomas Corwin's speech of February 11, 1847, on the Senate floor is recognized as one of the greatest in American political history. While in the Senate he was a courageous minority of one, his words may have been representative of the nation's silent majority. This is but a small segment of that courageous speech:

". . . You have taken from Mexico one-fourth of her territory, and you now propose to run a line comprehending about another third, and for what? I ask, Mr. President, for what? What has Mexico got from you, for parting with two-thirds of her domain? She has given you ample redress for every injury of which you have complained. She has submitted to the award of your commissioners, and, up to the time of the rupture with Texas, faithfully paid it. And for all that she has lost . . . what requital do we, her strong, rich, robust neighbor, make? Do we send our missionaries there "to point the way to heaven"? Or do we send the schoolmasters to pour daylight into her dark plans, to aid her infant strength to conquer, and reap the fruit of the independence herself alone had won? No, no; none of this do we.

But we send regiments, storm towns, and our colonels prate of liberty in the midst of the solitudes their ravages have made . . .

. . . Sir, had one come and demand[ed] Bunker Hill of the people of Massachusetts, had England's lion ever showed himself there, is there a man over thirteen and under ninety who would not have been ready to meet him? Is there a river on this continent that would not have run red with blood? . . .

. . . If I were a Mexican I would tell you, "Have you not room enough in your own country to bury your dead? If you come into mine, we will greet you with bloody hands, and welcome you to hospitable graves."

[88]Justin H. Smith, *The War With Mexico,* 2 vols. (Gloucester, Mass.: Peter Smith Press, 1963).

Why, says the Chairman of this Committee on Foreign Relations, it is the most reasonable thing in the world! We ought to have the Bay of San Francisco! Why? Because it is the best harbor on the Pacific! It has been my fortune, Mr. President, to have practiced a good deal in criminal courts in the course of my life, but I never yet heard a thief, arraigned for stealing a horse, plead that it was the best horse he could find in the country! . . .

"Mr. President, if the history of our race has established any truth, it is but a confirmation of what is written. "The way of the transgressor is hard." Inordinate ambition, wantoning in power, and spurning the humble maxims of justice ever has ended and ever shall end in ruin. . . .

". . . Let us abandon all ideas of acquiring further territory and by consequences cease at once to prosecute this war . . . Let us here, in this temple consecrated to the Union, perform a solemn lustration; let us wash Mexican blood from our hands, and on these altars, and in the presence of that image of the Father of his Country that looks down upon us, swear to preserve honorable peace with all the world, and external brotherhood with each other."*

And what of the Mexicans? How did they view the war? As in the United States there are also varying interpretations. But the tragedy of the event speaks loudly and clearly. Most often quoted are the words of Mexican scholar-philosopher, Justo Sierra:

"The United States had from the early days of the Mexican Republic attempted to acquire the zone between Louisiana and the entire course of the Bravo, from its source to its mouth. . . . The partisans of Democratic politics, which the Southern states of the Union always supported, never lost sight of the possibility of acquiring this territory by purchase or by force. To these designs was soon added the acquisition of the entire Mexican Pacific zone, north of the tropical line, in order to avoid, it was claimed, that another nation, England for example, take possession of it. In short, the doctrine was as follows: all the territory neighboring on the United States which Mexico could not control ought to be, in fact, North American."[89]

Justo Sierra indicts equally the actions of his own country. He blames political squabbling and instability as a basic factor:

"If blind and foolish patriotism, or rather, if the contending factions in Mexico had not converted the question of Texas into a political weapon to disparage each other by mutual accusations of treason, the great calamities could have been avoided. This could have been done by exploiting the needs of the North American political parties, and by recognizing the indisputable right of Texas to secede once the federal pact was broken. We would have salvaged at least the zone between the Nueces and the Bravo, and perhaps California. We would have obtained a better indemnity than

*David Brewer, ed., *The World's Best Orations* (Metuchen, N.J.: Mini-Print Corp.), pp. 1407-1417; as quoted from U.S. Senate Documents speech of Feb. 11, 1847.

[89]Justo Sierra, *Evolución Política del Pueblo Mexicano.* (Mexico, 1940 as quoted from: Ramón Eduardo Ruiz, *The Mexican War: Was it Manifest Destiny?* (New York: Holt, Rinehart, and Winston, 1963) p. 112.

that of the 1848 treaty, and above all, we would have shaken off the nightmare of war with the United States—which, even before it erupted, by its menace alone sucked dry the resources of our treasury."[90]

But Justo Sierra is philosophical about the event and its results; particularly the idealistic relations between the two countries.

> "In Mexico, Congress turned its attention to the American problem, tiresome, solemn, and terrible. It was the iron gauntlet around the collar of a weak and anemic nation; a brutal knee on its belly; jaws ready to gnaw, mangle and devour while at the same time talking about humanity, justice, and law."[91]

The poet-politician and historian concludes with a sense of resignation of the past—but with a note of hope for the future:

> "Mexico, a country weak because of its scanty and scattered population, one frequently cut off from intellectual currents and often unaware of the full meaning of nationhood, has been defeated in its international struggles, but never conquered."[92]

And so the controversy continues—not only over the war, but over the treaty that ended the war, the Treaty of Guadalupe Hidalgo which was signed in a suburb of Mexico City by that name. It was finally concluded and signed in a back room at the most Holy Shrine of Guadalupe. The Treaty essentially drew a dividing line between the United States and Mexico at the Rio Grande—sometimes called the Rio Bravo del Norto. In addition, it ceded all territory belonging to Mexico generally north of the Gila river. In other words, the United States gained practically 50% of all Mexican territory. But the controversy over the treaty rests not in territory, but in its philosophical interpretation—and whether or not the spirit of the treaty was observed in the United States. According to articles eight and nine of the Treaty of Guadalupe Hidalgo, Mexicans living in the ceded territory were given a year to decide whether to become citizens or to remain as resident aliens. Regardless of their choice, their private property was to be fully recognized under the protection of the United States Constitution.

But over the years, Mexicans in these territories generally lost their land titles, sometimes from adverse court decisions but mostly from the expense of proving the validity of their titles. The Treaty of Guadalupe Hidalgo generally recognized Spanish and Mexican land grants as valid. But as laws of implementation were passed, the land holder was placed in the position of proving his ownership—sometimes through three costly

[90]Ruiz, *The Mexican War*, p. 113.
[91]Ruiz, p. 114.
[92]Ruiz, p. 116.

trials in alien courts against a government with unlimited resources. By placing the burden of proof on all the landowners, the American government said "you are guilty until proven innocent" rather than "you are innocent until proven guilty." This was particularly true in California where gold was discovered on the eve of the signing of the treaty. Because of the insecurity of ownership, California land became the object of squatters whose disdain for the Mexican landowner appeared to be sanctioned or even promoted by the actions of the United States government.

And the conflict was not limited to California. In south Texas, the King ranch of more than one million acres was carved out of territory which included many small Mexican ranches. The Mexicans who were driven out by King's aggressiveness were harrassed by the Texas rangers—who took the side of the Anglos.

The same applied to New Mexico, where in 1870 Governor William A. Pile ordered the state librarian to remove old documents to make room for more office space. The result? Documents which could have clarified land claims were used as wrapping paper, or sold, or thrown out as trash. Some have suspected Pile of being in collusion with a so-called Santa Fé Ring. The Ring was bent on defrauding Mexicans of their land but there is no clear evidence. Nevertheless, the result was the same.

As the decades of the 1960's and 1970's approached, individuals and organizations representing Americans of Mexican descent have attempted to re-examine the impact—the very essence of the Treaty of Guadalupe Hidalgo. Years will pass before the full effect of the war and the treaty will finally unfold.

CHAPTER 26

"La Reforma"

There is a massive stone mosaic standing on the roadway just outside of the town of Oaxaca close to the birthplace and home of Mexico's hero-president Benito Juárez. The mosaic relates the life story of this noted politician. At the far left, he is a shepherd boy. Then he is shown studying for the priesthood. A radical change takes place as he turns to the law and enters the legal profession. From there, his knowledge of the law is applied to politics and the presidency. His most outstanding legal accomplishments? The Law of Juárez; and the Constitution of 1857!

At the close of the Mexican-American War there had been a peaceful transfer of government, but internal dislocation and turbulence remained. Intrigues and pronouncements by generals continued. The state of the treasury reflected the economic depression of the populace. Political uprisings brought on by the national state of affairs were common; as were Indian uprisings and racial wars within the Mexican republic. In the Sierra Gorda region of the mountains surrounding Oaxaca, there was a series of Indian rebellions. The government finally controlled them by executing their leader, Quiros. As punishment, several hundred of his followers were sent to the uninhabited northern frontier regions. And these were afflicted with turbulence of their own from the vengeful Apaches. Americans from the southern states offered "blood contracts," offering two hundred dollars per head for the killing of "troublesome

Indians." Actions such as these encouraged American adventurers and filibusterers to conduct raids across the border—not to subdue the 'savage' Indian but to acquire more territory. There was still talk among Americans—and in the American press—of annexing all of Mexico. The natural reaction to all of this was for Mexico to appropriate even more money for the military from an already defunct treasury.

But probably the most serious threat to the stability of the republic was the outbreak of racial or caste war in the Yucatan Peninsula. For some time there had been a continuing struggle between the Indians of the Yucatan and the Spanish settlers. In 1848, white settlers had successfully pushed the Indians into the hinterland and occupied several cities located in the north central portion of the peninsula. But the Indians regrouped and laid siege to several towns, particularly the town of Tihosuco. Their campaign was so successful that it encouraged other Indians on the peninsula to revolt and initiate guerrilla warfare. To make matters worse, Mexico accused the British traders in Belize, or British Honduras, of supplying the Indians with arms in exchange for saleable products. And it appears that the British traders were doing just that. However, protests to Great Britain were filed away in the drawer marked bureaucracy—and the struggle continued. In several engagements, government troops were overwhelmed by Indian insurgents and the outcome appeared very bleak. Over twenty thousand troops were employed in the counter offensive with the costs in life and money skyrocketing. When the government passed a decree which authorized the exile of belligerent Indians for a period of ten years; Cuba responded with an offer of twenty-five pesos for any able bodied person who could work on a plantation. The government in Yucatan accepted the offer, and hundreds of Indians were sent to Cuba on servitude contracts. The efforts of the federal government to stop this slave trade were weak and ineffectual. Numerous attempts were made to quiet the war in the Yucatan, but all that could be accomplished was a reduced war of attrition. Clearly, the central government was unable to effectively cope with this and a number of other uprisings throughout the republic. The effect was not only a greater drain on an empty treasury but the abatement of agricultural development as well. Instead of tilling the fields, much of the agricultural force was engaged in revolution or counter-revolution.

Added to all of this social and political upheaval was renewed unrest caused by a convention with the United States. In 1850, it was proposed that the United States should build a canal or a railroad across the Isthmus of Tehuantepec. Fear spread throughout Mexico over a clause in the agreement that permitted the United States to militarily protect the operation. What would stop the United States from using this as a pretext for more territorial aggrandizement? So even more money was expended to beef up Mexico's military defenses around the approaches to the Isthmus of Tehauntepec. Scarcely anything was left of the fifteen million dollars that the United States had paid to Mexico as idemnity for the Mexican-American War.

And internal political turmoil continued. After the Mexican-American War, the Federalists were in control of the reins of political power; but they were neither able to solidify their power base with the people nor with the Church and the military. Five presidents occupied that office from 1848 to 1853 and it is mute testimony to the political instability following the Treaty of Guadalupe Hidalgo. Manuel de la Peña y Peña remained in office scarcely long enough to conclude and sign the Treaty of Guadalupe Hidalgo since José Joaquín de Herrera was elected in June of 1848. During the five year interval of Santa Anna's absence, Herrera's presidency lasted the longest, two and one half years. And some gains were made: There were increased agricultural and mining yields and increases in building starts and small manufacturing. But these positive gains could not offset the negative effect of continued political upheaval. While elections were being held in January of 1851 for a new president, the clerical conservative monarchists continued their conspiracy. Thus it was that General Mariano Arista's election to the presidency in 1851 lasted only two years, and he was forced to resign early in January of 1853. Perhaps it was Arista's inability to stem the tide of liberalism and anti-clericalism that ultimately led to his downfall. In several states, particularly Oaxaca, Michoacán, Nuevo León, and Tamaulipas, liberal governors were attempting to eliminate clerical interference in government and education. Some were even attempting to tax the Church in order to secure support for public education. The governor of Oaxaca, Benito Juárez; and the governor of Michoacán, Melchor Ocampo, both attempted to abate the power of the Church and to initiate religious toleration. Arista's inability to cope with these national problems led to the usual *cuartelazo* or barracks revolt, and finally to his resignation. As provided by the Constitution, the government was turned over to the Chief Justice, Juan Bautista Ceballos. But the anti-Aristas were seeking more than the president's resignation. What they really wanted was to overturn the federalist form of government—to institute a centralist government. They preferred a monarch or at the very least a dictator. And who was their choice? Who would be brought back to Mexico after five years of a permanent exile? None other than Antonio López de Santa Anna!

Almost immediately President Ceballos clashed with the chamber of deputies and the senate. So he promptly dissolved them. Revolutionary activities were already under way in the south and in the north. Facing an impossible task, Ceballos resigned on February 7, 1853, almost one month to the day after taking the presidential oath. The presidency now fell to one of the chief revolutionaries—and a major supporter of Santa Anna—General Manuel María Lombardini. On the following March 17, eighteen of the twenty-three states voted for Santa Anna as president of Mexico. A dispatch was immediately sent to Santa Anna at his exile in Turbaco, Venezuela; and on April 1, 1853, the "Napoleon of the West," once again disembarked at Veracruz. The color and pomp of his arrival did little to induce a sense of confidence in the populace. Although some spoke about his maturity, many viewed him with great suspicion. His march to Mexico City was full of splendor and pomp—an attempt to prove the glory of his return. After spending three days at the Shrine of Guadalupe, Santa Anna took the oath of office for the fifth time in his turbulent political career on April 20, 1853. Although the reception for the new president was resplendent and costly—more than twenty thousand pesos were expended—there were no popular demonstrations of joy on the part of those attending or the residents of the capital.

If the Federalists thought they would receive an approving ear for their demands—they were sadly mistaken. Even the old freedom fighter, Juan Alvarez, had supported the return of Santa Anna, believing there was a measure of federalism left in his heart. But the plan for government had already been laid out by the intellectual conservative, Lucas Alamán. The ground rules were clear: There would be a strong central government; there would be a strong executive; there would be a strong army; and there would be a strong Catholic church. What about federalism and popular elections? They would be abolished as destructive to Mexico.

Within one week Santa Anna had established a centralist republic; adjourned all state legislatures; made state governors responsible to him; appointed a conservative cabinet including Lucas Alamán; and prohibited any attacks on the government by the Mexican press. Within a month, he dissolved congress; formed a Council of State; abolished town councils; appointed military bosses in larger towns; and centralized all tax collections. Within two months, he had sought out all political opposition leaders and either jailed them or sent them into exile. Among these leaders was Benito Juárez, who was thrown into a dungeon on San Juan de Ulúa to await his exile.

To insure success, Santa Anna showered favors upon the military. He rewarded ninety thousand troops with brilliant uniforms, colorful certificates, ribbons, awards and gawdy military orders. At the bottom of the certificates was Santa Anna's signature followed by his titles; "Savior of the Fatherland, General of Division, Knight of the Great Cross of the Royal and Distinguished Spanish Order of Charles III, President of the Mexican Republic, Grand Master of the National and Distinguished Order of Guadalupe, etc." But all the titles in the world could not insure the success of Santa Anna. In fact the death of Lucas Alamán, in June of 1853, eliminated all restraints on the president and the regime became increasingly corrupt and bureaucratic as officials high and low were required to attire themselves in uniforms consistent with their rank. Demonstrations, parades and parties became more and more resplendent. And the government took on the trappings of an empire. As the gawdiness increased so did the expenditures. So new taxes were levied; on dogs, horses, carriages, windows, doors, and rain spouts on homes. But still there was not enough.

December 30, 1853, a treaty was concluded with James Gadsden, United States Minister to Mexico. Mexico would sell a strip of land bordering on Southern Arizona to the United States for ten million dollars. When the Mexican people protested, Santa Anna responded that the sale was made under duress. He explained that if he had not sold to the United States, they would have taken the land by force.

The ten million dollars was soon squandered on the military, ostensibly to protect Mexico from further encroachments by the "American mutilators." The explanations that Santa Anna offered did little to quiet the rumblings of revolution. Yet in the midst of all this, Santa Anna acquired the title of *"Su Alteza Serenisima,"* or His Most Serene Highness forever, along with the right to name his successor.

But an ideological storm was brewing, and a major rebellion commenced on March 1, 1854, in the town of Ayutla in the area of Guerrero. The Plan of Ayutla had nine provisions which were designed to end the rule of Santa Anna; re-establish state and territorial government; form and assemble a new congress; select an interim president; and re-establish a Federalist Republic.

Santa Anna's response was to lead an army to personally crush the rebellion. He issued orders to burn rebellious towns and execute all those who had weapons. But it soon became apparent that the revolution was not the work of a few liberals; it had widespread support.

Santa Anna found it expedient to feign illness. Then he tried to rebuild his image by making many public appearances. Finally he rigged a plebiscite. Should the president continue? Or should he bestow the office on someone else? And if so, on whom? However, the ballot required signatures insuring there would be no secrecy. A lopsided victory for Santa Anna was reported; and many of those who had signed in opposition were jailed. By June of 1855, it became clear that the revolution of Ayutla, as it was popularly called, was just that—popular. Santa Anna hastily made preparations to escape. He shipped money out of the country and sent his family to his ranch at El Encero. To safeguard his escape, he posted loyal troops along the road to Veracruz. On the 16th of August, 1855, "His Most Serene Highness" hurriedly boarded the ship *El Guerraro*

which was towed by the *Iturbide* and sailed into exile. This finally was his
political demise. Santa Anna was to make several pleas to return—and was
permitted to do so in the latter years of his life. He returned to die
penniless and unnoticed in a Mexico that he had failed and that he could
not understand.

Santa Anna is one of many vivid personalities associated with the
history of Mexico. But the forces of change that now were sweeping
Mexico were not personal in nature. They were the forces of *La Reforma,*
or the Reform. And those who carried out the ideals of the Reform, were
appropriately called "The men of the Reform." A number of them were
learned men—lawyers, doctors, scholars, poets, economists, and scientists. Not all of them agreed; some were more radical than others, and
some wanted only minor changes in government to evolve slowly.

But Mexico had experienced major changes over which no politician
could have control. By 1850, the dominant population group was that of
the mestizo. Even those leaders who were pure Indian, such as Benito
Juárez, adopted the mestizo way of thinking. Their intellectual base was
French, and they represented a modified revival of eighteenth century
enlightenment. Much of what the reformers wanted to accomplish had
already been articulated by the old liberal, Valentín Gómez Farías. In
general, the Reform movement was bent upon eliminating feudalism in
its symbolic sense. This would mean the end, or at least the limitation on
the size of large estates. Somehow, the worker, the peasant, the *peone,* had
to be liberated from the landowner, from the hacendado. Somehow, the
peasant must have a share in the land—he *must* own a part of it. But in
order to accomplish this there had to be massive distribution of large
estates, and some of the largest estates were owned by the Church. There
lay a most difficult problem. How does one attack the economic and social
standing of the Catholic Church without being accused of attacking the
dogma, the very foundation of the religion? The answer is simple, one
doesn't. The men of the Reform believed that by instituting a strict
constitutional government, they could limit the political power of not only
the Church but the army as well. It appears that they wished to institute a
free capitalistic economy of a purely Mexican nature. Originally, it was a
moderate plan—and they believed it would be achieved by moderate
means. But as resistance to their plan grew; as the Church and the military
placed obstacles in the way of their progress, moderation gave way to
radicalism. Many of the goals of the Reform Era were not accomplished;
yet accomplishments are not always immediately realized. The real accomplishment of the men of the Reform was that they laid the foundation
for twentieth century liberalism that violently surfaced in the Revolution
of 1910.

The first aim of the reform was to overthrow the dictatorship of Antonio López de Santa Anna, and this was accomplished. The men of the reform included Melchor Ocampo, a scientist and a scholar who turned to politics. Ocampo had read throughly the words of Rousseau and he was completely committed to the French enlightment. Ocampo had been the governor of Michoacán and even in the face of clerical sanctions against him, he had formed a department of public education; and he had even succeeded in taxing the Church to support it. He would be selected as Secretary of State in the interim administration of Juan Alvarez.

Santos Degollado was also a member of the liberal camp. A fiery orator and a man of fighting spirit, he was nonetheless deeply committed to the law. Degollado had been a law professor at Morelia who had become interested in clerical limitations; and of all things, scientific agriculture.

In the new administration, another liberal took the impossible office of Secretary of the Treasury. He was Guillermo Prieto, whose talents had given emotional impetus to the Reform movement. Preito was a poet —in fact, he was considered Mexico's national poet—and he was a balladeer. Prieto wrote about heroes who fought in the movement for independence—and heroes who would fight in the movement for reform.

The most fiery anti-Catholic wrote under the pseudonym of "Necromancer." His writings were biting and hostile. He spared neither Catholicism nor Christianity itself. Both were evil! Both had brought no value to the nation! The real glory of Mexico lay in its Aztec ancestry, in the beauty of its Indian heritage, in the virtue of the Indian way of life. To the clergy he was blasphemous; he was Satan.

Probably one of the best-known men of the Reform was the economist, Miguel Lerdo de Tejada. Lerdo de Tajada was neither a political nor an economic radical. He truly believed in a reform capitalism that would eventually turn Mexico into a modern capitalistic nation. While Lerdo de Tejada did not see Mexico as a country of solely small property owners as did Melchor Ocampo, he did believe that some land distribution had to take place. It was to this end that he wrote his now famous *Ley Lerdo*, or the Law of Lerdo.

Two men who were part of the movement had in common their lack of ideological commitment to the ideals of the Reform. In time, each would turn against the movement and the people they represented. One was Ignacio Comonfort a mild reformer who had previously been the chief of the Acapulco Customs House. Because he issued the famous Plan de Ayutla, he was to have the distinction of the "man who overthrew

Antonio López de Santa Anna." In the government of Juan Alvarez, Comonfort was appointed Secretary of War. The other was none other than Porfirio Díaz. Although he never completed his studies, he had been a law student in his native state of Oaxaca. Díaz was an outstanding soldier, strong-willed, courageous, and unafraid. He came to be called "The Man of Stone."

But probably the most famous of all the men of the Reform was the pure-blood Indian from Oaxaca, Benito Juárez. Juárez is undoubtedly the major symbol of the Reform itself. Born of Zapotecan parents in 1806, Juárez was a young orphaned shepherd who spoke no Spanish at all until he was twelve years old. Thus, he was considered an *analfabeto,* or an illiterate. And he might have remained a shepherd for the rest of his life but for an incident that took place on Wednesday, December 16, 1818. Benito Juárez tells of the incident:

> "I was in a field, as usual, with my flock, when some muleteers chanced to pass, at eleven in the morning, leading their mules on the road to the Sierra. I asked them if they came from Oaxaca. They replied that they did, and at my request they described some of the things they had seen there and went on their way."

But they did not go empty handed. Benito Juárez, continues his story:

> ". . . another boy, who was much older than I and whose name was Apolonio Conde, approached and told me, on learning the cause of my grief, that he had seen one of the muleteers make away with the sheep.. . .
>   . . . fear and my natural desire to amount to something decided me to walk to Oaxaca."[93]

His arrival in Oaxaca meant a parting from his uncle and his tenure as a shepherd. For Benito Juárez, age twelve, it was a new society and a new life. Juárez went to work as a domestic for a bookbinder who was also a lay brother of the Third Order of Saint Francis. It was here that his education began. His first instruction was from the priesthood, although Juárez was never a deeply religious person. His decision was based on practical rather than spiritual reasoning:

> "It was an opinion generally accepted then, not only among the vulgar but in the upper classes of society, that clerics, and even those who were merely students without being ecclesiastics, knew a great deal, and I noticed that they were respected and considered for the knowledge attributed to them. This circumstance rather than any thought of becoming a cleric, for which I felt an instinctive dislike, decided me to beg my godfather to let me study in the Seminary. . . ."[94]

[93]Roeder, *Juárez,* p. 7.
[94]Roeder, pp. 10-12.

At age twenty-one, Juárez had to make a decision. Should he stay with the study of the priesthood or move into an area which would be more satisfying to him? The decision was made, and at age twenty-two, Juárez entered the Institute and began the study of law. He studied a variety of subjects, including physics—a subject which he taught in 1830. The following year, he was elected as Municipal Alderman—this was his first entry into politics.

Juárez was moved by the national events which surrounded him, the liberalism of Valentín Gómez Farías, the secession of Texas; foreign intervention from both Spain and France, the war with the United States, and amidst all of this the dictatorship of Antonio López de Santa Anna.

The poverty and helplessness of the poor moved him deeply and his ideological philosophy began to take form. In 1841, Benito Juárez, "the lawyer who took poor clients," was appointed to a judgeship.

Two years later he married Margarita Mazza, a daughter of a highly respected gachupin family in Oaxaca. Of Benito Juárez, Margarite wrote: "He is very homely but very good. . . ." His marriage increased the status of his social position; and this coupled with his abilities, placed him in the limelight. After serving a term on the Supreme Court of Oaxaca, he was appointed provisional governor of that state in 1847. The following year, he was elected to a four-year term.

During the five years he was governor of Oaxaca, Juárez accomplished the impossible. Exerting his liberal philosophy, he reduced the power of the Church and the landed aristocracy. He refused bribes and attempted to apply the law equally. Juárez initiated public works projects, especially the construction of roads, which would connect the state of Oaxaca with the heartland of Mexico. Although education was close to his heart, he did not see it as a panacea or cure-all. He felt that poverty had to be eliminated and that man liberated from the burden of poverty would by his own nature learn and grow. But the cause of man's "shortcomings" clearly was poverty:

> "That cause is the poverty of the people. The man who lacks the where-withal to feed his family considers the education of his children a very remote benefit or an obstacle to providing their daily bread. If that man had some advantages, if his daily labor were of some little value to him, he would provide his children with solid instruction in some one of the branches of human knowledge. The desire to learn and improve is innate in the heart of man. Relieve him of the fetters which poverty and despotism impose on him, and he will awaken naturally, even without direct protection."

During his tenure as governor, he believed that poverty could be abated by public works—particularly road construction and communications—Juárez was very effective in these areas. He was not a radical; and he was certainly not a iconoclast. But as he developed and learned, the elimination of poverty became deeply associated with the destruction of quasi-feudalism. The large landed estates had to be divided; and this meant conflict with the Church. Equality under the law meant conflict with not only the Church but the military as well. Benito Juárez and the men of the Reform met that conflict head-on as they assumed power after the final departure of Antonio López de Santa Anna.

CHAPTER 27

The Constitution of 1857

One hundred and fifty-five deputies met in the National Palace, in the Hall of Sessions late in 1856. They drew up a new constitution for Mexico that permitted freedom of religion and limited the political and economic power of the Catholic Church. On December 15, 1856, two months before the document was ratified and officially published, Pope Pius IX, issued a statement. "We raise our pontifical voice with apostolic liberty on this your full assembly, in order to condemn, to reject, and to declare irritating and of no value the above mentioned decrees. . . ."

For those who would sign or take oath to the constitution, the threat of excommunication faced them. One third of the delegates absented themselves from the signing in early February of 1857, but enough remained to make the constitution official. On Easter day, the doors of the National Cathedral were barred to the new president and his cabinet. The Church had officially declared war on the constitution and on the government which supported it.

By mid 1855, Mexico had for the last time experienced a power play by the perennial political dictator, Antonio López de Santa Anna. Now the men of the reform, the liberals—mostly mestizos, were faced with holding the reins of power which they had won in the revolution of Ayutla. They also had an opportunity to restructure the government and to initiate a political philosophy that could change the foundation of the

Mexican economy. Generally, they believed in political and personal equality; ideals which had been stated by one of their leaders, Valentín Gómez Farías as early as 1833. To accomplish this, they felt they must limit the power of the Church and the military—the two most powerful national institutions. Obviously, neither would voluntarily relinquish its power and authority. The men of the Reform also believed that they could best serve the national welfare by creating a country of small farmers. This would lead to agricultural reform and could initiate a development toward modern capitalism. The large landed estates—the haciendas—whether privately owned or owned by the Catholic Church, had to be distributed among the peasant farmers. The task was of gargantuan dimensions.

Upon the abdication and exile of Santa Anna, the liberal army moved toward Mexico City in November of 1855. The main forces and their leaders halted at Cuernavaca long enough for the delegates to name the old warrior of Independence, Juan Alvarez, as interim president of the Republic. By late November, the capital was occupied. While Alvarez' presidency lasted only a short time, it was long enough to incorporate some of the most talented men in Mexico into his cabinet. Melchor Ocampo—the scientist scholar—was appointed Minister of Interior and of Foreign Affairs. Ignacio Comonfort, Alvarez' chief political advisor and top general, became Minister of War. The poet and balladeer, Guillermo Prieto, was assigned to be Minister of Treasury. And the Ministry of Justice and Public Instruction was given to the lawyer-statesman, Benito Juárez.

It appeared that many of the ideals of the Ayutla Revolution would be rapidly enacted into law since the reformers were now in power. But the men of the Reform were by no means united. In the waning years of the Santa Anna power play the liberals had developed into two distinct camps: the puros and the moderados. The puros were the more radical. They wanted not only the abdication of Santa Anna, but also a complete restructuring of the government and economy—particularly as related to the military and the Church. Melchor Ocampo was the spokesman for the puros, although their titular head was Valentín Gómez Farías. The moderados, or moderates, wanted government to be democratic and representative—but they were compromisers. Hence, if the die-hard conservatives were forced to support one or the other, it would be the moderados, and their leader Ignacio Comonfort. It was clear that the liberals could not harmoniously assume governmental power and authority. Conflict was inevitable; and it came.

In December, after just one month, President Juan Alvarez, the object of attack by the clergy and "more genteel folk," offered to resign in favor of Ignacio Comonfort on the condition that legislation passed under his short tenure in office would remain in force. He was of course referring to *Ley Juárez* or the Law of Juárez, passed on November 23, 1855. The law of Juárez abolished the special privileges of the Church and military, and it restricted the jurisdiction of the Church courts. From now on, members of the clergy and the armed forces would no longer be exempt from paying taxes, and they would be subject to arrest and punishment as any other citizen. While the immediate reaction to Ley Juárez was the cry of *Religíon y fueros*—religion and privileges—the resignation of Alvarez cooled the heat of reaction. Nonetheless, the ardor of the puros such as Ocampo and Prieto, was not cooled by Comonfort's desire for compromise. Within a few weeks, they both resigned—in sharp disagreement with the new president, Ignacio Comonfort. Juárez, in order to permit the president to completely restructure his cabinet, also resigned and returned to his ranch in Oaxaca. Comonfort appointed him governor of Oaxaca, and it appeared then that the national contribution of Benito Juárez would end with *Ley Juárez*. In retrospect, Juárez admitted that the law he had conceived and executed was imperfect and only a beginning. Yet that is exactly why it was so important, it was a beginning. Juárez said:

> "Imperfect as this law was, it was received with great enthusiasm by the Progressive party; it was the spark that kindled the fire of Reform, which later consumed the rotten structure of abuses and privileges. It was, in short, a challenge flung to the privileged classes, and one which General Comonfort and all the others, who for lack of faith in the principles of the revolution or for personal advantage sought to check its course, compromising with the demands of the past, were forced to maintain in spite of themselves, pressed on by the all-powerful arm of public opinion."

In spite of the conservatives' feeling of relief at Juárez' departure, liberal legislation continued to be passed in the Capitol. Alongside of *Ley Juárez,* the most important law passed by the liberals was *Ley Lerdo* or the Law of Lerdo.

While President Ignacio Comonfort was attempting to reconcile the clergy and conservatives, the Secretary of the Treasury, Miguel Lerdo de Tejada, sponsored a law which would rock the foundations of the nation. Passed in June of 1856, *Ley Lerdo* was designed to achieve the economic goals of the Reform just as *Ley Juárez* had been designed to achieve the judicial goals. Capsulized, *Ley Lerdo* would permit the peasant farmer to "denounce" unused corporate property and to purchase plots of land at auction for a minimal price. A small transfer tax would accrue to the government which would help fill the need for federal revenue. While the law was directed against the massive land holdings of the Church, it was not so worded.*

*Ley Lerdo spoke not of Church property but of "Corporate property." But since the Church was the largest holder of corporate property, it stood to lose the most.

Ley Lerdo also established governmental authority over the Church, for it challenged the traditional canon law of *mortmain*. Literally "the dead hand," *mortmain* made all land acquisitions by the Catholic Church inalienable. Yet here was *Ley Lerdo*. The vision of the liberals was not to confiscate Church property, but to distribute it through legitimate sales. The vision was to make Mexico that nation of small farmers. But the reality had little co-relation to the vision. Few of the peasants could scrape enough money together to purchase even the smallest plots of land; and those woo could purchase land were threatened by excommunication if they were to denounce Church property. Thus the peasants refused to purchase land, while foreign investors and wealthy Mexican land speculators added to their holdings at bargain prices. The most tragic aspect of *Ley Lerdo* was its failure to draw a distinction between Church owned lands and Indian communal lands under Church control. Much of the ancient *ejido* land, or Indian communals, fell within the scope of *Ley Lerdo*. And these lands too, became the object of foreign and Mexican land speculators. Peasant Indians who were supposed to be aided by *Ley Lerdo* now viewed the government as their enemy. Indian uprisings, supported by members of the clergy, challenged the government of Ignacio Comonfort.

There was a serious rebellion in the state of Puebla led by the conservative-monarchist Governor Joaquín de Haro Y Tamáriz. By late 1856, the rebellion had spread to Queretaro, San Luis Potosí, Michoacán, Tlaxcala, and part of Veracruz. Comonfort's design for reconciliation had failed miserably. His presidency at stake, he faced continued Indian uprisings, spurred on by members of the clergy. He warned the clergy that its acts would bring reprisals, and thus he was forced to act. Some clerics were arrested and imprisoned while others were deported—and in some cases, Church property was even confiscated. Probably his most serious act was to order the closure and destruction of the great convent of San Francisco in the center of Mexico City; and only the church of this historic Franciscan sanctuary was spared. By mid 1857, Comonfort had brought the major portion of the rebellion to an end—but the conspirators continued to foment revolution.

In light of what it was designed to achieve, *Ley Lerdo* was a total failure. It did not break up the landed estates. It did not end quasi-feudalism. And it did not create a nation of small farmers. Only after the Revolution of 1910, and the Constitution of 1917, were advances made in those directions. Yet there were measures of success in the law. It did establish the principle of the nation's authority over the Church, especially in matters of vital national welfare. In this sense, national law became paramount over Church or canon law. And it did establish a philosophical precedence that was to become a central theme of the

Revolution of 1910, "land and liberty." Land distribution and redistribution has become almost a part of the Mexican political ethos. This probably is the greatest legacy left by the era of the Reform.

While Mexico was wracked by rebellion, and by economic and political confusion, one hundred and fifty-five delegates gathered in the Hall of Sessions of the National Palace with the express object of rewriting the supreme law of the land. The delegates to the constitutional convention were primarily liberals—puros and moderados. The conservatives received only token representation since the clergy and the military were barred. The delegates not only worked under the pressure of continued rebellion; but even before the document was completed, Pope Pius IX issued a statement declaring it null and void, and threatening excommunication to anyone who signed it or publically took allegiance to it. Even within the Hall of Sessions the debate was far from calm and agreeable. There were some who felt the restrictions placed on the clergy were not strong enough—and there was one delegate who objected to any reference to God at all. Ignacio Ramierz spoke out against the preamble because it began with "In the name of God. . . ." He chided:

> "I well know how much of the fictitious, the symbolic, the poetic, there is in all known legislation . . . but I consider it even more dangerous than absurd to suppose ourselves the interpreters of Divinity. . . . The name of God has been written by the hands of the oppressors in the blood and sweat of the peoples. And we who think ourselves free and enlightened, are we not combating Divine Right even now? Do we not tremble like children when we are told that, if we discuss religious toleration, a phalanx of old women will attack us, armed everyone of them with Divine Right? If a revolution hurls us from the tribune, it will be Divine Right that will drive us to prison, exile, and execution. . . . Gentlemen, for my part, I declare that I have not come here prepared by ecstasy or revelation. . . . The duty of forming a Constitution is too respectable to begin it by lying."[95]

Nevertheless, the preamble remained as written. The issue of freedom of religion, of total religious tolerance was also a hotly debated item. And those in the galleries waved banners, cheered, booed, or shouted threats as the debate met with their approval or disapproval. The puros wanted a statement insuring total freedom of religion. The moderados warned it could lead to civil war. They said the nation needed time. A puro delegate, Francisco Zarco, answered with an impassioned plea for immediate action:

> "To those who say that the time is not yet, I put the question, when will it come? When the people are enlightened, they reply; when there is prosperity; when there is well-being. But this is to close the question in a vicious

[95]Roeder, p. 131.

circle. . . . If they wish the reform of society to precede religious liberty, we have only to consider what Catholic exclusiveness has produced in three hundred years to abandon all hope. It has produced poverty, abjection, and slavery, it was an element of colonial domination, and it stubbornly opposed Independence."[96]

From the galleries came the cry of "Death to the sacristans." Zarco raised his hand to silence the outburst, he looked into the galleries and answered: "Jesus Christ never wished to kill." Some delegates argued that intolerance was an evil, but a necessary one. They pointed out that the constitution should be a reflection of the face of the nation—and the nation was decidedly Catholic. Still others argued that the delegates had gone beyond their expressed authority; and that they misrepresented the people. Zarco answered that from Moses to the first American Congress, legislators and leaders had to be courageously ahead of their time; and that they had to overcome public resistance. After all the arguments and counter-arguments, the vote was sixty-five to forty-four to shelve the article on religious tolerance. People in the galleries whistled, applauded and issued cries of "Long live religion! Death to the heretics! Long live the clergy!" The puros were defeated but not demoralized. They fought on tenaciously for the incorporation of military and religious restrictions; and for the addition of a bill of human rights.

Many of the guarantees for which the puros fought were incorporated; but many were watered down or lost, such as trial by jury. Universal suffrage was included even though it was watered down by indirect elections. Under the proddings of Francisco Zarco, total freedom of the press was incorporated. To the delight of the puros, both *Ley Juárez* and *Ley Lerdo* were also placed in the document that was to become the supreme law of the land. And there were other restrictions placed on the religious establishment. Nuns and priests were permitted to renounce their vows without government penalty. The constitution provided for secular education by promoting a department of public education. While the document did not call for complete religious tolerance, the offending clause in the Constitution of 1824, that which enforced the singularity of Catholicism, was removed. Freedom of religion was tacitly accepted. The most idealistic and yet unenforceable clause—made peonage illegal.

Almost a year of debating; of argument; of boos and cheers from the galleries made the delegates anxious to bring the congress to a close. In the midst of open rebellion in Puebla; and facing the specter of excommunication, the document was proclaimed. On February 5, 1857, the old dean of the puros, Valentín Gómez Farías, was carried on a litter into the Hall of Sessions. He was the first to affix his signature. Gómez Farías

[96]Roeder, p. 132.

leaned over a Bible and swore his allegiance to the new constitution; and one hundred delegates—all that remained—swore their allegiance.

Under the new constitution, national elections were held in September of 1857. But they were far from conclusive or representative. The conservatives stayed away from the polls, and Comonfort was elected by a slim majority. The election of Benito Juárez to President of the Supreme Court and Vice President of the Republic was even less conclusive. Neither Juárez nor his challengers received a constitutional majority. Therefore it devolved on congress to make the final selection. They chose Benito Juárez. At the same time Juárez' name appeared on the ballot in his home state of Oaxaca. There his popularity fared much better for he received ninety percent of the votes cast for state governor. In addition, Juárez' national office as President of the Supreme Court also made him Vice President of the Republic. If this were not enough to draw him away from his home state of Oaxaca, Comonfort also appointed him to the cabinet post of Minister of Interior. Comonfort asked congress to permit Juárez and two other justices to hold cabinet posts while simultaneously sitting as justices of the Supreme Court. The dispensation was granted.

If the congressional elections constituted a barometer of public reaction to the new constitution, then it was a repudiation. Out of the 155 deputies in the convention, only twenty-one were elected to the first congress under the new constitution; and of the puros that were the prime movers of the instrument, only one was returned.

The opposition of the Church and the military was considerably more direct, and certainly more organized. The clergy attacked what they called inconsistancies in the constitution. They warned the populace that the liberals were Godless men who were trying to destroy the Catholic religion. Using these and other arguments, they organized what were called spontaneous petitions by the people against the constitution. Bringing out its most powerful weapons, on November 13, 1857, the clergy issued a circular signed by the Archbishop of Mexico. For those who supported the instrument, no confession would be heard from the transgressors, there would be no Christian burial, and no money would be received for their souls. However, if one refused to support the constitution—or if one repented and retracted his support, absolution would be granted and full privileges in the Church would be restored.

However, the Church does not always speak with a single voice. As in the movement for independence, while the Church officially deplored the concept of independence, two Church fathers, Hidalgo and Morelos stepped forward as fathers of Mexican Independence. Especially among the lower clergy, priests openly and courageously told their parishes that no issue of religion or religious doctrine was involved in the constitutional controversy. Even among the higher clergy, there were dissenters.

On March 22, 1857, the Bishop of Oaxaca acceded to the government's request for a *Te Deum* in the cathedral. The clergy of Tobasco agreed only to preach the gospel and not to interfere with the government's authority. In Jalisco, a priest wrote a pamphlet in which he said that bishops are not infallible. He pointed out that in the past—citing the movement for Independence—they erred from "ignorance, malice, envy, and fear." He wrote that ". . . the voice of the bishop does not teach the doctrine of the Church directly, it has only the force of the reasons on which it is based."

But the forces of opposition to the constitution—the Church, the military, the conservative-monarchists, the owners of landed estates— marshalled their forces and continued the pressure. The greatest amount of pressure was exerted on President Ignacio Comonfort. True, Comonfort was a liberal, but he was not a puro. And he did not subscribe to the restrictive portions of the constitution that applied to the Church. Comonfort was a devout Catholic who nevertheless wanted to place limits on the Church, but he did not want to see it crushed. He had taken an oath to uphold the constitution; yet he was deeply shocked by the national division it had caused. Indeed, his closeness and love for his mother also caused him deep concern. Heeding the advice of her father confessor, Father Miranda, she urged her son to either reform or abandon the constitution. Comonfort felt he was torn between maintaining the *status quo* and initiating constitutional reforms with which he philosophically disagreed. He vacillated and then decided upon a middle course. He would institute those changes which appeared just, and he would maintain those aspects of the society for which the conservatives clamored the most. His decision to satisfy both camps was to be disasterous for him and for Mexico.

On December 15, 1857, Comonfort told Juárez that he was unable to govern any longer under the constitution. He said that the situation was "unbearable." He told Juárez that he would attempt a *coup d'etat* against his own liberal government; and then attempt to institute a conservative government. Purportedly, Juárez' answer was "I wish you a good outcome and much happiness in the course you are taking, but I do not accompany you."

The following day congress disbanded; and on the seventeenth, General Félix Zuloaga, leading the garrison of Tacubaya rose in rebellion. Conservatives and Church officials quickly rallied to the Plan of Tacubaya, and a confused Comonfort accepted. Ever since Mexico's independence, revolutionary groups have always issued plans under which the revolution or coup was to be fought. This plan said that the constitution would be set aside; that Comonfort would have dictatorial authority. It called for a new constitution to be ratified by the people and for the president to have a consultative council until the new document could be ratified. On the same day, Comonfort placed Juárez, President of the Congress Isidoro Olvera, and several deputies under arrest.

Seventy deputies of the congress assembled in Queretaro to register their official protest. Some towns throughout Mexico, however, accepted the plan; while still others joined in the protest organized in Queretaro. Comonfort, who sincerely thought he could bring the conservatives and liberals together, suddenly saw governmental order turn into sheer anarchy. He accepted and then rejected the plan, only to change his mind again. But for him it was too late, and he realized it. As more garrisons joined the conservatives, Comonfort decided to rejoin the constitutionalists. He knew his position was untenable, so he released Juárez, who as president of the Supreme Court was next in line to become president of the nation. The conservatives now ordered Comonfort's resignation, and they voted Félix Zuloaga as President of the Republic by an *ad hoc* conclave of priests and generals. Comonfort, defeated politically and emotionally, was permitted to exile himself to New York.

At Guanajuato, Juárez was installed as the Constitutional President of the Mexican Republic. He asked for the aid and commitment of the Mexican people; and for divine guidance. From Guanajuato, the constitutionalists moved and established their headquarters at Guadalajara, beginning a campaign of escape from capture and certain death. The adherents of Tacubaya relentlessly attempted to capture and annihilate the moving Juárez government. Finally, the constitutionalists found protection in Veracruz; a city which offered swamp-like refuge and the money collected from the port customs office. The War of Reform, or the Three Years War had started. Before it was over, thousands would die on both sides; and the Church and nation would be left in a shambles.

The conservatives controlled Mexico City, but by no means did they have full support, even among their own backers. Wealthy land owners who had purchased Church lands at bargain prices were dismayed at the repeal of *Ley Lerdo.* They balked at the prospect of having to return their valuable gains.

But the conservatives did have a strong and diciplined military force. And although Zuloaga was generally considered to be a mediocre leader, he was blessed with generals of outstanding ability. Miguel Miramón and Tomás Mejía were courageous and able. Both were strong adherents to the conservative cause. And within ten years both would die at the hands of a firing squad alongside of Maximilian. The conservatives won most of the battles but were unable to penetrate the defenses of Veracruz. Morally, the war was on the side of the constitutionalists for most were committed to a cause for which they were willing to die. Singular acts of heroism brought them renewed courage and determination. Even the wife of Benito Juárez, doña Margarita, became a legend in her own time. Escaping from Oaxaca with her eight children— one a babe in arms—she and a small escort climbed mountain trails and passes that seemed impossible. Her arrival in Veracruz was viewed as a remarkable act of heroism.

The constitutionalists were sustained by the revenues collected from import duties. They too had some excellent military minds. The army was commanded by a professor, Santos Degollado who did an admirable job. There was also a new rising star who Juárez called the "man of Oaxaca." He was also called the "man of stone," Porfirio Díaz. But the advantage of the constitutionalists was more political and moral than military. In 1859, at the height of the war, they passed a series of laws designed to implement the Constitution of 1857. There would be complete separation of Church and State; and all religious monasterial orders would be dissolved and turned over to parish priests. Religious corporations would be abolished as would be nunneries and convents. All except voluntary Church tithes were abolished. And all real Church property would be nationalized. Unlike *Ley Lerdo,* this law was confiscatory—and it made a strict distinction between Church lands and Indian communal lands under Church control. The *ejidos* would not be disturbed. Francisco Zarco's call for religious freedom at the convention of 1856 was finally decreed. Obviously, the purpose of the Juárez government in issuing these decrees in mid-conflict was to announce to the nation and the world that constitutional law would prevail. If the Juárez government could not enlist the active aid of foreign governments, possibly he could at least neutralize them.

By the end of 1860, the tide of battle had turned in favor of the constitutionalists. And in mid December, General Miguel Miramón the conservatives leading general, surrendered Mexico City and fled to France with whatever loot he could carry. On the evening of December 23, while attending an opera, Benito Juárez was notified of the surrender. As he stood silent, the orchestra played *Le Marseillaise* which had become an international anthem marking the triumph of Democracy. Crowds filled the streets in spontaneous demonstrations. The war was over.

On January 11, 1861, the famous black carriage of Benito Juárez, entered Mexico City. The constitutionalists were successful, but they gained political control of a nation that was weak and anemic. The treasury was bankrupt. The national and foreign debts were astronomical; and the clergy and conservatives continued to plot and conspire. To them, the new government was only temporary. If they could not succeed from within, possibly they could gain aid from abroad. They looked to France; they conspired, they waited.